ACTS OF THE APOSTLES

The Storyteller's Companion to the Bible™

Dennis E. Smith and
Michael E. Williams, editors

VOLUME TWELVE

ACTS OF THE APOSTLES

Abingdon Press
Nashville

ACTS OF THE APOSTLES

Copyright © 1999 by Abingdon Press

This book is printed on recycled, acid-free paper.

Library of Congress Cataloging-in-Publication Data

The Storyteller's companion to the Bible.
   Includes indexes.
   Contents: v. 1. Genesis—v. 2 Exodus-Joshua—[etc.]—v. 12. The Acts of the Apostles

   1. Bible—Paraphrases, English. 2. Bible—Criticism, interpretation, etc. I. Williams, Michael E. (Michael Edward), 1950–
BS550.S7664   220.9'505   90-82498
ISBN 0-687-39670-0 (v. 1: alk. paper)
ISBN 0-687-39671-9 (v. 2: alk. paper)
ISBN 0-687-39672-7 (v. 3: alk. paper)
ISBN 0-687-39674-3 (v. 4: alk. paper)
ISBN 0-687-39675-1 (v. 5: alk. paper)
ISBN 0-687-00838-7 (v. 6: alk. paper)
ISBN 0-687-00120-X (v. 7: alk. paper)
ISBN 0-687-05585-7 (v. 10: alk. paper)
ISBN 0-687-08249-8 (v. 12: alk. paper)

Unless otherwise noted, scripture quotations are from *The Revised English Bible*. © Oxford University Press and Cambridge University Press 1989. Used by permission.

99 00 01 02 03 04 05 06 07 08—10 9 8 7 6 5 4 3 2 1

MANUFACTURED IN THE UNITED STATES OF AMERICA

To
The Right Reverend Mark S. Sisk,
Bishop Co-adjutor of New York

(R.I.P.)

To
Barbara and Adam

(D.E.S.)

Contributors

Richard I. Pervo, who holds a Th.D. in New Testament from Harvard University Divinity School, is Professor of New Testament and Patristics at Seabury-Western Theological Seminary and is an Episcopal priest. A specialist in early Christian narrative, he has written or co-authored three books on the Acts of the Apostles.

Donald Davis, a graduate of Duke University Divinity School, was formerly an ordained Methodist minister and chairperson of the Board of Directors of the National Storytelling Association. He is currently a featured storyteller at festivals and concerts throughout the world and is the author of numerous books on storytelling. He was also a contributing storyteller for *The Storyteller's Companion to the Bible, Volume Five: Old Testament Wisdom.*

Margie Brown holds an M.Div. and an M.A. in Religious Education from United Theological Seminary in Dayton, Ohio, and a Ph.D. in Arts, Worship and Proclamation from the Graduate Theological Union in Berkeley, California. She is a storyteller and performer as well as an adjunct seminary professor at Pacific School of Religion. She is also author of numerous articles and books on storytelling and religion.

Michael E. Williams is pastor of Blakemore United Methodist Church in Nashville, Tennessee. He earned his Ph.D. in oral interpretation from Northwestern University and formerly directed the Office of Preaching for The United Methodist Church. He is also a member of the National Storytelling Association and can be heard practicing the art of storytelling at storytelling festivals throughout North America.

Dennis E. Smith is Professor of New Testament at Phillips Theological Seminary, Tulsa, Oklahoma. He holds the M.Div. degree from Princeton Theological Seminary and a Th.D. in New Testament from Harvard University Divinity School. He is also the editor and commentator for *The Storyteller's Companion to the Bible, Volume Ten: John.*

Contents

A Storyteller's Companion

Dennis E. Smith

Narrative analysis of the Bible has come into its own since the 1970s and now dominates the interpretation of the Gospels and Acts. At the same time, narrative preaching has also begun to receive greater prominence as a form of proclamation. Add to this the resurgence of storytelling during this same period and you have the ingredients that have gone into this series. It is an opportune time to reexamine the riches of the biblical stories.

The stories in the Acts of the Apostles have been revered throughout Christian history as a resource for the origins of the church. The author of Acts was a skilled storyteller who used the models of popular storytelling of his day to make his account compelling and inspirational for his audience. He provides an example for us of the power of storytelling in presenting the Christian message. It is hoped that this volume will aid the modern storyteller in appreciating and emulating the ancient storyteller who wrote the Acts of the Apostles.

The Stories

The starting point for our study is the biblical story itself. Any interpretation of the text should start with a fresh re-reading. These stories have survived for so long because of their power as stories. That power still comes across to us as we read them today. And each close reading of the text can bring new insights into its meaning. It is especially helpful to try to come to the text afresh, listening to it as if for the first time.

The Acts of the Apostles has been divided into thirty story segments, which make up the thirty chapters of the book. Virtually all of Acts is included. In this way, we are able to follow the narrative from beginning to end. The translation used is *The Revised English Bible*. You are encouraged to utilize a variety of modern translations to give you a perspective on the range of possibilities for translation that the original language of the text presents.

Comments on the Stories

The commentator for this volume is Richard I. Pervo, Professor of New Testament and Patristics at Seabury-Western Theological Seminary. Pervo has long been a leader in the narrative analysis of Acts. He brings an expertise in ancient narrative to his study of the text, enabling us to hear these stories once more with the magic they held for the ancient listener.

Retelling the Stories

To help you in developing your own stories, we have provided a sample story with each biblical text. These are intended to serve as models for how a retelling can be done, but they are not expected to exhaust the possibilities in each story. Various approaches have been used in the retellings. Sometimes the retelling will take the point of view of a character in the original story and develop it further. The retelling may follow the original plot line of the biblical story, or it may expand on one detail of the plot, or it may explore the after-effects of the original story. Retellings may utilize the first-century setting as their starting point, or they may be placed in modern settings. In some cases, a folktale or family story may be found to offer a retelling of a biblical story. The possibilities are many, and you are encouraged to develop your own retellings according to a format and style that works for you.

Four storytellers have contributed stories for this volume. The first ten stories were written by Michael E. Williams and myself. We also serve as co-editors of the series.

Donald Davis has contributed stories for chapters 11–20. As an ordained minister and storyteller, he describes his task as seeking stories that might help him to create parable experiences in preaching and teaching. "A parable experience happens in storytelling when a story that we hear pulls another story from our memory or experience and each of the two stories, side by side, informs, enlarges, and expounds upon the other," he says. Using the story segments from Acts as one point of comparison, Davis attempts to lay alongside them stories that will provide parable experiences for the listener/reader.

Margie Brown has contributed stories for chapters 21–30. She brings to the task her skills as an adjunct seminary professor, storyteller, and author. Her retellings of the biblical stories are fresh and creative, and spiced with pathos and humor.

Parallel Stories

None of the biblical stories developed in a vacuum. They came out of a rich storytelling culture. The parallel stories are provided to bring to our attention the storytelling milieu out of which these stories came. Here are collected a wide variety of stories that provide insights into storytelling models that might have been used in Acts as well as later Christian variations on the stories in Acts. The purpose is to acquaint us with the ancient world of storytelling so that we can better understand how these stories in Acts were heard by their original audience.

The parallel stories in the New Testament volumes take the place of the midrashim that are provided in the Old Testament volumes of the Storyteller's Companion to the Bible. The midrashim are traditional Jewish interpretations, in story form, of biblical texts. There are no such traditions for New Testament texts.

How to Use This Book

Bible stories share many characteristics with traditional stories. As every storyteller knows, there is no one way to tell a story, but a storyteller cannot tell a story any way he or she wants.

On the one hand, it is often difficult for people of faith to think that Bible stories can be retold imaginatively. We tend to think of the Bible in rigid terms—as having one, clear, divine meaning. But the plurality of the Gospels, for example, in which stories about Jesus were told and retold in different ways, teaches us to think of Bible stories differently—as imaginative retellings that showcase the art of the storyteller.

On the other hand, the possibilities are not endless; you can tell a story in a form that is inappropriate to the original. Successful storytelling involves a delicate balance between the meanings inherent in the original tradition, the parameters of understanding in the community within which the story is told, and the imagination of the storyteller. Bible stories have a range of meanings that are considered appropriate based on our sense for a balance between how they were understood then and how they can best be understood now. But we are remiss if we overlook the medium as a component part of the message, for the biblical narratives present stories that function as stories—they always have and always will. New Testament stories are created out of the tradition of the church, but retold in an imaginative form that is constructed to fit the needs of the storyteller's community.

This book is intended to be a resource to promote the telling of Bible stories. But there is an important component that is not present within these pages. That is what you, the reader, bring to the text. Your experiences and understandings are vital to your own creation of viable retellings of the biblical stories. Only in this way can these ancient stories become real and pertinent to our lives today.

A Narrative Introduction to the
Acts of the Apostles

Richard I. Pervo

The book of Acts may be as close as the New Testament comes to a story-teller's dream. "Ordinary" believers and children have long enjoyed many of its stories, such as the famous tale of Paul's shipwreck (chap. 27). Many scholars and clergy, however, have tended to view good stories with some suspicion. Just as medicine ought to be bitter, and the best education requires rigorous discipline, so writings designed to improve one's moral or spiritual life ought not be adorned with sugar coatings. Dissatisfaction with the tendency of scholarship to give insufficient account of the—by no means exclusive—importance of entertainment in Acts led me to launch my scholarly career with a detailed study of this factor and its significance. This is to say that my *entrée* to this project has come less from experience with storytelling or exposure to the contemporary revival of the art than from years of seeking to learn what ancient people viewed as a pleasing, "popular" story. The comments following have drawn heavily from two works, *Profit with Delight,* and, in particular, *Luke's Story of Paul,* both now out of print. The former contains abundant references to primary and secondary literature.

If the entertaining features of Acts have sometimes experienced official neglect, its success in presenting a story of Christian origins needs no endorsement. Not until recent times, when pluralism and diversity have become qualities to admire, has there been a challenge to this picture. Much of this success is due to the skill of its author as a creator of convincing narrative. One measure of that success is the spate of imitations, parallels, and sequels that followed. Among the earliest of these are "The Apocryphal Acts of the Apostles" (Pervo, "Ancient Novel"; Elliott).

Recent decades have witnessed several scholarly trends conducive to the appreciation of Acts as "story" and of the stories of Acts. The most obvious would appear initially to be an obstacle. Viewing a work as a source of stories reduces texts to fragments. Current scholarship emphasizes works as wholes, rather than as collections of "passages," or "pericopes." The Gospels and Acts must be analyzed as *narratives.* This, in turn, demands the study of narrative techniques, including not just what individual sections mean, but how meaning is achieved and stories told. Stories are not just skeletons for ideas. Much of the message comes through the medium of their telling.

In the case of Acts, narrative interest has produced a change of orientation.

At one time, the primary basis for comparison came from the epistles of Paul, data from which were inserted into, harmonized with, or placed against the text of Acts as a means for describing Christian origins. The project remains legitimate, of course, but at the present time the major point of comparison with Acts is the Gospel according to Luke. Both of these books were written by the same author, whose name is unknown, for, like many biblical books, they were written anonymously. The name "Luke" represents a tradition of the second century linking the writer to Paul (cf. Col. 4:14; 2 Tim. 4:11; Philem. 24). The titles are also of later date. (The writer would certainly not have called his work "The Acts of the Apostles," for his leading subject, Paul, was not, by the definition of Acts, an apostle.) Like most scholars, then, I employ "Luke" to identify the author and use "Acts" for its title as matters of convenience. "Author" is used without a difference in meaning. As a reminder that early Christian texts were heard aloud, I alternate "hearers" with "readers."

Another term, "the narrator," is somewhat different. Contemporary study distinguishes an actual author from the one or more narrators who appear within a text. Narrators "tell the story." There are different types of narrators. The principal narrator of (Luke and) Acts is a type known as "omniscient" and "reliable." The narrator is reliable because what is said is to be regarded as true. This narrator does not play tricks on the readers. When we read in 10:2 that Cornelius was a "devout man," we may be sure that this is true, not ironic or misinformed. The narrator is omniscient because he (Luke 1:3 in the original Greek identifies the narrator as a male) can go anywhere, into closed rooms and private meetings. He can even read minds. Many biblical books display omniscient narration. (For an example, see Gen. 1:1. Could a limited human narrator claim to be reporting on events that she or he has witnessed?)

Reference to the narrator seeks to distinguish between an event and a story about an event by reminding readers that narrators have choices about what they will describe in detail, summarize, or omit, and about how they will report things. A narrator who introduces Cornelius with the adjective "devout" intends that the reader will view him with favor. When texts are studied as narratives, the methods used are those applied to fiction. Does "narrative," then, mean "fiction"? In the case of Acts this is complicated by more than one hundred fifty years of scholarly debate, ranging from those who find nearly every word in the text absolutely "factual" to scholars who are highly skeptical. I happen to be one of the latter. Since the object of this series is not "bible history" but storytelling, it makes little difference to the reader what the commentator thinks actually happened. The historical information or judgments occasionally supplied have two major goals: to alert the reader to the danger of contaminating the story of Acts with that contained elsewhere, and to provide historical or social details for those who wish to endow a particular character or scene with accurate coloration.

The object of the following commentary on the stories is, therefore, not to relate early Christian history, but to help storytellers by elucidating the narrative of Acts. At points I raise questions. These seek to remind those for whom the outcome of the stories is well-known that there are alternatives. There is a great deal of suspense in Acts, much of which can be overlooked. I try very hard to prevent such oversight. Luke is a splendid teller of stories, a model to all who would undertake the task. Many of the comments attempt to illustrate his techniques, as example and for inspiration.

The role of context is a more difficult question. As stated above, contemporary scholarship reads Luke and Acts together. At issue is whether this is a unified work, conveniently divided, or whether Acts should be viewed as a "sequel" to the Gospel. (Related to this is the question of whether the two books together represent one or two literary genres and what this or they might be.) Acts presents *one* story. I believe that appreciation of the individual stories gains greatly from understanding their part in the larger story. In any case, I make references to the wider context, references tellers of individual stories may find otiose.

Users of this commentary deserve to know where its writer stands on such matters as the author, date, and location of the work. Statements about the author are, strictly speaking, observations about the narrator. The narrator of Acts has benefited from some Greek education, roughly on the level of one who can write good technical or business prose. The narrator is also thoroughly at home in the Greek translation of Jewish scriptures, which he can not only cite but also imitate. His perspective is that of a gentile.

As Acts 20, in particular, indicates, the narrator looks back upon the events described. For a number of reasons, I am inclined to posit a date of about 100 C.E. The narrative celebrates the heritage of the Pauline mission around the Aegean Sea, embracing Greece and the western part of modern Turkey. From the narrative one is tempted to suggest Ephesus as the place of origin. (See the comments on Acts 19–20.) Many of the issues addressed in the text remain important today: the church's social mission, inclusion of diverse groups, conflicts over doctrine, and controversies about the nature and style of leadership. Two of these elicit particular comment.

Luke is a promoter of inclusion: male and female, Greek and "barbarian," rich and poor. He also is something a snob, one who can make snide remarks about backward "natives" and leave more humble believers nameless. In the matter of Jews and women, the text displays deep ambivalences. Women played leadership roles in the emergent Christian movement. By Luke's time such leadership was under pressure in certain circles. Roman imperial society as a whole had become more conservative about the emancipation of women, and their prominence was a characteristic of religious sects often viewed as vulgar or subversive. The result is a "double message" (Seim). While seeking to express continuity with the message of Israel and proudly emphasizing the Jewish credentials of, for example, Paul, the narrator is quite willing to portray Jews as so jealous of Christian success among gentiles that they will stoop to any means in order to defeat them. This is another complex "double message." Tellers of the story of Acts will have to take considerable pains if they wish not to reinforce racism, sexism, and anti-Semitism, since the plots of many stories spring from what look like these perspectives. In short, these stories do not belong to our social world. Pretending that the Bible exists in a timeless vacuum has made no small contribution to the general fund of human evil and brought discredit upon the Christian church.

What Are New Testament Parallel Stories?

Dennis E. Smith

If a story is told about a modern day president in which he eventually says, "I cannot tell a lie," we might think immediately of the first such story, the one about George Washington and the cherry tree. Stories are like that. They often draw on traditional formats or motifs or plots. It is the stock-in-trade of a good storyteller to utilize shared cultural data to make her stories come alive.

The stories in the New Testament work the same way. They are often adapted to standard plots from the culture. The stories in Acts draw primarily from adventure tales of the first century, especially those of martyrs. Themes such as arrest and trial, imprisonment and miraculous escape, persecution and martyrdom are common in such tales. These kinds of stories are found in the Jewish tradition (such as in the stories of the Maccabees in 1–4 Maccabees), in the pagan tradition ("Acts of the Pagan Martyrs"), and in the developing Christian tradition ("Acts of the Christian Martyrs"). Acts of the Apostles is a part of this literary tradition.

"Parallel stories" are provided here to help us trace some of the background and foreground of these stories about the apostles. They are intended to give us a sense for the different ways these stories would have been heard by different Christian groups at different times in early church history. The parallel stories collected here offer a variety of types of information.

Jewish Traditions

In some cases, similar stories are found in the Jewish tradition. In this way, we can see how the stories being told about the apostles would be similar to stories being told about heroes in the Jewish tradition. Such stories are found in the hellenistic Jewish authors Philo and Josephus, and in other Jewish writings from the hellenistic and Roman periods, such as 1–4 Maccabees, *Joseph and Asenath,* and *Testaments of the Twelve Patriarchs.* Stories in the rabbinic tradition often present the rabbis as heroes as well.

Christian Traditions

Acts of the Apostles is a part of a tradition in early Christian literature that extended for several centuries: the tradition of stories about apostles and martyrs. This includes such writings as *Acts of Paul, Acts of Peter,* and *Martyrdom of Polycarp.* These stories tell of miracles, trials and imprisonment, and martyrdom. They often take on the aura of adventure tales, with the apostles and martyrs being the heroes of the stories.

"Pagan" Traditions

As a storyteller, the author of Acts seems to have been widely read in the literature of the day. He knows how to write like a historian, presenting speeches with the skill of a Thucydides, for example, and like a novelist, presenting adventure tales that would rival those of the pagan novelists Apuleius and Chariton. He knows how to use motifs from a variety of literary resources and traditions in order to tell a good story. The parallel stories from the pagan tradition help remind us of the kinds of stories this audience was accustomed to and how they would have heard this story. They also help us to appreciate the skill with which this author was able to present the stories about the apostles so that they would compare favorably with heroic figures in any stories of the day.

The stories in Acts were skillfully put together not only to entertain but also to instruct the listener in the basics of the faith. They present their teachings with such a power that the listener is drawn in to be a part of the story itself. The modern storyteller seeks for no less. The parallel stories are provided to illustrate the skill with which these stories have been constructed and the complex ways in which they would have been heard. It is our hope that this knowledge will help you to retell the Bible stories for today's world with an immediacy that rivals the ancient tellings.

Learning to Tell Bible Stories

A Self-Directed Workshop

1. Read the story aloud at least twice. You may choose to read the translation included here or the one you are accustomed to reading. I recommend that you examine at least two translations as you prepare, so you can hear the differences in the way they sound when read aloud.

Do read them *aloud*. Yes, if you are not by yourself, people may give you funny looks, but this really is important. Your ear will hear things about the passage that your eye will miss. Besides, you can't skim when you read aloud. You are forced to take your time, and you might notice aspects of the story that you never saw (or heard) before.

As you read, pay special attention to *where* the story takes place, *when* the story takes place, *who* the characters are, *what* objects are important to the story, and the general *order of events* in the story.

2. Now close your eyes and imagine the story taking place. This is your chance to become a playwright/director or screenwriter/filmmaker because you will experience the story on the stage or screen in your imagination. Enjoy this part of the process. It takes only a few minutes, and the budget is within everybody's reach.

3. Look back at the story briefly to make sure you haven't left out any important people, places, things, or events.

4. Try telling the story. This works better if you have someone to listen (even the family pet will do). You can try speaking aloud to yourself or to an imaginary listener. Afterward ask your listener or yourself what questions arise as a result of this telling. Is the information you need about the people, places, things, or language in the story? Is it appropriate to the age, experiences, and interests of those who will be hearing it? Does the story capture your imagination? One more thing: You don't have to be able to explain the meaning of a story to tell it. In fact, those of the most enduring interest have an element of mystery about them.

5. Read the "Comments on the Story" provided for each passage. Are some of your questions answered there? You may wish also to look at a good Bible dictionary for place names, characters, professions, objects, or worlds that you need to learn more about. *The Interpreter's Dictionary of the Bible* (Nashville: Abingdon Press, 1962) and *The Anchor Bible Dictionary* (New York: Doubleday, 1992) are the most complete sources for storytellers.

6. Read the "Retelling the Story" section for the passage you are learning to tell. Does it give you any ideas about how you will tell the story? How would you tell it differently? Would you tell it from another character's point of view? How would that make it a different story? Would you transfer it to a modern setting? What places and characters will you choose to correspond to those in the biblical story? Remember, the retellings that are provided are not meant to be told exactly as they are written here. They are to serve as springboards for your imagination as you develop your telling.

7. Read the "parallel stories" that accompany each passage. These give you insights into how the story was heard or retold at various times in the early church. Do these variations on the story respond to any of your questions or relate to any of your life situations or those of your listeners? Do the alternative stories parallel cultural "stories" from today that you know of? Sometimes you may find that experiences and points of view from the past are mirrored fairly closely in the modern setting.

8. Once you have the elements of the story in mind and have chosen the approach you are going to take in retelling it, you need to practice, practice, practice. Tell the story aloud ten or twenty or fifty times over a period of several days or weeks. Listen as you tell your story. Revise your telling as you go along. Remember that you are not memorizing a text; you are preparing a living event. Each time you tell the story, it will be a little different, because you will be different (if for no other reason than that you have told the story before).

9. Then "taste and see" that even the stories of God are good—not all sweet, but good and good for us and for those who hunger to hear.

A New Departure: The Ascension

After telling the disciples to await empowerment that will make them worldwide witnesses, the risen Christ departs.

The Story

IN the first part of my work, Theophilus, I gave an account of all that Jesus did and taught from the beginning until the day when he was taken up to heaven, after giving instructions through the Holy Spirit to the apostles whom he had chosen. To these men he showed himself after his death and gave ample proof that he was alive: he was seen by them over a period of forty days and spoke to them about the kingdom of God. While he was in their company he directed them not to leave Jerusalem. 'You must wait', he said, 'for the gift promised by the Father, of which I told you; John, as you know, baptized with water, but within the next few days you will be baptized with the Holy Spirit.'

When they were all together, they asked him, 'Lord, is this the time at which you are to restore sovereignty to Israel?' He answered, 'It is not for you to know about dates or times which the Father has set within his own control. But you will receive power when the Holy Spirit comes upon you; and you will bear witness for me in Jerusalem, and throughout all Judaea and Samaria, and even in the farthest corners of the earth.'

After he had said this, he was lifted up before their very eyes, and a cloud took him from their sight. They were gazing intently into the sky as he went, and all at once there stood beside them two men robed in white, who said, 'Men of Galilee, why stand there looking up into the sky? This Jesus who has been taken from you up to heaven will come in the same way as you have seen him go.'

THEY then returned to Jerusalem from the hill called Olivet, which is near the city, no farther than a sabbath day's journey. On their arrival they went to the upstairs room where they were lodging: Peter and John and James and Andrew, Philip and Thomas, Bartholomew and Matthew, James son of Alphaeus, Simon the Zealot, and Judas son of James. All these with one accord were constantly at prayer, together wth a group of women, and Mary the mother of Jesus, and his brothers.

Comments on the Story

Because ancient books largely lacked such format features as punctuation, paragraphs, and chapter headings, their authors had to incorporate more information in the text than must modern writers. Prefaces are one way to summarize, provide previews, and mark divisions. The preface to Acts looks two ways, marking a new book and referring to the Gospel preface (Luke 1:1-4). Dedications were likewise embedded in the text. What of this "Theophilus" ("friend of God")? "Your excellency" (Luke 1:3) intimates high status. Scholars debate whether he was a real or symbolic person. For those who tell the story and stories of Acts, Theophilus may be construed as the ideal reader, informed and attentive. The narrator "breaks the rules" of preface-writing in that the normal preview of the coming book is disrupted by the sudden irruption of direct speech in verse 4 (smoothed over by the translation). This produces vividness, the voice of the Risen One overriding, as it were, conventions of discourse. By this means, readers are swept from detached observation into direct engagement as auditors.

The beginning of Acts both overlaps and conflicts with the end of Luke (see Luke 24:36-53). Various theories seek to explain this conflict. In any event, these verses establish Acts as a different book with new leading characters, among them the apostles mentioned in verse 2, who engage in a six-week course of instruction. Early Christians devoted considerable attention to the Savior's post-Easter appearances and teaching. Some claimed that he remained for a year or more and revealed many mysteries. Forty days is a modest period and not without precedent: Moses sojourned with God for the same span (Exod. 24:18). Jesus, who opened his earthly ministry with forty days of fasting, closes it with a forty-day feast. Merriment aside, these meals ("in their company" refers to dining), like those in the Gospel, were occasions for teaching. The relatively new gift, John's baptizing, will be superseded by the newer gift of the Spirit. For the disciples, all this looks good. Once more they have the opportunity to reveal their dullness: "Are we about to set up a kingdom, to return to the good old days of David?" Newness is not easy to grasp. Jesus' response (vv. 7-8) would expand their horizons while quashing their expectations. The ends of the earth, not the end of the world, is the theme of this book. The preview that properly belongs in a prosaic preface issues from the risen Christ. Old boundaries, Israel and its constitution, and old centers of the universe, Jerusalem, are no longer adequate.

What can this mean? Samaria is the region of "the other," people who are by nature hostile, wrong-headed, and alien (cf. Luke 9:52-56; 10:25-37; and 17:11-10). What are "the farthest corners of the earth"? What challenges and adventures will they bring? Dragons, gentiles, Babylon on the Tiber? Let "farthest corners" conjure up all the mystery and potential excitement they should evoke.

Following this astonishing statement by Jesus, the narrator provides a corresponding surprise. All this has been taking place on the momentous Mount of Olives, where Jesus was arrested (cf. also Zech. 14:4). These words are a speech of farewell. Like a film director, the narrator slowly pulls back to unveil a setting. Readers view the ascension from the perspective of the apostles rather than from a neutral angle. Vividness is not all. The Ascension is an Easter story, complete with interpreting "angels" who, like those of Luke 24:4-5, provoke their audience with a question and deliver a promise. The cloud is not a biblical taxicab but a trope for divine power and glory. Ascension is less a departure than a prelude to empowerment. The Risen One, detached from earthly limits, will touch those distant corners. This is a beginning that foreshadows an end, the return in ultimate power.

Rapt in breathless expectation, hearers are plunked back on solid ground with a map reference in verse 12, followed by an inventory of personnel. Lists of names in Acts foreshadow important events. Comparison with Luke 6:13-16 shows continuity and change. The twelve have become eleven. Moreover, the women disciples and members of Jesus' family are part of the inner circle. In this way Luke intimates changes in leadership (the family includes James) and boundaries (women are disciples).

Retelling the Story

'Men of Galilee, why stand there looking up into the sky? This Jesus who has been taken away from you up to heaven will come in the same way as you have seen him go.' (Acts 1:11)

As I lie here looking toward the same ceiling under which I have slept for sixty-eight years, I am preparing never to see it again. It will become transparent; then the sky will open, and I will become part of the great beyond. This world and this house, both of which I have called home, will be like a dream from which I am waking. I await the doctor who will make my demise official with a stroke of the pen on a state certificate. I have often imagined this moment, and it is just as I thought it would be so far.

I was brought to The Village of the Second Advent when I was seven years old. My parents had been converted at one of the millennial revival meetings that seemed to spring up everywhere at the close of the twentieth century. They both had worked in the computer industry, my mother as a designer of hardware and my father as a developer of software. Neither were likely candidates for a religious transformation of any kind.

Neither had been raised in any church and both had an attitude toward organized religious groups that exhibited less the disdain common of their time than indifference. That is, until they were hired to work with a very wealthy man who had become interested in devising a means of computing the date of Christ's return. He hired them at double the going salary in the industry to help him create a processor and program that would predict the Second Coming of our Lord. Of course, they would not have used those exact terms at the time, since Jesus would not have been considered by either of them as Lord.

That came later. The further they got in their work on this project the more they wanted to learn of the substance of their work. Their employer told them of Jesus and his promise to return in the same way he had gone from those first disciples. He told them of how those followers had stared into the sky after Jesus has ascended on a cloud. "Watch the sky," he told them again and again. "The sky will tell you all you need to know." He had worked out a complicated scheme based upon the Hebrew calendar and other astrological phenomena. By this he hoped to calculate the time of our Lord's return. His work was not contaminated by the desire to make money as so many of those who had attempted such predictions before. He had more money than he needed. Besides, he really believed that our Lord would return, which would make distinctions based on money or anything else irrelevant.

My parents were still skeptical. They asked him why, if the angel in the story had told the disciples that they were not to know the times of the seasons, he was seeking to discover such a time. He explained that the angel had told those ancient followers that it was not for *them* to know the time of the return. Nowhere did it say that later disciples, like himself, could not know it, especially with the advent of new technology. Little by little his aspirations began to make sense to my parents. After a period of several years they became followers. As others joined with them it finally became clear that the group's work would require all of them to work even more closely. So, the wealthy man bought an apartment complex where they all lived. He named it The Village of the Second Advent and the clubhouse was renovated to house the computer and the labs in which all the followers worked. I attended school within the village, as did all the children who lived there. Our entire curriculum was based upon the work our parents did and our education was technologically more advanced than we would have received in the outer world. Several times during my life span the computer predicted that the date of Christ's return was imminent. Each time it passed, and we were all sent back to our calculations. Each time a few of the followers would drift away from the community.

I was a true believer because my parents were true believers. After their deaths I took over their work. I managed both the project and the village. After several dates had passed without our Lord's return so many of the followers had gone that it was no longer economically feasible to keep the village open without help. The decision was made to lease apartments to outsiders. In a very few years after this decision was made, all the apartments but mine were being leased to outsiders. Or perhaps I, as the only remnant of the original inhabitants left, was the outsider. The computer system became so antiquated that it could no longer be repaired. The clubhouse became a place for birthday parties and wedding receptions again. My income was assured from the rentals so I spent most of my time sorting through the religious or

24

technical materials I had access to through the Cosmonet (the successor to the Internet). You might say this was my way to continue to search the skies. But I was no longer sure of that for which I searched.

Then one day the city came with a proposal to turn the entire housing complex into housing for group homes for children whose parents had died or abandoned them. It seemed to be a good cause, so after brief negotiations and assurances that all the present tenants would be cared for, the deal was closed.

The first day the children and their guardians moved in I had the strangest feeling of peace and satisfaction, as if something I had waited for all my life had finally fallen into place. Then as I knelt to talk to one of the five year olds, I looked her in the eye and a voice came to me, clear as could be. It said, "I am the one you have waited for." And at that moment I felt a sinking feeling, like hearing that your flight had departed from a different gate from the one at which you were waiting. This child was the one I had waited for. And that experience repeated with each child I greeted. I felt rather foolish that while I had been searching the skies for my Lord, he had come to me as a little child.

The preface was widely used in the literature of antiquity. It gave a sense of authenticity to the material it introduced and so was used especially in historical writings. It could also be used in other kinds of writings, such as in ancient novels. When more than one book was written, probably because the limited size of the scroll required that a lengthy work be broken up into parts, the content of the previous work would be summarized, as Luke does here in repeating the information he presented in his preface to the Gospel of Luke. The Jewish historian Josephus has a similar preface for Book 2 of his *Against Apion* (late-first-century C.E.): "In the first volume of this work, my most esteemed Epaphroditus, I demonstrated the antiquity of our race, corroborating my statements by the writings of Phoenicians, Chaldaeans, and Egyptians, besides citing as witnesses numerous Greek historians. . . . I shall now proceed to refute the rest of the authors who have attacked us."

So I go to meet Christ, no longer a true believer, but one who has seen his face in the face of his children. Perhaps it was not for us to know the time or the season. All I do know is that these children were his second advent for me. Any other mysteries will await his explanation or simply dissolve in his presence. *(Michael E. Williams)*

The ascension of a semi-divine human to dwell with the gods was a frequent theme in Greek and Roman religion and mythology. Hercules, Romulus, and Proculus are among the mythological figures who were said to have ascended to the heavens. This was also commonly attributed to Roman emperors. Augustus, for example, is said to have been seen "ascending to heaven after the manner of which tradition tells concerning Proculus and Romulus" (Dio Cassius 56.46 [early-third-century C.E.]). Justin, the second-century Christian apologist, used this data to lend credibility to the Christian claim that Jesus ascended: "We propound nothing different from what you believe regarding those whom you esteem sons of Jupiter. . . . And what of the emperors who die among yourselves, whom you deem worthy of deification, and in whose behalf you produce some one who swears he has seen the burning Caesar rise to heaven from the funeral pyre?" (*Apology* 1.21 [mid-second-century C.E.]; from Boring, nos. 215, 217, 219, 485)

Equipment for Ministry

After Peter sets forth the criteria for an apostle, Matthias is chosen by lot to complete the number.

The Story

It was during this time that Peter stood up before the assembled brotherhood, about one hundred and twenty in all, and said: 'My friends, the prophecy in scripture, which the Holy Spirit uttered concerning Judas through the mouth of David, was bound to come true; Judas acted as guide to those who arrested Jesus—he was one of our number and had his place in this ministry,' (After buying a plot of land with the price of his villainy, this man fell headlong and burst open so that all his entrails spilled out; everyone in Jerusalem came to hear of this, and in their own language they named the plot Akeldama, which means 'Blood Acre'.) 'The words I have in mind', Peter continued, 'are in the book of Psalms: "Let his homestead fall desolate; let there be none to inhabit it." And again, "Let his charge be given to another." Therefore one of those who bore us company all the while the Lord Jesus was going about among us, from his baptism by John until the day when he was taken up from us— one of the those must now join us as a witness to his resurrection.'

Two names were put forward: Joseph, who was known as Barsabbas and bore the added name of Justus, and Matthias. Then they prayed and said, 'You know the hearts of everyone, Lord; declare which of these two you have chosen to receive this office of ministry and apostleship which Judas abandoned to go where he belonged.' They drew lots, and the lot fell to Matthias; so he was elected to be an apostle with the other eleven.

Comments on the Story

This episode, which provides an interlude between the Ascension and Pentecost, is not mere filler. By contrast, it heightens the following story. In this, the first of those orations that show one important formal difference from the Gospel of Luke, it is clear that the author uses speeches more to communicate with the reader than to create dramatic plausibility. Note, for example, the summary of Judas's death, of which the dramatic audience would have been informed, and the translation of an Aramaic word from "their" language. Aramaic would, in fact, have been the language of both speech and audience.

As often is the case, the narrator shows rather than tells. Peter is shown exercising leadership over the group, now reported to consist of 120, a corporation of respectable size. Moreover, the narrator does not simply say that the community began to put into place the model of scriptural interpretation set forth in Luke 24, but depicts Peter practicing it. That model envisions Scripture (the "Old Testament," for Luke the Greek translation known as the Septuagint) as promise fulfilled in the events of redemption. In effect, believers begin with fulfillment and peruse the Scripture to find promises of that fulfillment. Behind this theory, and beyond it, is a theology of divine providence that makes sense of mysterious or disturbing events and empowers believers to act. God is in charge.

Another particularity of Acts emerges in this account: stories of how God punishes the wicked. These people are, of course, wholly responsible for their fate. On the positive side, such stories hold up the possibility of judgment, always a good curb to nascent or virulent triumphalism. Nonetheless, they produce discomfort, and rightly so, for human conclusions about divine judgment can be rather cheap. Contemporary theology does not regard threat as an appropriate evangelistic tool. In Luke's time this was not the case.

Within a few verses the narrator achieves much. While describing the fate of Judas, Luke not only exhibits the mandated approach to interpretation and at theology of providential direction; he also defines the office of apostle in a manner that creates a link between the past of Jesus and the future of the church. The use of Scripture is another element of this sense of continuity with the history of Israel, an important Lucan theme. Moreover, although the twelve constitute a one-time group (future vacancies are not filled), the speech envisions issues of later times, including our own, one of which is the use of money.

The casting of lots, easily developed into a moment of suspense, was a technique familiar to the original audience. Luke does not wish to establish it as a permanent method. After Pentecost, choices are made by the Spirit (cf. 13:1-3). What kind of story is this? In essence it is a story about decision making and leadership, including the consequences of self-serving decisions.

Retelling the Story

After buying a plot of land with the price of his villainy, [Judas] fell headlong and burst open so that all his entrails spilled out. (Acts 1:18)

REPORT OF THE CORONER'S JURY

in the Death of **JUDAS ISCARIOT**

The circumstances of the death of our subject, Judas Iscariot, are disputed. It was the task of this coroner's jury to hear testimony in the case and come to some determination concerning the facts surrounding the demise of the deceased. First, we wish to relate certain information from his life. This we know: Said Judas Iscariot was a follower of the Nazarene rabbi, Jeshua, and had been in the company of this teacher and that teacher's other disciples for some time. Second, he was clearly a trusted member of this collection of disciples, since there is clear evidence that he was involved in the finances of the group. Third, though he did sell certain information about his rabbi, Jeshua of Nazareth, to the Temple authorities, there was no indication that he ever renounced his membership in the rabbi's following nor did he personally deny or denounce his teacher.

The jury heard two basic lines of evidence concerning the death of Judas Iscariot. The first, held by the disciple of the same rabbi named Matthew, contended that his death was a suicide, committed by hanging himself after his failed attempt to return the money to the Temple authorities who had first given it to him. The second theory, put forth by the followers of a certain writer (also a disciple of the rabbi) whom we shall call Luke, suggests that the death was either accidental or providential depending on your interpretation of the events surrounding it. This theory states that Judas simply fell, swelled up and popped open like an overfilled sack of grain spilling his entrails onto the ground.

There is no physical evidence to support either version of his death, so we will have to base our decision on the secondhand testimony of witnesses, none of whom were present at the time of death. In short, we have to reach a conclusion based entirely on hearsay, not a firm basis for such an important decision.

As you can readily see, the two theories of Judas's death are contradictory. The one implies that he was repen-

> It was traditional in stories about evil men to relate how they died awful and disgusting deaths. Acts has two such accounts, this one about Judas and the death of Herod (12:3). There is more than one account of the death of Judas. Matthew says he repented and hanged himself (Matt. 27:5). Papias, a first-century church father, says he swelled up so much that he blocked the way of a horse and cart. (Haenchen 160, n. 5)

29

tant and despondent over circumstances that had not turned out the way he had planned. Had Judas intended for his rabbi to die? This first theory would suggest that he did not. What was his purpose for turning his teacher in to the authorities? This is not clear. Perhaps he wanted to force his rabbi's hand. If he truly believed that this Jeshua was a reluctant messiah, he may have thought that turning him in was the better way to make him declare and show himself as the one who would overthrow the Roman occupation.

The other theory holds that Judas turned in his rabbi for the monetary gain or perhaps he had become disaffected with his teacher's teachings. Those who follow this line of thought see Judas as a clear villain in the case and view his death as righteous punishment for such a betrayal, since no one but God can plumb the depths of the human heart in its devotion or its capacity for deception.

It seems the followers of Rabbi Jeshua of Nazareth are divided in their opinions on this matter. Since they are a small sect among the Jewish people and will likely disappear into the constant flow of history, we are not convinced that a complete determination concerning the death of said Judas Iscariot will ever be possible. Nor do we believe that it is ultimately of any great significance.

Casting lots was a traditional means for determining God's will (1 Chron. 26:14) and was used not only by Jews but also by Romans and others. One method was to place the names written on stones into a vessel and then shake it until one of the names fell out. (Foakes Jackson and Lake, 4.15).

Therefore it is the finding of the coroner's jury that Judas Iscariot died of undetermined causes. I wish to express the gratitude of the High Priest and the Temple hierarchy to this jury for your service in this capacity.

THE OFFICE OF THE RECORDER OF DEATHS

(Michael E. Williams)

The Power of the Tongue

The coming of the Spirit foreshadows the world mission and leads to the conversion of three thousand in a single stroke.

The Story

THE day of Pentecost had come, and they were all together in one place. Suddenly there came from the sky what sounded like a strong, driving wind, a noise which filled the whole house where they were sitting. And there appeared to them flames like tongues of fire distributed among them and coming to rest on each one. They were all filled with the Holy Spirit and began to talk in other tongues, as the Spirit gave them power of utterance.

Now there were staying in Jerusalem devout Jews drawn from every nation under heaven. At this sound a crowd of them gathered, and were bewildered because each one heard his own language spoken; they were amazed and in astonishment exclaimed, 'Surely these people who are speaking are all Galileans! How is it that each of us can hear them in his own native language? Parthians, Medes, Elamites; inhabitants of Mesopotamia, of Judaea and Cappadocia, of Pontus and Asia, of Phrygia and Pamphylia, of Egypt and the districts of Libya around Cyrene; visitors from Rome, both Jews and proselytes; Cretans and Arabs—all of us hear them telling in our own tongues the great things God has done.' They were all amazed and perplexed, saying

to one another, 'What can this mean?' Others said contemptuously, 'They have been drinking!'

But Peter stood up with the eleven, and in a loud voice addressed the crowd: 'Fellow–Jews, and all who live in Jerusalem, listen and take note of what I say. These people are not drunk, as you suppose; it is only nine in the morning! No, this is what the prophet Joel spoke of: "In the last days, says God, I will pour out my Spirit on all mankind; and your sons and daughters shall prophesy; your young men shall see visions, and your old men shall dream dreams. Yes, on my servants and my handmaids I will pour out my Spirit in those days, and they shall prophesy. I will show portents in the sky above, and signs on the earth below—blood and fire and a pall of smoke. The sun shall be turned to darkness, and the moon to blood, before that great, resplendent day, the day of the Lord, shall come. Everyone who calls on the name of the Lord on that day shall be saved."

'Men of Israel, hear me: I am speaking of Jesus of Nazareth, singled out by God and made known to you through miracles, portents, and signs, which God worked among you through him, as you well know. By the deliberate will and plan of God he was given into your power, and you killed him, using heathen men to crucify him. But God raised him to life again, setting him free from the pangs of death, because it could not be that death should keep him in its grip.

'For David says of him:

I foresaw that the Lord would be
   with me for ever,
with him at my right hand I cannot
   be shaken;
therefore my heart is glad
and my tongue rejoices;
moreover, my flesh shall dwell in
   hope,
for you will not abandon me to
   death,
nor let your faithful servant suffer
   corruption.
You have shown me the paths of life;
your presence will fill me with joy.

'My friends, nobody can deny that the patriarch David died and was buried; we have his tomb here to this very day. It is clear therefore that he spoke as a prophet who knew that God had sworn to him that one of his own direct descendants should sit on his throne; and when he said he was not abandoned to death, and his flesh never saw corruption, he spoke with foreknowledge of the resurrection of the Messiah. Now Jesus has been raised by God, and of this we are all witnesses. Exalted at God's right hand he received from the Father the promised Holy Spirit, and all that you now see and hear flows from him. For it was not David who went up to heaven; his own words are: "The Lord said to my Lord, 'Sit at my right hand until I make your enemies your footstool.' " Let all Israel then accept as certain that God has made this same Jesus, whom you crucified, both Lord and Messiah.'

When they heard this they were cut to the heart, and said to Peter and the other apostles, 'Friends, what are we to do?' 'Repent,' said Peter, 'and be baptized, every one of you, in the name of Jesus the Messiah; then your sins will be forgiven and you will receive the gift of the Holy Spirit. The promise is to you and to your children and to all who are far away, to everyone whom the Lord our God may call.'

He pressed his case with many other arguments and pleaded with them: 'Save yourselves from this crooked age.' Those who accepted what he said were baptized, and some three thousand were added to the number of believers that day. They met constantly to hear the apostles teach and to share the common life, to break bread, and to pray.

Comments on the Story

Pentecost, a harvest festival later associated with the giving of the Torah at Sinai, provides the setting for "the birthday of the Church." Our nomenclature reflects the understanding that the church is not simply a group of disciples but the body of those incorporated and empowered by the Spirit. The narrative pattern is one often used in Acts: a wondrous event that gathers a crowd who learn its meaning in an accompanying speech. This, in turn, reflects the understanding that events, even stories of events, are ambiguous. They require interpretation. Much of this transpires, of course, in how the story is told. Verse 13, "Others said contemptuously, 'They have been drinking!' " makes the point.

Unlike some of his later representatives, Jesus had not set a particular day for fulfillment. While assembled for prayer, the company experience an irruption of signs suggesting motifs familiar from biblical theophanies: sound, wind, thunder. (The cloud of 1:9 and the earthquake of 4:31 finish the list and serve to frame this section.) The background of this, already "demythologized" in Hebrew Scripture, is the epiphany of a storm god upon a mountaintop. Fiery flames rest upon all and each. This is a gift that unites individuals into a body. In this event the prophecy of John the Baptizer (Luke 3:21-22) finds fulfillment, not in a fiery end but as an illuminating overture. Observe how the narrator seizes our attention in a breathless series of arresting images. These set forth the origin and nature of the gift. Spirit, speech, and water evoke Genesis 1. New creation is the subject here. Fire is not the focus, for they "began to talk in other tongues." Is this ecstatic speech, that glossolalia that was a source for both pride and embarrassment to early Christians?

Before one can even begin to ponder this question, the narrator discards the house. Were this a film, the scene would dissolve to be replaced by another. The focus is now outdoors, where a large crowd of devout residents and tourists appear to investigate the sound (the same word as the "voice" of Luke 3:23). The following scene vividly foreshadows the course of Acts. Representatives of "the farthest corners of the earth" (1:8) can hear the message in their native tongues. Babel (Genesis 11) has fallen; the original unity of the human race can be restored. What is the real miracle, the tongues or the ability to hear? The latter. This wind will not cease to roar until its stormy gusts propel Paul to Rome.

This was a cosmopolitan crowd, however, including some urbane enough to attribute the hullabaloo to holiday spirits. Peter then steps in, flanked by his colleagues, to clarify the situation in an inaugural sermon. The subject, like that of Jesus' first speech in Luke 4:16-30, is the Spirit. The utopian words of Joel, cited in detail, have come to pass. Young and old, male and female, are added to the national groups previously mentioned.

The main section (vv. 22-36) of the sermon exhibits careful structure: initial and concluding creedal summaries framing the central proclamation of the resurrection, which is itself encased between scriptural quotations. Dialogue colors the close (vv. 37-42). Pierced to the quick, the hearers raise the question of all potential converts: "What next?" Peter has an answer to their inquiry, but the narrator is content to summarize his words. The results? Three thousand new members, not a bad day's work for a community that started with one hundred twenty. The casual mention of large numbers at the end is characteristic of miracles stories. Pentecost is a miraculous explosion of new life.

From the critical perspective, Pentecost is a foundational story. Like many such, it is written to explain the present in light of the past. Whatever story stands behind it, the account reveals sophisticated reflection. From the Christian perspective this is not a story about "them" (the apostles), but a story about us, how it became possible for us to hear of and embrace that new life given by the Spirit.

Retelling the Story

They were all filled with the Holy Spirit and began to talk in other tongues, as the Spirit gave them power of utterance. (Acts 2:4)

To this very day she would tell you that they were angels, dressed in khaki and speaking in languages from the world to come. For a long time I thought my grandmother was off her rocker, if you know what I mean. Not that I blamed her after what she had been through. It was still weird, the things she would tell a little kid. I don't think my parents ever knew, or maybe she told my mom the same thing when she was a girl and she just thought such stories were normal.

They were my fairy tales, these strange narratives of Nana's childhood. They all began in the never-never land of the village of her earliest memories. Her father had been a student and had loved that life in the city. After the money ran out, though, he returned to his hometown to help in his father's store. Still he spent most of his days with his nose in a book. Nana always told that part of the story with obvious pride, emphasizing her father's studious nature. "He didn't have a head for business," she would say. "He should have been a professor."

> The Pentecost story is related to the utopian concept in ancient literature in which there would be a common language for all humanity. A third-century B.C.E. novel by a certain Jambulos told of an island people with the amazing ability to speak every language. Plutarch, a contemporary of Luke, spoke of a belief in a future time in which "there shall be one manner of life and one form of government for a blessed people who shall all speak one tongue" (*Isis and Osiris* 47). In biblical tradition, the time of one language ended with the tower of Babel (Gen. 11:1-9). (Boring, no. 486)

In a way, he was a teacher because his love for literature, history, and philosophy was communicated to his daughter, and his inquisitive spirit must have been infectious because she caught it and it remained with her all of her days. He taught her everything that captured his imagination, telling her stories from Herodotus and Aesop, teaching her words and phrases in the languages of other peoples and reading her poems from across the ages.

My great-grandfather's approach to educating his daughter did not sit well with everyone in the village. The good religious folk took special exception to his subject matter as well as his choice of student. You see, he taught the Bible alongside other works, which offended those who thought that the Bible, and only the Bible, should be taught to children (or adults for that matter). Also, he scandalized his neighbors, religious and not-so-religious, by choosing to educate his girl-child, which went against long-standing custom in the village. When people would bemoan the fact that he had no sons he would quickly retort, "But I have a daughter who is smarter than seven sons." He meant seven of *their* sons, and they knew it.

So my great-grandfather was not an outwardly religious man, perhaps because he saw the religious folk intentionally cutting themselves and their children off from much knowledge and insight he found valuable. When the soldiers came, though, they made no distinction between religious and non-religious. All the people of the village, including my grandmother and her father, were packed into railroad cars so tightly that there was no room to sit and hardly room to breathe. When they arrived at the camp my grandmother was sent with the women and her father with the men.

Lists of nations like the one given here were often found in writings of historians and geographers of the time. Such lists are intended to represent the entire world by listing its major races or kingdoms. Luke's list here bears some similarity to lists of astrologers, who condensed to twelve—the same number as in the zodiac—the basic kingdoms of the world. This list includes legendary kingdoms from the past (Parthians and Medes) as well as national identities current in Luke's day. A similar list, intending to represent in a comprehensive way the kingdoms of the world conquered by the Romans, appears in Curtius Rufus 6.3.3 (mid-first-century C.E.): "We have made ourselves masters of Caria, Lydia, Cappadocia, Phrygia, Paphlagonia, Pamphylia, the Pisidians, Cilicia, Syria, Phoenicia, Armenia, Persia, the Medes, and Parthiene." (Haenchen, 14-15)

My grandmother told me that there was one man at the camp, a physician who was supposed to promote life and health, who, whenever he arrived in his white, starched-lab coat, was referred to as "the angel of death." His touch was death, his look was death, she would tell me. While other children grew up with ogres and trolls, the figure who appeared to me in nightmares was this angel of death.

Even those whom the angel of death passed over were underfed and overworked. They slept without mattress or covers on hard wooden bunks. "We looked like firewood stacked there waiting to be burned," she told me. "In fact," she said, "we were waiting for the angel of death to come and call our number; we were waiting to be burned. And they gave us no more consideration than a stick of wood. We were not human; we were fuel. We used to joke and ask if anyone knew why we didn't celebrate Passover in the camps? The answer was that it was our blood over the doors and even that could not stop the angel of death. It was a cruel joke—but true."

By the time the end of the war came my grandmother was so weak that she could hardly get out of her bed. One day she saw a vision—angels dressed in khaki speaking in unknown tongues. Yet she understood every word. She thought at first she was hallucinating, because she understood what they were saying. The language they spoke was neither Yiddish nor any other language with which she was familiar. She heard life. She heard freedom.

"Some said they were American soldiers," she told me, "but I say they were angels speaking in angelic tongues. When I tell my Christian friends about it," she continued, "they say it was Pentecost. But for me it was another holy day. For me Passover had finally come."

As I grew up I decided that Nana was not crazy after all. In fact, she is the sanest person I know.

(Michael E. Williams)

> Philo, the first-century C.E. Jewish philosopher, also envisioned a supernatural voice having an appearance like a flame of fire when he retold the story of God speaking to the people from Mount Sinai: "Then from the midst of the fire that streamed from heaven there sounded forth to their utter amazement a voice, for the flame became articulate speech in the language familiar to the audience, and so clearly and distinctly were the words formed by it that they seemed to see rather than hear them." (*Decalogue* 46)

ACTS 3:1–4:24, 31

Giving and Receiving

Peter and John heal a crippled man in the temple, which leads to their arrest and examination by the court.

The Story

ONE day at three in the afternoon, the hour of prayer, Peter and John were on their way up to the temple. Now a man who had been a cripple from birth used to be carried there and laid every day by the temple gate called Beautiful to beg from people as they went in. When he saw Peter and John on their way into the temple, he asked for alms. They both fixed their eyes on him, and Peter said, 'Look at us.' Expecting a gift from them, the man was all attention. Peter said, 'I have no silver or gold; but what I have I give you: in the name of Jesus Christ of Nazareth, get up and walk.' Then, grasping him by the right hand he helped him up; and at once his feet and ankles grew strong; he sprang to his feet, and started to walk. He entered the temple with them, leaping and praising God as he went. Everyone saw him walking and praising God, and when they recognized him as the man who used to sit begging at Beautiful Gate they were filled with wonder and amazement at what had happen to him.

While he still clung to Peter and John all the people came running in astonishment towards them in Solomon's Portico, as it is called. Peter saw them coming and met them with these words: 'Men of Israel, why be surprised at this? Why stare at us as if we had made this man walk by some power of godliness of our own? The God of Abraham, Isaac, and Jacob, the God of our fathers, has given the highest honour to his servant Jesus, whom you handed over for trail and disowned in Pilate's court—disowned the holy and righteous one when Pilate had decided to release him. You asked for the reprieve of a murderer, and killed the Prince of life. But God raised him from the dead; of that we are witnesses. The name of Jesus, by awakening faith, has given strength to this man whom you see and know, and this faith has made him completely well as you can all see.

'Now, my friends, I know quite well that you acted in ignorance, as did your rulers; but this is how God fulfilled what he had foretold through all the prophets: that his Messiah would suffer. Repent, therefore, and turn to God, so that your sins may be wiped out. Then the Lord may grant you a time of recovery and send the Messiah appointed for you, that is, Jesus. He must be received into heaven until the time comes for the universal restoration of which God has spoken through his holy prophets from the beginning. Moses said, "The Lord God will raise up for you a prophet like me from among yourselves. Listen to every thing he says to you, for anyone who refuses to listen to that prophet must be cut off from the people." From Samuel onwards, every prophet who spoke predicted this present time.

'You are the heirs of the prophets, and of the covenant which God made with your fathers when he said to Abraham, "And in your offspring all the families on earth shall find blessing." When God raised up his servant, he sent him to you first, to bring you blessing by turning every one of you from your wicked ways.'

They were still addressing the people when the chief priests, together with the controller of the temple and the Sadducees, broke in on them, annoyed because they were proclaiming the resurrection from the dead by teaching the people about Jesus. They were arrested and, as it was already evening, put in prison for the night. But many of those who had heard the message became believers, bringing the number of men to about five thousand.

Next day the Jewish rulers, elders, and scribes met in Jerusalem. There were present Annas the high priest, Caiaphas, John, Alexander, and all who were of the high-priestly family. They brought the apostles before the court and began to interrogate them. 'By what power', they asked, 'or by what name have such men as you done this?' Then Peter, filled with the Holy Spirit, answered, 'Rulers of the people and elders, if it is about help given to a sick man that we are being questioned today, and the means by which he was cured, this is our answer to all of you and to all the people of Israel: it was by the name of Jesus

Christ of Nazareth, whom you crucified, and whom God raised from the dead; through him this man stands here before you fit and well. This Jesus is the stone, rejected by you the builders, which has become the corner-stone. There is no salvation through anyone else; in all the world no other name has been granted to mankind by which we can be saved.'

Observing that Peter and John were uneducated laymen, they were astonished at their boldness and took note that they had been companions of Jesus; but with the man who had been cured standing in full view beside them, they had nothing to say in reply. So they ordered them to leave the court, and then conferred among themselves. 'What are we to do with these men?' they said. 'It is common knowledge in Jerusalem that a notable miracle has come about through them; and we cannot deny it. But to stop this from spreading farther among the people, we had better caution them never again to speak to anyone in this name.' They then called them in and ordered them to refrain from all public speaking and teaching in the name of Jesus.

But Peter and John replied: 'Is it right in the eyes of God for us to obey you rather than him? Judge for yourselves. We cannot possibly give up speaking about what we have seen and heard.'

With a repeated caution the court discharged them. They could not see how they were to punish them, because the people were all giving glory to God for what had happened. The man upon whom this miracle of healing had been performed was over forty years old.

As soon as they were discharged the

apostles went back to their friends and told them everything that the chief priests and elders had said. When they heard it, they raised their voices with one accord and called upon God.

. . . .

When they had ended their prayer, the building where they were assembled rocked, and all were filled with the Holy Spirit and spoke God's word with boldness.

Comments on the Story

The pattern of chapter 2 continues: a miracle brings a crowd to whom a sermon is addressed. (Such stories are synecdoches of the early Christian mission, condensed reports of growth.) There is an important difference from Pentecost: the first signs of official opposition. Mission and opposition will grow in tandem.

On their way to prayer at the time of the evening sacrifice, Peter and John encounter a crippled beggar. Temple gates were good "pitches" for such unfortunates, both because of the crowds who flowed through them and the propriety of a good deed while engaged in worship. The temple was also the center of Luke 1–2, so that the new story recapitulates the old. Just as Jesus had taught in the temple, so will his apostles. Moreover, they, too, can heal. As the stories of exorcism (cf. Mark 5:1-20; Acts 19:13-17) indicate, names convey power. Among those who utilized this power were magicians who provided numerous personal services—for, of course, a suitable fee. The apostles do not carry money, but they share what they have, and it terminates a career: this petitioner will never have to beg again. Reference to "silver or gold" sets a dramatic contrast, while distinguishing apostles from magicians. Community money is not their property.

The language of the healing evokes what it symbolizes: rising to new life. The one restored responds with ecstatic praise, in words (v. 8) that recall Isa. 35:6 (cf. Luke 7:22). Fulfillment continues. When a crowd gathers, Peter has a sermon to hand, like that of chapter two, but with appropriate focus on the name and titles of Jesus. The people of Jerusalem were ironically responsible for killing the author of life. They can repent and gain forgiveness and the promised "universal refreshment," reinforced by reference to Abraham, through whom God had promised universal beatitude.

Just as Peter is about to climax his sermon with an appeal, the forces of evil burst upon him. Not only the temple police, but also their supervisors, the priests, and representatives of a party, the Sadducees, make the arrest. Acts represents the early believers as allied with Pharisees in a partisan quarrel with the Sadducees. Since it is too late in the day, the hearing must be postponed until tomorrow. Suspense rises.

When that day arrives, the pair are arraigned before the Sanhedrin, a fate Jesus had also experienced. The Council is portrayed in all of its power and solemnity. What can two humble Galileans do against such authority and prestige? At stake are not the facts of the case, but its grounds (cf. Luke 11:14; 20:2). Magic is the charge. "Oh," says Peter, in effect, "Do you wish to condemn us for well–doing?" Having rebutted the charge, he proceeds to lay before them the creed proclaimed earlier to the crowd. The result is different.

The eloquence of these two presumed yokels, former fishermen without a trace of professional education or social standing, takes the Sanhedrin aback. With these few strokes the narrator manifests the power of Pentecost. By ineptly including the healed man in the proceedings, the Sanhedrin is at a disadvantage. The circumstances call for an executive session that, through the omniscient narrator, hearers can attend. Their question, "What are we to do?" is the same as that of the crowd in 2:37, but the motive differs. The Council opts for damage control, imposing a gag order.

This classic example of locking the barn door once the horse has bolted won't work. Peter and John, who had, like philosophers, taught in the temple portico (3:11), now take the role of philosophers in the face of ruthless tyrants. Each side has shown its cards. The frustrated Sanhedrin can do no more than utter shrill threats, since public opinion inhibits them from anything more drastic. The once hapless apostles now imitate their master in stirring sermons and mighty deeds, receiving, like Jesus, popular acclaim and official scorn. Verse 22 reports the age of their beneficiary. Such data, which serve to prove that this was no short-term malady but a life-long affliction, properly belong in the healing account. By delaying the information until this moment, the narrator has heightened its impact. More important, he has made of 3:1–4:22 one lengthy miracle story.

Verses 23-31 ratify this understanding in a communal context. Peter and John have had things very much their own way. Their very similarity to Jesus is thrilling, but it also raises suspense for any who remember the outcome of Jesus' confrontation with the Sanhedrin. The community does not ask for deliverance from danger, but for courage and healing power. The earth shakes. Indeed, before the story is done, the farthest corners of the earth will tremble.

Retelling the Story

> Peter said, 'I have no silver or gold; but what I have I give you: in the name of Jesus Christ of Nazareth, get up and walk.' (Acts 3:6)

The light of dawn was sifting through the morning mist as the old man began his journey toward waking. In his dreams he was being chased but was unable to flee. He was immobilized as one can be only in dreams, beyond any waking debilitation. As consciousness crept upon him it was the ache that woke him. It had worsened over the past few years and offered no promise of improvement. It was not the memory of lost loves or passing strength that brought him back to the waking world but the plain, biting pain that accompanied his every move.

His still-strong hands pulled each leg to the edge of the pallet and forced his feet to make contact with the floor. The muscles of his arms engaged to pull his body up to a seated position. There he paused until the world within his vision stopped whirling like some ecstatic dancer. He slipped on his sandals, then stood slowly and carefully, holding onto the wall as he made his way toward the door and the sun that had by now completely burned away the mist.

As soon as he passed from the darkness of the interior of the house into the sunshine, the children left their games and emerged from doorways and shadows to surround him. "Good morning, Grandfather. Let us help you sit down." They called to the old man. Mostly, though, they begged, "Tell us a story."

The old man knew many stories and told them all with little provocation. There was one story, though, that he always told, especially now that the aches and pains were such constant companions.

"My legs hurt me something terrible this morning," he began. He always started this particular story with an allusion to his legs and how poorly they worked these days. "Which reminds me of a gift I once received."

"What was it?" the children shouted with the confidence of those who already know the answer. In truth, they had heard this story so often they not only knew their responses by heart, most could have picked up the narrative in midsentence if the old man had needed them to.

"It was the middle of the afternoon on a day like any other day," he said. "I was sitting at the gate called Beautiful asking for alms as I had every day of my life since I was younger than most of you. Unable to walk or even stand without help, I depended on the generosity of others. On a good day, from time to time, a kind soul would press a coin into my hand. On a bad day people would look away when I spoke to them as if I wasn't there at all. This day would turn out like no other day in my life.

"As I sat there I saw two men walking toward me. I cast my eyes down and cried, 'Alms for the poor, alms for a poor lame man.' I could see from their feet that they both had stopped in front of me and were looking my way. I tilted my head back and when their eyes caught mine they locked my gaze with theirs. They made no move to look or move away, nor did they press a coin in my hand. I was confused and not a little frightened by their behavior.

"The taller of the two men, the one they called Peter, took my right hand in his as if he might give me something. Instead, though, he told me, 'I have no money to give you, but what I have to give you will find so much more precious than silver or gold.'

41

"I tell you I was confused and getting more frightened with every breath. Then the man said to me in a voice that was commanding, 'In the name of Jeshua of Nazareth stand up and walk.' And before I remembered that I couldn't walk, I was standing with only the slight pressure of his hand on mine. Then I was leaping and dancing. Everyone must have thought me quite the fool for the way I behaved as I walked along with my two new friends. But I didn't care. Every movement was a new experience for me.

"It was the finest gift I ever received, far more valuable than silver or gold, just as Peter had said. You would think that people who could give such good gifts would be honored and rewarded, but it was not so for my friends. Their kindness toward me brought them nothing but hostility and suspicion.

"Every ache and pain in my legs each morning is a reminder of that gift. I thank God for every one of them. And I thank God for every one of you. Now, I will tell you a story I learned from that same Peter about Jeshua of Nazareth. . . ."

> The reply of Peter and John to the court that they cannot refrain from obeying and speaking about God is reminiscent of the reply of Socrates to the Athenian court in Plato's *Apology* 29 C-D (fourth-century B.C.E.): "Men of Athens, I respect and love you, but I shall obey the god rather than you, and while I live and am able to continue I shall never give up philosophy, or stop exhorting you and pointing out the truth to any one of you whom I may meet." (Boring, no. 494)

The old man's voice had taken on an energy of youth that defied his age. From time to time as he told his stories he would rise and leap and dance like the man who thought himself foolish on that afternoon so many years ago.

(Michael E. Williams)

> Just as in Acts 4:31, pagan literature also represented answers to prayer by means of an earthquake: "I was paying homage to the god's temple. . . . 'Grant, father, an omen, and inspire our hearts!' Scarcely had I thus spoken, when suddenly it seemed all things trembled, the doors and laurels of the god; the whole hill shook round about and the tripod moaned as the shrine was thrown open. Prostrate we fall to earth, and a voice comes to our ears." (Virgil, *Aeneid* 3.84-89 [first-century B.C.E.]; Boring, no. 495)

Life in the Spirit

The early Christians subscribe to an ancient social ideal, the sharing of resources, and when Ananias and Sapphira do not comply, they are punished by God.

The Story

A sense of awe was felt by everyone, and many portents and signs were brought about through the apostles. All the believers agreed to hold everything in common: they began to sell their property and possessions and distribute to everyone according to his need. One and all they kept up their daily attendance at the temple, and, breaking bread in their homes, they shared their meals with unaffected joy, as they praised God and enjoyed the favour of the whole people. And day by day the Lord added new converts to their number.

. . . .

THE whole company of believers was united in heart and soul. Not one of them claimed any of his possessions as his own; everything was held in common. With great power the apostles bore witness to the resurrection of the Lord Jesus, and all were held in high esteem. There was never a needy person among them, because those who had property in land or houses would sell it, bring the proceeds of the sale, and lay them at the feet of the apostles, to be distributed to any who were in need. For instance Joseph, surnamed by the apostles Barnabas (which means 'Son of Encouragement'), a Levite and by birth a Cypriot, sold an estate which he owned; he brought the money and laid it at the apostles feet.

But a man called Ananias sold a property, and with the connivance of his wife Sapphira kept back some of the proceeds, and brought part only to lay at the apostles' feet. Peter said, 'Ananias, how was it that Satan so possessed your mind that you lied to the Holy Spirit by keeping back part of the price of the land? While it remained unsold, did it not remain yours? Even after it was turned into money, was it not still at your own disposal? What made you think of doing this? You have lied not to men but to God.' When Ananias heard these words he dropped dead; and all who heard were awestruck. The younger men rose and covered his body, then carried him out and buried him.

About three hours passed, and his wife came in, unaware of what had happened. Peter asked her, 'Tell me, were you paid such and such a price for the land?' 'Yes,' she replied, 'that was the price.' Peter said, 'Why did the two of you conspire to put the Spirit of the Lord to the test? Those who buried your husband are there at the door, and they will carry you away.' At once she dropped dead at his feet. When the young men came in, they found her dead; and they carried her out and buried her beside her husband.

Great awe fell on the whole church and on all who heard of this.

Comments on the Story

The various "summaries" in Acts, such as 2:43-47, are like hinges. They point two ways, rounding off one section and introducing the next. Unison prayer (4:23-31) is remarkable, unison property even more so. The activity described is not properly called "communism," for it does not involve common ownership of the means of production but the liquidation and distribution of capital. Unlike wealthy benefactors, who gave freely but controlled what they gave, these donors surrender their goods to the church, epitomized in its leaders. Luke thus depicts how early Christians prevented the more wealthy members of the community from taking power by making "clients" of others. The language proclaims this miracle as a realization both of Greco-Roman ideals (society as a circle of friends sharing all) and of an Israelite commandment (Deut. 15:4; Acts 4:34). Here is another kind of "Pentecost," making one new culture from old forms.

Two case histories give the summaries specific color. The first example is that of Barnabas, provided with an introduction so elaborate that one may expect to hear of him again. The nickname, as interpreted (Barnabas may mean something like "Son of Nebo," a Babylonian deity), intimates preaching ability (13:15; Heb. 13:22). He is a Levite, thoroughly Jewish, and a representative of the Diaspora (Cyprus).

Ananias and Sapphira are the subject of the second case, which begins well enough. They, however, wished to enjoy the renown of perfect generosity while retaining something for a rainy day. That day comes rather soon, and their cash reserves won't help. The narrative assumes that the practice would have been acceptable. What was not acceptable was their deceit. Spiritual power is not limited to healing those who can't walk or by opening ears. In this instance the Spirit serves as both financial auditor and executioner, through the hand of Peter. The identical fate of Sapphira does much to enhance the quality of the narrative. At the theological level, her demise eliminates any possibility that Ananias's expiration was a piece of particularly bad luck.

The narrative is not particularly realistic. Is one to envision an assembly, as the "youth group" suggests? Does this remain in session for some hours? The coincidence of the return of "young men" with Sapphira's departure is both dramatically effective and theologically apt. The Spirit of God is directing this scene. The author of this deception is Satan, of course. The fate of Ananias and Sapphira is a timely reminder that Satan can find other agents than wicked officials and evil priests. Some of them are close to home. The couple who falsely claimed to have deposited all at Peter's feet were promptly deposited six feet under.

Distilled of thrills and chills, the essence of this story is that the Spirit works in the community to produce both blessing and curse. Christians for very many centuries found such tales particularly edifying (cf. 1 Cor. 5:3-5). Today these must be handled with some profundity and much delicacy. Among the refinements in the tale are many cross-references, including the ubiquitous and ironic "feet," the contrast between God and mortals (5:4), which binds this with the previous (4:19) and subsequent (5:29) trials, and parallels with the story of Judas. There are two miracles here: the generosity of Barnabas and the "executions" of the deceiving couple. Readers are invited to choose.

Retelling the Story

> The younger men rose and covered his body, then carried him out and buried him. (Acts 5:6)

It was the weirdest job the young men had ever been asked to do. When they were asked if they wanted to be a part of a young-adult group, they had thought it meant social gatherings and Bible studies. Never in their wildest dreams had any of them even considered the possibility of what they were being asked to do now.

Giving all their worldly possessions into the care of Peter and the others had been no problem. Most of them were young enough that they hadn't acquired enough to be loathe to give it up. The only one with any property to speak of was Barnabas, and he gave that up without uttering so much as a peep. He was a good example for the rest who sacrificed so little to become a part of this group. In fact, he exemplified the best the group had to offer, always ready to offer a hand to those who stumbled and a second chance to those who fell.

The young adults had returned that day thinking this would be an ordinary evening of coffee and store-bought cookies when one of the servants called them over to speak with them privately.

The ideal that comrades should share goods in common was widely known in the ancient world. Aristotle expressed it in this way: "The proverb says, 'Friends' goods are common property,' and this is correct, since community is the essence of friendship. Brothers have all things in common, and so do members of a comradeship; other friends hold special possessions in common, more or fewer in different cases, inasmuch as friendships vary in degree." (*Nicomachean Ethics*, 8-9 [fourth-century B.C.]; Boring, no. 492)

"I have something of a delicate matter to discuss with you," said the servant. "Tell me, do any of you know how to use a shovel? You're obviously strapping young men. Peter has a job for you."

"What are you talking about?" the young men asked.

"Remember the late Ananias?" the servant inquired.

"What do you mean?" said one. "I saw Ananias this morning. There was nothing 'late' about him then."

"Well, there will be from now on," replied the servant. "After this he'll be late for everything. In fact he won't be showing up at all."

"Tell us what this crazy talk is all about," they demanded.

When Josephus described the common life of the Jewish sect of Essenes he idealized their communal lifestyle, just as Luke idealized the communal life of the early Christians. "Riches they despise, and their community of goods is truly admirable; you will not find one among them distinguished by greater opulence than another. They have a law that new members on admission to the sect shall confiscate their property to the order, with the result that you will nowhere see either abject poverty or inordinate wealth; the individual's possessions join the common stock and all, like brothers, enjoy a single patrimony." (*Jewish War* 2.122 [late-first-century C.E.]; from Boring, no. 491)

"Just a little while ago," the servant began, "Peter called Ananias in to ask him about a piece of property he and Sapphira had sold. Ananias had said that they had entrusted all the proceeds into the care of the apostles, but it seems they weren't telling the truth, the whole truth, and nothing but the truth. And Peter knew it. Of course, they didn't have to give everything to the group. But they wanted to claim that they had, so that everyone would be impressed that they were big givers. But when Peter investigated the matter, it became clear to him that the figures just didn't add up. So Peter informed Ananias and Sapphira that they had not just lied to him and the whole community—they had lied to God."

"Wow," said one of the young men. "So I guess Ananias confessed and threw himself on the mercy of the apostles?"

"Not exactly," the servant replied.

"I know," said another of the young men. "He offered to give the rest of the money into the care of the apostles and make amends to the community."

"Well, no," said the servant.

"So what happened?" they all inquired.

"Well," said the servant, "you might say that this is where you come in. Looking back on it, I think maybe Ananias was nervous. After all, sometimes nerves can make us say things before we think. Or maybe he thought a little humor would lighten the tension of the situation. I don't know. But when he opened his mouth, he just said the wrong thing."

"Which was?" they asked.

The servant replied: "He said, 'If I'm lyin', I'm dyin.' " So he did."

"Did what?" they asked.

"Died," said the servant.

"Ananias died?" they asked incredulously.

"Yes," said the servant. "Fell down and died and is lying in the next room as we speak."

So the young men, stunned that their group meeting had turned into a burial detail, followed him into the next room where Ananias was, indeed, lying in a heap on the floor. Though it was difficult and dirty work, the young men saw to it that Ananias was given a burial. And as for the money he had cherished so deeply—well, it turned out to be of no avail to him at all.

The young men returned tired but satisfied that they had done the community—and, in a way, Ananias—a service. As they made ready for a bath and bed the servant approached them once more.

"Don't change your clothes," he said.

(Michael E. Williams)

The Jewish community of Qumran, which was probably a sect of Essenes, defined penalties for lying about one's property that had been turned over to the common store: "If one of them has lied deliberately in matters of property, he shall be excluded from the pure meal of the congregation for one year and shall do penance with respect to one quarter of his food" (1QS 6:24-25 [first-century B.C.E.]; Boring, no. 496). Luke's account here in Acts, however, is closer in form to the Old Testament account of divine punishment in 1 Kings 14:1-18, in which the prophet Ahijah predicts the death of the son of Jereboam in a form similar to the story of Ananias and Sapphira.

Who Is in Charge?

Increasing success kindles official rage, which is twice thwarted.

The Story

Many signs and wonders were done among the people by the apostles. All the believers used to meet by common consent in Solomon's Portico; no one from outside their number ventured to join them, yet people in general spoke highly of them. An ever-increasing number of men and women who believed in the Lord were added to their ranks. As a result the sick were carried out into the streets and laid there on beds and stretchers, so that at least Peter's shadow might fall on one or another as he passed by; and the people from the towns round Jerusalem flocked in, bringing those who were ill or harassed by unclean spirits, and all were cured.

Then the high priest and his colleagues, the Sadducean party, were goaded by jealousy to arrest the apostles and put them in official custody. But during the night, an angel of the Lord opened the prison doors, led them out, and said, 'Go, stand in the temple and tell the people all about this new life.' Accordingly they entered the temple at daybreak and went on with their teaching.

When the high priest arrived with his colleagues they summoned the Sanhedrin, the full Council of the Israelite nation, and sent to the jail for the prisoners. The officers who went to the prison failed to find them there, so they returned and reported, 'We found the jail securely locked at every point, with the warders at their posts by the doors, but on opening them we found no one inside.' When they heard this, the controller of the temple and the chief priests were at a loss to know what could have become of them, until someone came and reported: 'The men you put in prison are standing in the temple teaching the people.' Then the controller went off with the officers and fetched them, but without use of force, for fear of being stoned by the people.

When they had been brought in and made to stand before the Council, the high priest began his examination. 'We gave you explicit orders,' he said, 'to stop teaching in that name; and what has happened? You have filled Jerusalem with your teaching, and you are trying to hold us responsible for that man's death.' Peter replied for the apostles: 'We must obey God rather than men. The God of our fathers raised up Jesus; after you had put him to death by hanging him on a gibbet, God exalted him at his right hand as leader and saviour, to grant Israel repentance and forgiveness of sins. And we are witnesses to all this, as is the Holy Spirit who is given by God to those obedient to him.'

This touched them on the raw, and they wanted to put them to death. But a member of the Council rose to his feet, a Pharisee called Gamaliel, a teacher of the law held in high regard by all the people. He had the men put outside for a while, and then said, 'Men of Israel, be very careful in deciding what to do with these men. Some time ago Theudas came forward, making claims for himself, and a number of our people, about four hundred, joined him. But he was killed and his whole movement was destroyed and came to nothing. After him came Judas the Galilean at the time of the census; he induced some people to revolt under his leadership, but he too perished and his whole movement was broken up. Now, my advice to you is this: keep clear of these men; let them alone. For if what is being planned and done is human in origin, it will collapse; but if it is from God, you will never be able to stamp it out, and you risk finding yourselves at war with God.'

Convinced by this, they sent for the apostles and had them flogged; then they ordered them to give up speaking in the name of Jesus, and discharged them. The apostles went out from the Council rejoicing that they had been found worthy to suffer humiliation for the sake of the name. And every day they went steadily on with their teaching in the temple and in private houses, telling the good news of Jesus the Messiah.

Comments on the Story

Growth, marked by both the first recorded Christian expansion to the suburbs and the intensification of miraculous power, encapsulated in the potency of Peter's very shadow, brings the light of hope to many and lengthens the shadow of gloom in which the authorities sit. They will not sit still for long.

"Goaded by jealousy," the authorities jail the Twelve. As in 4:1, a night will intervene. Day will cast the shadow of judgment upon the apostles, who have no reason to expect leniency. So the Sadducees can sleep, perchance to dream of vengeance. Meanwhile, an angel foils their plans, not merely to spring some apostles out of jail, but to allow the spring of new life to flow freely. Without a thought for angelic intervention—they do not believe in angels (23:8)—the assembly gathers in all its pomp and majesty to exorcise this threat to their security and dignity. The constables return to report a difficulty: the scrupulously guarded prisoners have disappeared. Their news throws the stately chamber into disarray, a state scarcely abated by the arrival of a messenger to tell them what the hearers know. Guards must then be sent to extricate the insurgent apostles from the temple, tactfully, of course, lest the crowd prevent the arrest by stoning the police. (This is not the last time we shall hear of stones.)

That task accomplished, the trial may now proceed. The chief priest can do no more than underscore his earlier warning. Led by Peter, the Twelve vigorously reassert the precedence of divine will over human command. His words are in full accordance with Jewish thought. They also echo the defense of Socrates before his accusers. Heaven, Peter says, has not sanctioned this trial.

49

He goes on to affirm that the Sanhedrin is, in fact, responsible for the death of Jesus. That does it. In their fury the judges determine upon the death penalty. This sentence would doubtless have been promptly carried out had not, at the last moment, a learned and venerable Pharisee asked for an executive session, to which he delivers a few well-chosen sentences, the burden of which is that decision should be left in God's hands. He supports this by two examples of terrorist movements. In short, Gamaliel and Peter share the same view: what God endorses cannot be extinguished. Said to be convinced, the Sanhedrin is clearly unrepentant, for they repeat their somewhat tattered admonitions, punctuated with a touch of the whip. The unrepentant apostles return to their duties.

How much Luke has packed into twenty-five verses: another foreboding arrest, a wondrous delivery, an exciting trial, comedy, and bountiful suspense! Two finely crafted little speeches color the narrative. As violence looms larger, mission increases. Through the mouth of a theoretical opponent, Gamaliel (historically known as one of the formative teachers of what would become rabbinic Judaism), the vast chasm between the Jesus movement and advocates of violent resistance is affirmed. Gamaliel urges his colleagues to wait and see which side God is on. Readers have no doubt about God's position on this matter.

Retelling the Story

The officers who went to the prison failed to find them there, so they returned and reported, 'We found the jail securely locked at every point, with the warders at their posts by the doors, but on opening them we found no one inside.' (Acts 5:22-23)

Miraculous prison escape stories were widespread in ancient literature. An example is found in Euripides' *Bacchae* (fifth-century B.C.E.): "The bonds [of the prisoners] loosed themselves from their feet and the bolted doors opened themselves without mortal hands" (455). This story in Acts takes a different tack by having the divine being actually appear and lead the prisoner to safety.

"They're out of jail again," reported the officer.

"Not again!" said Gamaliel. "How do you know?"

"I saw them preaching at the Temple this morning," replied the officer.

"How did they get out?" asked Gamaliel. "I thought you saw to it yourself that they were locked securely in the jail last night?"

"I did, sir," said the officer sheepishly.

"Then how could they have gotten out?" asked Gamaliel. "And don't tell me an angel did it."

"Would you believe an angel did it, sir?" gulped the officer.

"I told you not to tell me that!" bellowed Gamaliel. Glancing up at the heavens, he continued, "Why am I surrounded by such incompetents?" Then he turned back to the officer. "Can't you carry out a simple order—just put the prisoners in the cell and lock the door. Is that too hard? Is that too much to ask?"

The officer said nothing. He continued to stare straight ahead and looked very uncomfortable.

"Come with me," said Gamaliel. "I want to check this out for myself."

Gamaliel and the officer walked across the plaza to the jail and went in. They came upon the jailer who was leaning against the wall snoring softly. Gamaliel walked over to him, put his mouth next to the man's ear, and bellowed: "Attention!" The man started, lost his balance, and fell in a heap to the floor. When he finally got his feet underneath him, he jumped to attention, saluted, and yelled out, "*Sir!* At your service, *Sir!*"

Gamaliel glared at him and asked demandingly, "Where are the prisoners?"

"Why, in the jail, sir," said the jailer.

"Are you sure?" asked Gamaliel.

"Yes, sir. I locked them in myself last night," replied the jailer.

"Show me," said Gamaliel.

"Yes, *Sir!* Right this way, *Sir!*" said the jailer. He led Gamaliel and the officer down a hallway to a dark, dank cell. The huge, oaken door was shut tight.

"Open it," demanded Gamaliel. The jailer hesitated, then got a blank expression on his face. "Well?"

"I can't, sir," said the jailer, "I don't have the key."

"Well, where *is* it?" Gamaliel yelled, getting more agitated by the minute.

"It's in my desk drawer, sir," said the jailer, in a meek, whiny voice.

"Then *get it!*"

"Yes *Sir!*" said the jailer, and he immediately scurried off down the hall. Gamaliel and the officer stood in front of the cell impatiently as they heard in the distance drawers opening and closing and small items being scattered on the floor. Finally the jailer returned with a triumphant grin on his face and the keys tightly grasped in his hand.

"Now, show me the prisoners!" Gamaliel urged.

The jailer opened the lock and, with a great deal of huffing and puffing, pushed back the heavy door. "Here they are, sir."

"Here who are?" asked Gamaliel.

"Why the pris . . . they're gone!" shouted the jailer.

"Right, Sherlock," said Gamaliel. "Give me those keys!" Gamaliel took the keys and checked the door, opening and closing it several times until he was satisfied that the lock was in working order. Then he turned to the two men and glared at them. "I need answers," he said. "I need to know how you can let a measly group of peasant prisoners escape from this prison every time we put

> Imprisonment works in the story not as an embarrassment but rather as a form of verification. Such stories of persecution were often found in religious propaganda of various sects. Juvenal, the satirist, refers to such stories with typical disdain: "Fellows like these are believed if they've been in some far-off prison, shackled hand and foot: if he hasn't a prison record, then he has not renown, but a sentence to one of the islands, a narrow escape from death, procures him a reputation." (*Satire* 6.560-64 [early-second-century C.E.]; Pervo, *Profit*, 25)

them in it." The jailer and the officer began sweating profusely. "Was this door opened at all during the night?" asked Gamaliel.

"No, sir," they replied in unison.

"Was it opened this morning?"

"No, sir."

"Can the door be opened without a key?"

"No, sir."

"Look around. Do you see any holes in the wall? Do you see any loose bars in the window? Do you see any tunnels in the floor?"

"No, sir."

"Then tell me," said Gamaliel, "How did they get out? I want an answer, and I want it now. And don't tell me an angel did it."

No answer.

"Well?" repeated Gamaliel.

No answer.

"I'm waiting."

"Would you . . . would you believe an angel did it?" replied the jailer, in a meek voice.

"I told you not to tell me that!" bellowed Gamaliel, hitting them both over the head with the keys. "You two are in real trouble. You haven't heard the last of this. What are your names?"

"Laurel, sir," said the jailer.

"Hardy, sir," said the officer.

"Well, I am going to report this to your superiors," said Gamaliel. "But first, I have to report to *my* superiors. How am I going to explain this to them?"

"Tell them an angel did it, sir?" said Jailer Laurel.

Gamaliel's face turned red and he struggled to say something to Jailer Laurel, but the words just would not come out. Finally, he threw the keys to the floor and stalked off, leaving Jailer Laurel and Officer Hardy standing sheepishly at the door to the empty cell.

"Tell them an angel did it, sure," muttered Gamaliel, as he strode angrily to the council hall. "They'll love that. We're having a bloody angel's convention here—angels showing up everywhere! And with no respect for law and order! It's not fair. They get angels—I get Laurel and Hardy. You would think those people had God on their side or something!" *(Dennis E. Smith)*

ACTS 6:1-7

New Occasions Teach New Duties

When growth leads to potential conflict, the apostles quickly propose an acceptable solution. The result: more growth.

The Story

DURING this period, when disciples were growing in number, a grievance arose on the part of those who spoke Greek, against those who spoke the language of the Jews; they complained that their widows were being overlooked in the daily distribution. The Twelve called the whole company of disciples together and said, 'It would not be fitting for us to neglect the word of God in order to assist in the distribution. Therefore, friends, pick seven men of good repute from your number, men full of the Spirit and of wisdom, and we will appoint them for this duty; then we can devote ourselves to prayer and to the ministry of the word.' This proposal proved acceptable to the whole company. They elected Stephen, a man full of faith and of the Holy Spirit, along with Philip, Prochorus, Nicanor, Timon, Parmenas, and Nicolas of Antioch, who had been a convert to Judaism, and presented them to the apostles, who prayed and laid their hands on them.

The word of God spread more and more widely; the number of disciples in Jerusalem was increasing rapidly, and very many of the priests adhered to the faith.

Comments on the Story

Growth that includes diversity can lead to conflict. An influx of Greek-speaking Jews (like Barnabas) leads in this case to the charge that "widows" of non-Judean origin were being neglected in the daily administration of aid, which was evidently in the charge of native Aramaic speakers. For more than a century, scholars have attempted to elucidate thorny issues: was this an ethnic conflict, a problem in communication, or the result of theological differences? Whatever his sources, Luke views the issue from the perspective of his own day, which includes the desire to maintain unity among believers of different backgrounds. Widows, a disadvantaged group in most societies, had, by Luke's time, acquired some of the characteristics of a "religious order" with certain privileges and responsibilities. For centuries, widows would inspire and frustrate male leaders (cf. 1 Tim. 5).

Whatever the specific nature of the problem, the response is rapid and apt.

53

Summoning the entire community, the apostles suggest that (fuller?) attention to the matter on their part would detract from their "religious" obligations. They propose the selection of seven persons with spiritual and intellectual qualifications. The plan is deemed good. Seven, all with Greek names, are chosen and presented. The apostles qualify them by prayer and the imposition of hands. To Luke's first readers this would look like an ordination. Lists of names presage significant transitions in Acts (cf. 1:13; 13:1-3; 20:3-4). First on this list comes Stephen, whose particular gifts receive notice, then Philip. Last is Nicolas from Antioch, a gentile by birth. The significance of these facts will become apparent in due time.

What kind of story is this? In the first place it is a story about how to manage conflict, not by brushing aside complaints but through addressing them in the presence of all involved. *All* of those selected for administration seem to be Greek speakers. The solution thus involves not a token "Hellenist" or two, but assignment of the entire program to the minority group. This is also a tale about continuity and change. Change includes diversity: Greek speakers (who are the wave of the future). Continuity is less apparent until one observes how closely the text models itself upon Num. 11:4-26 and Exod. 18:7-13. Renewed Israel is like the Israel of old. Finally, this is a story of growth, notes about which bracket the narrative (vv. 1 and 8). Properly managed conflict will enhance growth rather than simply ease an impediment to it.

Retelling the Story

DURING this period, when disciples were growing in number, a grievance arose on the part of those who spoke Greek, against those who spoke the language of the Jews; they complained that their widows were being overlooked in the daily distribution. (Acts 6:1)

The church dinner was finally drawing to a close. Dishes clattered as the clearing of tables began. Suddenly, the people clearing the tables were at it again, bickering over who was going to handle the kitchen chores. Sometimes you had to wonder if this new Christian group was ever going to get off the ground.

"I'm not going to do the dishes," said one.

"Well, I'm certainly not going to do the dishes—it's not my turn," said another.

"Let's get Stevie to do it—he will do anything!" said the first. "Hey, Stevie!"

Stephen looked up from the table he was clearing and nodded. Yes, he would do the dishes. The others brought their stacks of dirty dishes over to him and left early. They knew they could depend on Stephen. He looked at the huge stack of dirty dishes and began to calculate how many hours it would take him. Then a coworker came over. "I'll help," said Philip. And the two of them rolled up their sleeves and got to work.

Starting up a soup kitchen had been a great idea. Everyone agreed it was the right thing to do. And, heaven knows, it sure was needed. Times were tough, and a lot of people were going hungry.

But keeping the soup kitchen going was another thing altogether. It seemed to bring out the worst in everyone.

Organized relief for the poor was a regular part of Jewish tradition. The Mishnah refers to a pauper's dish, which was a provision of food for poor travelers, and a poor basket, which was a weekly distribution of food and clothing to the poor in the community. Such practices must have been a model for the early Christians. (Jeremias, 131)

First there had been the disagreement about who was going to do the serving.

"I am not sure I have the strength," said one. "Those dishes are awfully heavy."

"I would help out, but something has come up at work," said another. "Maybe next time."

Then there was the problem about who deserved to be served.

"What are those people doing here?" they would say. "You are not going to serve them too, are you? What will people think? Look at how dirty they are. And such table manners! Why, we will never be able to live this down. Besides, listen to them talk—such a foul-sounding language. Why can't they speak our language if they want to come to our dinner?"

And so, the arguments continued. Finally the apostles decided they had to intervene.

"Look, people," said Peter, speaking for the other apostles, "we have to get organized."

"First, nobody is going to be turned away from this table. Jesus never turned anyone away, and neither are we.

"Second, it's a dirty job but somebody has to do it. We need some volunteers to take charge of this task and make sure it is done right. Matthias over here will form a committee and come up with a job description."

Within a few days the committee held its first meeting. Levi asked what

Justin Martyr described Christian relief activities as a normal activity of the church: "Those who are prosperous and willing give what each thinks fit, and what is collected is deposited with the president, who gives aid to orphans and widows and those who are in want on account of illness or any other cause, and to those also who are in prison and to strangers from abroad, and, in a word, cares for all who are in need." (*Apology* 1.67 [mid-second century C.E.])

qualifications they were looking for. He suggested they find people who were thrifty, so that they could be depended on to get the most out of each bowl of soup. Martha pointed out that there was an art to serving at the table. They needed people with food service experience.

But Matthias set them all straight. "Remember what brought about the problem in the first place," he said. "It was not lack of experience nor wastefulness. It was selfishness. We need people who will be willing to serve everyone, who won't play favorites."

"So moved," said Martha. "I second the motion," said Levi. It passed unanimously.

The next day the ad appeared in the church newsletter. It read: "Wanted: seven table servants. No previous experience necessary; training will be provided. Primary qualifications: compassion, generosity, a hospitable nature, a willingness to serve."

They were *not* swamped with applications.

But there were some obvious people for the job, the kind of people who could always be depended on when something needed to be done, the little people of the church who were willing to do the basic tasks that kept the church going. Among them were Philip and Stephen. *(Dennis E. Smith)*

Lucian, the second-century Greek satirical writer, described early Christians as gullible and easy touches, as exemplified by the way in which they responded to the needs of the charlatan Peregrinus: "So it was then in the case of Peregrinus; much money came to him from them by reason of his imprisonment, and he procured not a little revenue from it. The poor wretches (i.e., Christians) have convinced themselves, first and foremost, that they are going to be immortal and live for all time, in consequence of which they despise death and even willingly give themselves into custody, most of them. Furthermore, their first lawgiver persuaded them that they are all brothers of one another after they have transgressed once for all by denying the Greek gods and by worshiping that crucified sophist himself (i.e., Christ) and living under his laws. Therefore they despise all things indiscriminately and consider them common property, receiving such doctrines traditionally without any definite evidence. So if any charlatan and trickster, able to profit by occasions, comes among them he quickly acquires sudden wealth by imposing upon simple folk." (*The Death of Peregrinus* 13; Boring, no. 493)

The Death of an Expert Witness

Stephen is arraigned on trumped-up charges and delivers a lengthy
speech of justification, at the climax of which he is stoned to death.

The Story

Stephen, full of grace and power, began to do great wonders and signs among the people. Some members of the synagogue called the Synagogue of Freedmen, comprising Cyrenians and Alexandrians and people from Cilicia and Asia, came forward and argued with Stephen, but could not hold their own against the inspired wisdom with which he spoke. They then put up men to allege that they had heard him make blasphemous statements against Moses and against God. They stirred up the people and the elders and scribes, set upon him and seized him, and brought him before the Council. They produced false witnesses who said, 'This fellow is for ever saying things against this holy place and against the law. For we have heard him say this Jesus of Nazareth will destroy this place and alter the customs handed down to us by Moses.' All who were sitting in the Council fixed their eyes on him, and his face seemed to them like the face of an angel.

Then the high priest asked him, 'Is this true?' He replied, 'My brothers, fathers of this nation, listen to me. The God of glory appeared to Abraham our ancestor while he was in Mesopotamia, before he had settled in Harran, and said: "Leave your country and your kinsfolk, and come away to a land that I will show you." Thereupon he left the land of Chaldaeans and settled in Harran. From there, after his fathers death, God led him to migrate to this land where you now live. He gave him no foothold in it, nothing to call his own, but promised to give it as a possession for ever to him and to his descendants after him, though he was then childless. This is what God said: "Abraham's descendants shall live as aliens in a foreign land, held in slavery and oppression for four hundred years. And I will pass judgement," he said, "on the nation whose slaves they are; and after that they shall escape and worship me in this place." God gave Abraham the covenant of circumcision, and so, when his son Isaac was born, he circumcised him on the eighth day; and Isaac was the father of Jacob, and Jacob of the twelve patriarchs.

'The patriarchs out of jealousy sold Joseph into slavery in Egypt, but God was with him and rescued him from all his troubles. He gave him wisdom which so commended him to Pharaoh king of Egypt that he appointed him governor of Egypt and of the whole royal household.

'When famine struck all Egypt and Canaan, causing great distress, and our ancestors could find nothing to eat, Jacob heard that there was food in Egypt and sent our fathers there. This was their first visit. On the second visit Joseph made himself known to his brothers, and his ancestry was disclosed to Pharaoh. Joseph sent for his father Jacob and the whole family, seventy-five persons in all; and Jacob went down into Egypt. There he and our fathers ended their days. Their remains were later removed to Shechem and buried in the tomb for which Abraham paid a sum of money to the sons of Hamor at Shechem.

'Now as the time approached for God to fulfil the promise he had made to Abraham, our people in Egypt grew and increased in numbers. At length another king, who knew nothing of Joseph, ascended the throne of Egypt. He employed cunning to harm our race, and forced our ancestors to expose their children so that they should not survive. It was at this time that Moses was born. He was a fine child, and pleasing to God. For three months he was nursed in his fathers house; then when he was exposed, Pharaohs daughter adopted him and brought him up as her own son. So Moses was trained in all the wisdom of the Egyptians, a powerful speaker and a man of action.

'He was approaching the age of forty, when it occurred to him to visit his fellow-countrymen the Israelites. Seeing one of them being ill-treated, he went to his aid, and avenged the victim by striking down the Egyptian. He thought his countrymen would understand that God was offering them deliverance through him, but they did not understand. The next day he came upon two of them fighting, and tried to persuade them to make up their quarrel. "Men, you are brothers!" he said. "Why are you ill-treating one another?" But the man who was at fault pushed him away. "Who made you ruler and judge over us?" he said. "Are you going to kill me as you killed the Egyptian yesterday?" At this Moses fled the country and settled in Midianite territory. There two sons were born to him.

'After forty years had passed, an angel appeared to him in the flame of a burning bush in the desert near Mount Sinai. Moses was amazed at the sight, and as he approached to look more closely, the voice of the Lord came to him: "I am the God of your fathers, the God of Abraham, Isaac, and Jacob." Moses was terrified and did not dare to look. Then the Lord said to him, "Take off your sandals; the place where you are standing is holy ground. I have indeed seen how my people are oppressed in Egypt and have heard their groans; and I have come down to rescue them. Come now, I will send you to Egypt."

'This Moses, whom they had rejected with the words, "Who made you ruler and judge?"—this very man was commissioned as ruler and liberator by God himself, speaking through the angel who appeared to him in the bush. It was Moses who led them out, doing signs and wonders in Egypt, at the Red Sea, and for forty years in the desert. It was he who said to the Israelites, "God will raise up for you from among yourselves a prophet like me." It was he again who, in the assembly in the desert, kept company with the angel, who spoke to him on Mount Sinai, and with our forefathers, and received the living utterances of God to pass on to us.

'Our forefathers would not accept his leadership but thrust him aside. They wished themselves back in Egypt, and said to Aaron, "Make us gods to go before us. As for this fellow Moses, who brought us out of Egypt, we do not know what has become of him." That was when they made the bull-calf and offered sacrifice to the idol, and held festivities in honour of what their hands had made. So God turned away from them and gave them over to the worship of the host of heaven, as it stands written in the book of the prophets: "Did you bring me victims and offerings those forty years in the desert, you people of Israel? No, you carried aloft the shrine of Moloch and the star of the god Rephan, the images which you had made for your adoration. I will banish you beyond Babylon."

'Our forefathers had the Tent of the Testimony in the desert, as God commanded when he told Moses to make it after the pattern which he had seen. In the next generation, our fathers under Joshua brought it with them when they dispossessed the nations whom God drove out before them, and so it was until the time of David. David found favour with God and begged leave to provide a dwelling-place for the God of Jacob; but it was Solomon who built him a house. However, the Most High does not live in houses made by men; as the prophet says: "Heaven is my throne and earth my footstool. What kind of house will you build for me, says the Lord; where shall my resting-place be?

Are not all these things of my own making?"

'How stubborn you are, heathen still at heart and deaf to the truth! You always resist the Holy Spirit. You are just like your fathers! Was there ever a prophet your fathers did not persecute? They killed those who foretold the coming of the righteous one, and now you have betrayed him and murdered him. You received the law given by God's angels and yet you have not kept it.'

This touched them on the raw, and they ground their teeth with fury. But Stephen, filled with the Holy Spirit, and gazing intently up to heaven, saw the glory of God, and Jesus standing at God's right hand. 'Look!' he said. 'I see the heavens opened and the Son of Man standing at the right hand of God.' At this they gave a great shout, and stopped their ears; they made a concerted rush at him, threw him out of the city, and set about stoning him. The witnesses laid their coats at the feet of a young man named Saul. As they stoned him Stephen called out, 'Lord Jesus, receive my spirit.' He fell on his knees and cried aloud, 'Lord, do not hold this sin against them,' and with that he died. Saul was among those who approved of his execution.

THAT day was the beginning of a time of violent persecution for the church in Jerusalem; and all except the apostles were scattered over the country districts of Judaea and Samaria. Stephen was given burial by devout men, who made a great lamentation for him. Saul, meanwhile, was harrying the church; he entered house after house, seizing men and women and sending them to prison.

Comments on the Story

New groups, including Greek speakers, new personalities, such as Stephen and Saul, and a new setting, the synagogue, come to the fore. Of Stephen's labor in poor-relief nothing is said. He begins to do what the apostles have been doing, working wonders and preaching convincing sermons. Although the general public of Jerusalem have been supportive of the apostles, Stephen's work finds no favor in synagogues made up of Diaspora Jews. Both this setting and the response to it will dominate much of Acts.

Unable to convict Stephen in a fair fight, "they" resort to slander, suborning witnesses to say that he has derided Moses and God. The charges, which resemble those framed against Jesus earlier and Paul later, ignite widespread opposition. Stephen answers these evident calumnies with the longest speech in Acts. Although this address seems to insult the complacent Sanhedrin with a Sunday school review of Bible history, he lends credence to the charges by defending the Jesus movement as one more family quarrel within the history of Israel, whose people have not tended to give their heroes proper respect. Stephen's address is not lacking in malice. He highlights the enmity of Joseph's brothers and the hostile reaction to Moses. Since the days in the wilderness, a period already marked by idolatry, all has been decline and fall. Even the temple, great as it is, is nothing that God needs. This provides an opening to the unity of gentile and Jew (with 7:48; cf. 17:24). Sins against Moses, Torah, and temple? Yes, they have occurred, committed by the people in general. The finale noticeably lacks an invitation to repent.

Throughout the story Stephen has been transfigured (6:15; 7:56), reflecting the glory of heaven. By ignoring that witness, the Sanhedrin aligns itself with the sinners Stephen has denounced. His transfigured oration transfixes them with wrath. The audience has had enough. Omitting such technicalities as the delivery of a verdict and the imposition of a sentence, they dissolve into a lynch mob. Stephen dies with a grandeur redolent of his sincerity and truth. Checking coats at these proceedings was a young man named Saul, who thus checks into a story in which he will play a progressively larger part. Stephen's death was the starting gun for a general persecution. The apostles alone have the courage to stand fast. Others flee. Nonetheless, some pious Jews see to the proper disposal of Stephen's remains, as kindred spirits had done for his Lord (Luke 23:50-56). Saul, for his part, did not check coats at the funeral. Instead he effervesced into the most pernicious and vicious of persecutors.

From a historical perspective, the story of Stephen's death leaves many questions. As narrative, the story is altogether thrilling, a typical martyrdom, happily biased and thoroughly vibrant. Through chapters 3–5 the narrator has been building tension, with repeated trials and threats. Now the rage has boiled over, and the thread has snapped. The Sanhedrin has done its most and worst.

As the pot boils over, its contents inundate the community. This is, in every sense, climactic, the culmination of a carefully developed narrative.

Acts 6:8–8:3 relates the parting of the ways, a bitter parting marked by violent deeds and violent prose. The time for repentance has passed, not because God has limited patience, but because the leadership refuses to listen and to see. For present-day Christians reading this story in light of their historic persecution of Jews, it is a painful tale. When it was written, Christians were not in the driver's seat. Luke will relate this schism more than once. It is not the kind of story that can simply be compressed into one account, but a story that reverberates through the ages, to good and ill, to Auschwitz no less than to the world mission.

Retelling the Story

> At this they gave a great shout, and stopped their ears; they made a concerted rush at [Stephen], threw him out of the city, and set about stoning him. (Acts 7:57-58a)

The disciples brought the news to Peter right after it happened. "Stephen is dead," they said.

"Oh, no!" cried Peter. "How did it happen?"

The messengers began to recount the events of the day leading up to the tragic death of Stephen. As they talked, Peter thought back on how he had first become aware of Stephen. It was when he was chosen as one of the seven to serve the tables. He and his friend Philip were among that group. They had seemed like obvious choices at the time; they were always volunteering to do the dirty work of the church.

> Martyrdom stories were quite popular in Greco-Roman culture, among Jews, Christians, and pagans. They always represented the point of view of the group for whom the martyr was a hero. It is common in these stories for the martyr to present a long speech prior to his death in which the case for his innocence and the rightness of his cause is presented.

But they had sure come a long way from being table servants. Both Philip and Stephen had begun to stretch their wings and get involved in more activist forms of ministry, and Stephen in particular had been getting himself into trouble as a result.

It was hard to imagine two men so unlike as Philip and Stephen. Philip was the easygoing, idealistic one of the two. Philip probably never met a man he didn't like. He was a natural at table service.

Stephen, on the other hand, had the penetrating eyes of a prophet. He could not countenance injustice. He was always championing the poor and downtrodden. But because of this he, too, was a natural at table service.

And now he was dead. Peter was distraught and wondered if he should blame himself. Had they failed Stephen in some way? How had he gone from table servant to martyr?

Peter thought back on recent conversations he had had with Stephen. Stephen was the kind of man who was intent on whatever he did. They had entrusted him with a basic task in the church, a task that really took place behind the scenes. There was no way that table service should have become a dangerous occupation.

But it became dangerous for Stephen. Peter knew it was because Stephen believed so strongly in his calling as a table servant that he began to speak out. He saw the table as a microcosm of the world at large. He could not imagine not providing a generous table to anyone who came to his community. He felt the world should work the same way. Justice in the world started with justice at the table, and vice versa. Stephen simply took everything about the church seriously, and for him table service was a model for the ministry of the church.

> Attributing an angelic visage to a religious hero is a common motif in Jewish and Christian literature. In the *Acts of Paul and Thecla* 3 (late-second century C.E.), Paul is described like this: "At times he looked like a man, and at times he had the face of an angel." (Haenchen, 48)

No one knows what set him off that day, the messengers were saying. He had rushed out from the kitchen to preach in the marketplace. Peter imagined how he must have seen some injustice that needed to be corrected. He was always wanting to make things right. He wanted society to be like the table where he served, open to everyone without distinction.

They described how his eyes were flashing as he pointed his finger at the crowd. "You claim to be worshipers of God, but you have forsaken God's ways!" he said. "God is a God of justice!" But there was to be no justice that day for Stephen.

> Criticism of the Temple is found in other Jewish polemic of the second Temple period, but always from the viewpoint of reforming the Temple. Only in Christian polemic, as here, does the idea arise that the Temple should perish. (Haenchen, 56)

They said he died while still wearing his waiter's apron. Peter thought a long time about that. He decided that somehow it was appropriate. For Stephen, the waiter's apron had become a holy garment, a symbol of his calling.

(Dennis E. Smith)

Great Power in Samaria

Philip, followed by Peter and John, converts many Samaritans and confronts Simon, a magician.

The Story

As for those who had been scattered, they went through the country preaching the word. Philip came down to a city in Samaria and began proclaiming the Messiah there. As the crowds heard Philip and saw the signs he performed, everyone paid close attention to what he had to say. In many cases of possession the unclean spirits came out with a loud cry, and many paralysed and crippled folk were cured; and there was great rejoicing in that city.

A man named Simon had been in the city for some time and had captivated the Samaritans with his magical arts, making large claims for himself. Everybody, high and low, listened intently to him. 'This man,' they said, 'is that power of God which is called "The Great Power".' They listened because they had for so long been captivated by his magic. But when they came to believe Philip, with his good news about the kingdom of God and the name of Jesus Christ, men and women alike were baptized. Even Simon himself believed, and after his baptism was constantly in Philip's company. He was captivated when he saw the powerful signs and miracles that were taking place.

When the apostles in Jerusalem heard that Samaria had accepted the word of God, they sent off Peter and John, who went down there and prayed for the converts, asking that they might receive the Holy Spirit. Until then the Spirit had not come upon any on them; they had been baptized into the name of the Lord Jesus, that and nothing more. So Peter and John laid their hands on them, and they received the Holy Spirit.

When Simon observed that the Spirit was bestowed through the laying on of the apostles' hands, he offered them money and said, 'Give me too the same power, so that anyone I lay my hands on will receive the Holy Spirit.' Peter replied, 'You thought God's gift was for sale? Your money can go with you to damnation! You have neither part nor share in this, for you are corrupt in the eyes of God. Repent of this wickedness of yours and pray the Lord to forgive you for harbouring such a thought. I see that bitter gall and the chains of sin will be your fate.' Simon said to them, 'Pray to the Lord for me, and ask that none of the things you have spoken of may befall me.'

After giving their testimony and speaking the word of the Lord, they took the road back to Jerusalem, bringing the good news to many Samaritan villages on the way.

Comments on the Story

Persecution leads to mission as the fugitives enter new fields. Philip quickly replaces Stephen. In the Gospels Samaritans are "the other" par excellence. Samaritans were (and are) Jews who were at that time locked in bitter enmity with Judea and rejected the Temple at Jerusalem. A mission to them goes one step beyond the traditional religion. Samaritans had rejected Jesus (Luke 9:52-56). The success of Philip will testify to the power of Pentecost.

Philip, like Stephen and the apostles, is both a convincing preacher and a worker of potent wonders. To indicate this, the narrator provides a brief review of the career of a certain Simon, whose proficiency at magic had once awed the populace. In fact, Simon received the epithet "The Great Power." Simon talked the talk; Philip walked the walk. Will this magician, in the face of business disaster, plot some vile vengeance? Surprisingly, he does not, but is himself added to the fold. At this point Philip disappears from the story.

The scene returns to Jerusalem, where the apostles, who had remained stalwart during the persecution, resolve to back this new enterprise with Peter and John. Through the ministrations of Peter and John, the new converts manifested the gift of the Spirit. The narrator does not explain this phenomenon. (For one early description see Gal. 4:6.) In Acts, the Spirit blows where it wills and may appear before, during, or after baptism. In the interest of portraying early Christian unity, Luke takes pains to link all missions with Jerusalem.

However the Spirit manifested itself—narrators do well to leave some mysterious elements unresolved—the magician Simon was quite impressed. This is a substantial professional endorsement. By offering to put cash on the line to obtain this secret, he exposes both his unrepentant character and the apostles' superior technique. The writer does not claim that magic does not work but that it is satanic. The conquest of demons and the humiliation of magicians actualizes the defeat of Satan. Miracle, magic, and money are elements of power. All three emerge in Simon's proposal. The episode is thus a lesson in the proper use of power.

Those who have learned of the demise of Ananias and Sapphira will expect Simon to perish at a word of Peter. To our surprise, this does not happen. Simon is "let off with a warning," and even seeks prayers. The story thus closes on an open note. Whatever Simon later did (he is a standard archvillain in early church history) was his own responsibility. Judgment, then, does not work "magically" in every instance.

Retelling the Story

[Simon] was captivated when he saw the powerful signs and miracles that were taking place. (Acts 8:13b)

"Come see a miracle! See snakes dance, rabbits appear out of nowhere, rabbits disappear inside snakes! See the two-headed woman! See the half-man, half-alligator! See minds being read, the future foretold, the secrets of the universe revealed! Bring money!"

It was festival time in the village. The great magician was visiting once more, and everyone was excited. His show was always spectacular. It was not to be missed.

"Simon the Magnificent," he was called. He had spent his entire life perfecting his craft, and it had paid off. He had become the most successful magician of the region. People came from far and wide to witness his power. And they were never disappointed. What a show! He appeared in a magnificent robe and dazzled everyone with his sleight of hand. Everyone always went away impressed and a little lighter in the pockets.

Then a new show came to town, calling itself "The Traveling Gospel Spectacle." And Simon's business began to drop off dramatically. He decided to pay a visit to this new magical revue.

Samaritans were viewed as archetypal enemies of Judaism, though they were a sect that had separated from Judaism and still utilized the same basic scripture, the Pentateuch. They had their own temple on Mount Gerizim and so did not acknowledge the Temple in Jerusalem. They even had a separate identity outside Samaria, as evidenced by the existence of a first-century B.C.E. Samaritan enclave on the Greek island of Delos, a group that identified itself as "Israelites who pay homage to Hallowed Argarizein (i.e., Mount Gerizim)." With such a heritage, as a distant but distinct and rival cousin of Judaism, they represented for the story in Acts the move of the gospel to regions and peoples beyond Jerusalem and traditional Judaism. (Adapted from White, 66)

Right away he could tell they were amateurs. First, their marketing was terrible; they set up their show in the worst part of town, where all of the riffraff of society hung out. That was no way to get the wealthiest customers. Also, they had no advertising to speak of; people found out about them only by word of mouth. And their stage presence definitely left something to be desired. They clearly knew nothing about costuming—no robes, no top hats, not even white gloves. And there was no flair at all to their act; they looked like country bumpkins; they didn't know the first thing about how to wow an audience.

Yet Simon had to acknowledge that there was something appealing about this new show. They pulled off some of the finest tricks he had ever seen, despite their poor technique. And the crowds they attracted from all levels of society were very impressive. Simon had never realized that there was such potential among society's outcasts. It was like an untapped reservoir of power! And he had completely overlooked it.

Well, Simon was quickly converted. He thought he had known all there was to know about the magical arts, but here was a fresh new act. He was determined to learn their methods.

After the show, Simon went backstage to talk to one of their leaders, a big, rustic-looking fellow whom they called Peter. "Peter, my boy," said Simon, shaking his hand vigorously, "glad to meet ya! What a show! What a show! You guys are really good! And I know what I am talking about, because I have seen them all. Yessir, Peter, old boy! I've seen 'em all! I saw Gargantua, Mover of Mountains, in his prime! I saw Percy the Great disappear before our very eyes! I saw Daedalini the Magnificent fly like a bird!

"But you, Peter, my boy, you put them all to shame. Healing the crippled, what a nice touch! And where did you get such a realistic wild man to cure of his, 'unclean spirit'? What a marvelous idea, to cure the world of impurity! Fits right in with the location, in the midst of the impure! A stroke of genius!

"But you have to move up to the high-rent district, if you know what I mean, Peter, old boy. You can't stay here—there is not enough money here to buy a barrel full of rotten olives, if you get my drift. No, this will not do. You have to move up—go where the money is.

"Now with my savvy and your skill, we can really make a killing. I'll put up the front money and provide the opening act. You can close with the crippled walking or the taming of the wild man, whichever. It'll bring the house down, and the money will come rolling in. What do you say, Peter, my boy?"

Peter had been staring at Simon dumbfounded, as if he were in a trance. When Simon finished his tirade and looked expectantly at Peter, there was a long pause. Then Peter shook himself back into reality, and looked quizzically at Simon.

"Let me get this straight," said Peter. "You want to buy our show?"

"No, no, no," said Simon. "Not buy—merge! Let's put our acts together. We can be the best thing since . . . since . . . since Barnum and Bailey! We'll call ourselves 'Simon the Magnificent and Associates.' What do you say?"

> Simon the magician (Simon Magus) became a stock villain in Christian legend. The *Acts of Peter* (late-second-century C.E.), for example, presents a contest of Peter against Simon when the two meet once more in Rome and perform their acts of magic and miracle before a paying audience of Roman officials. Simon's attempts to raise the dead are shown to be deceptions, whereas Peter demonstrates repeatedly his ability to perform such a miracle. Later, when Simon shows that he can fly, Peter, through the power of prayer, causes him to fall and break his leg. Simon, "the angel of the devil," then is carried away on a stretcher and dies soon after.

"Thanks, but no thanks," said Peter. "The gospel is not for sale." And he turned and walked away.

" 'Simon and Peter the Magnificent'?" Simon called to the departing figure. "Okay, okay, 'Peter the Magnificent and Company.' That's my last offer!" But Peter just kept walking.

Simon never did figure out what went wrong with his merger deal. And try as he might, he could not quite get the hang of the gospel magic. He even hired a wild man to add to his act as a, "man possessed with an unclean spirit," but somehow it wasn't the same. His profits dwindled and he was soon reduced to selling homemade elixirs from a medicine wagon.

Meanwhile, Peter and his traveling show got bigger and better. Their crowds grew larger, and their fame spread far and wide.

And Peter did learn something from his encounter with Simon—the power of advertising. Now when they came to a new village they announced their arrival like this:

"Come see a miracle! See the crippled walk, see the unclean made clean! See society change right before your very eyes! Come one, come all—no one will be turned away at the door—all are welcome. Bring your worries and anxieties, your pain and hardships, the deepest longings of your soul! No problem too great to be addressed!" *(Dennis E. Smith)*

A Hand Toward Ethiopia

Philip converts a court official from the distant and exotic kingdom of Ethiopia.

The Story

Then the angel of the Lord said to Philip, 'Start out and go south to the road that leads down from Jerusalem to Gaza.' (This is the desert road.) He set out and was on his way when he caught sight of an Ethiopian. This man was a eunuch, a high official of the Kandake, or queen, of Ethiopia, in charge of all her treasure; he had been to Jerusalem on a pilgrimage and was now returning home, sitting in his carriage and reading aloud from the prophet Isaiah. The Spirit said to Philip, 'Go and meet the carriage.' When Philip ran up he heard him reading from the prophet Isaiah and asked, 'Do you understand what you are reading?' He said, 'How can I without someone to guide me?' and invited Philip to get in and sit beside him.

The passage he was reading was this: 'He was led like a sheep to the slaughter; like a lamb that is dumb before the shearer, he does not open his mouth. He has been humiliated and has no redress. Who will be able to speak of his posterity? For he is cut off from the world of the living.'

'Please tell me,' said the eunuch to Philip, 'who it is that the prophet is speaking about here: himself or someone else?' Then Philip began and, starting from this passage, he told him the good news of Jesus. As they were going along the road, they came to some water. 'Look,' said the eunuch, 'here is water: what is to prevent my being baptized?' and he ordered the carriage to stop. Then they both went down into the water, Philip and the eunuch, and he baptized him. When they came up from the water the Spirit snatched Philip away; the eunuch did not see him again, but went on his way rejoicing. Philip appeared at Azotus, and toured the country, preaching in all the towns till he reached Caesarea.

Comments on the Story

Philip, offstage since 8:14, is featured in a story utterly unlike that of Simon. The anonymous "eunuch" (castrated officials were long able to hold high positions in Middle Eastern kingdoms because they could not conspire on behalf of their offspring) is an African Black of very high status, "Secretary of the Treasury" of the reigning queen. Greeks often idealized the kingdom of Ethiopia. This official typifies the ideal potential convert. He is a sincere and open-minded student of Scripture who wishes a guide to unravel its mysteries. Despite his piety and prestige, the official can come no closer than the margins of Judaism, since his physical state disqualifies him for circumcision and full conversion.

The narrator makes it clear that Philip did not come up with the idea of converting an Ethiopian "God-fearer" on his own initiative. Each step follows heavenly direction. The first command sends Philip toward the barren south, the desert habitat of pristine Israel, the place of testing and revelation. The scene then shifts to the perplexed official. His choice of Isaiah 53 was fortunate, for this text raises precisely the kind of questions that Philip can readily answer. The dialogue is thus exposition. When water, rare in the desert, opportunely appears, the eunuch has one more question. Torah may prohibit circumcision, but baptism is open to all. Once the sacrament has been administered, Philip is snatched away while the Ethiopian travels on, his journey lightened by Easter joy.

The appeal of the story, with its rapid action, sentimental content, exotic details, and pleasantly mysterious end, is patent. Beneath this attractive surface are numerous symbols and allusions. Here is the story of Acts in a nutshell— the story of Acts, and the story of every believer. The world of 8:14-25 is thus nowhere and everywhere. Structurally the passage resembles Luke 24:13-35. Both begin as a story about another's journey and end as the story of each Christian's journey.

The official has turned his back upon a place that will not give him full acceptance. Such "God-fearers" provide Luke with an important social group and a link between emergent Judaism and nascent Christianity. This story portrays early Christian hermeneutic as the exploration of Scripture by those seeking God and finding barriers. The Gospel is the offer of inclusion. For Luke this conversion is a kind of "foundation myth" for believers not reared as Jews. It is wholly characteristic of the author that this foundational tale is not only interesting in its own right but also advances the plot. The large story of Acts has come to a climactic point. The next journey will traverse the Damascus Road.

Retelling the Story

'Look,' said the eunuch, 'here is water: what is to prevent my being baptized?' (Acts 8:36b)

Philip, contrary to popular opinion, had not had an easy time of it. Ever since he got back from his excursion in the desert he had been in trouble. Now he had been summoned to appear before the Christian Caucus for Political and Moral Purity. Somehow they had heard about his meeting with the Ethiopian eunuch.

"He is a foreigner," said one.

"He is from the wrong race," said another.

"He has the wrong sexual identity," said still another.

"His kind are not allowed in the company of the politically and morally pure," added another.

"God does not allow it," they all concluded.

"But he can't help what he is. Doesn't God have some say in that?" asked Philip.

"We and God are just like this," said their spokesperson, raising his hand with two fingers upraised and pressed tightly together. "We know what God likes and we know he doesn't like those kinds of people."

Ancient Greeks were fascinated with exotic, faraway places, and Ethiopia was among the most exotic to their mind. For example, Homer referred to Ethiopians as "the most remote of men" (*Odyssey* 1.22-23). Pliny notes that "it is ruled by a woman, Candace, a name that has passed on through a succession of queens for many years" (*Nat. hist.* 6.186 [first-century C.E.]). Plutarch referred to their custom "to have mostly eunuchs as treasurers" (*Demetrius* 25.5 [early-second-century C.E.]). (Conzelmann, 68; Foakes Jackson and Lake, 4.96)

It was a strong argument, Philip had to admit. Before he met the eunuch from Ethiopia, he had agreed with all of them. God was a God of purity, and a God of holiness—this is what he had always believed. It was the job of religious people to protect God from impurity. And an Ethiopian eunuch was about as impure as they come—everybody knew that.

He thought back on how he had gotten into this mess. Now normally Philip didn't hear voices. But this time he did. Maybe yelling at him was the only way God could get his attention. The voice was clear and demanding: "Go down that road over there, the one that leads south out of town and into the desert." It was a strange command, like it came from a heavenly travel agent or something. And what a choice for a journey! Why go there of all places, on a desert road that led nowhere important?

At first, he was alone on the road, but then another pilgrim showed up. This man was obviously well-connected because he was riding in a chariot and reading from a scroll. As he passed, Philip got a good look at him, and automatically recoiled. He saw that he was a foreigner, an Ethiopian, and his dress betrayed him as one of the castrated servants of the Ethiopian queen. Philip turned aside and pretended to be busy adjusting his garments as the chariot passed. He wanted to avoid any contact with such a person so he could get on with God's business.

But then, to his utter surprise, he found himself being propelled, goaded really, by an invisible force. Without knowing how he got there, he found himself running alongside the chariot, listening to the eunuch reading aloud. The eunuch looked over at him, startled that a traveler on a desert road would suddenly break into a trot. Philip looked back at him sheepishly, also rather startled at his own behavior. "Can I help you?" asked the eunuch.

"Well," panted Philip, "maybe I can help you. I notice you are reading the Bible. I am a pretty good Bible scholar myself, and would be happy to help you understand what you are reading." Philip couldn't believe he said that. What he really wanted to do was get as far away from this person as possible. Besides, he hated chariot solicitors, and now he had become one.

"What luck!" said the eunuch. "I have just been puzzling over this passage here. I would appreciate some help."

"Well," said Philip, fading fast, "if you would just stop this chariot for a minute, I would be happy to oblige."

"Of course," said the eunuch, and gave the order to his driver to stop. "Why don't you get in and join me?" he said, extending a hand to Philip. Philip stood in the road a minute catching his breath and eyeing the eunuch suspiciously. He looked around and saw that

> Reading aloud was the common ancient practice even when one was reading privately to oneself. This was necessary since texts were written without any breaks between the words. Reading aloud helped the reader better determine the meaning of the text, since syllables and words could be distinguished by sound. Silent reading was so rare that Augustine remarked with astonishment at seeing Ambrose read silently: "As he read, his eyes scanned the pages and his heart searched out the sense, but his voice and tongue were silent" (*Conf.* 6.6.3 [early-fifth-century C.E.]) (Gamble, 203-4; 321-22, n. 1)

no one else was on the road—no one would see him—so maybe it was okay. After all, he had to be careful of his reputation—he was a representative of the church.

He climbed in and sat beside the eunuch. He felt humiliated—he had never been this close to one of *them* before. What had he gotten himself into?

Then the eunuch extended the scroll to Philip and said, "Here is the passage I was reading. What do you think it means?" Philip listened intently as the eunuch read. The passage was one he had heard many times before, but somehow today was different. It was like he heard it for the first time. "He was led like a sheep to the slaughter," read the eunuch. "He has been humiliated and has no redress." The eunuch finished the reading and handed the scroll to Philip, who began to study it closely. "Did it really say that?" thought Philip. The words echoed in his mind: "he has been humiliated."

The eunuch looked steadily at Philip and asked, "Whom is the prophet speaking about, himself or someone else?"

"Or is he speaking about me?" thought Philip, as he became acutely aware of his own sense of humiliation, but for all of the wrong reasons. He swallowed hard, looked back at the eunuch, and began to tell him the story of Jesus, a man who spent most of his time with the outcasts of the world, and who ended his life with a humiliating death. Yet from that life and death, God had fashioned a message for all of humanity. And Philip was just now beginning to understand how powerful that message was. For as he told that story, it worked on him as well. And by the time he had finished, he had lost all his nervousness in the presence of the eunuch. The eunuch took on a different form to him—he felt as if he was in the presence of a messenger from God. For although he had begun as the teacher, he had become the one who was taught.

The eunuch listened attentively and nodded approvingly as Philip told his story. Then, when they suddenly came to a watering hole, he presented his challenge to Philip. "Here is water," he said. "Is there any reason why you should not baptize me?"

Philip burst into a wide grin and nearly leaped out of the chariot. "No—not at all!" he cried. Together they went into the water, and Philip baptized the eunuch. Then, in his joy, Philip embraced the eunuch. There was no longer any difference between them at all, he knew. That was what that scripture meant—what God meant by the death of Christ! And until this moment in the desert, he had missed it.

And then suddenly, the eunuch was gone, and Philip was back in the real world. Was it all a dream? Had he just imagined such a brave new world? Certainly no one else here in Jerusalem had caught the vision.

Now he was being interrogated by the religious leaders. "What do you have to say for yourself?" they inquired.

The question awakened him from his musings about the events in the desert. And the answer came to him in a flash.

"The spirit made me do it," he said. *(Dennis E. Smith)*

72

Opening the Eyes of a Blind Man

A notorious persecutor joins his former foes and experiences persecution from the other side.

The Story

SAUL, still breathing murderous threats against the Lord's disciples, went to the high priest and applied for letters to the synagogues at Damascus authorizing him to arrest any followers of the new way whom he found, men or women, and bring them to Jerusalem. While he was still on the road and nearing Damascus, suddenly a light from the sky flashed all around him. He fell to the ground and heard a voice saying, 'Saul, Saul, why are you persecuting me?' 'Tell me, Lord,' he said, 'who you are.' The voice answered, 'I am Jesus, whom you are persecuting. But now get up and go into the city, and you will be told what you have to do.' Meanwhile the men who were travelling with him stood speechless; they heard the voice but could see no one. Saul got up from the ground, but when he opened his eyes he could not see; they led him by the hand and brought him into Damascus. He was blind for three days, and took no food or drink.

There was in Damascus a disciple named Ananias. He had a vision in which he heard the Lord say: 'Ananias!' 'Here I am, Lord,' he answered. The Lord said to him, 'Go to Straight Street, to the house of Judas, and ask for a man from Tarsus named Saul. You will find him at prayer; he has had a vision of a man named Ananias

coming in and laying hands on him to restore his sight.' Ananias answered, 'Lord, I have often heard about this man and all the harm he has done your people in Jerusalem. Now he is here with authority from the chief priests to arrest all who invoke your name.' But the Lord replied, 'You must go, for this man is my chosen instrument to bring my name before the nations and their kings, and before the people of Israel. I myself will show him all that he must go through for my name's sake.'

So Ananias went and, on entering the house, laid his hands on him and said, 'Saul, my brother, the Lord Jesus, who appeared to you on your way here, has sent me to you so that you may recover your sight and be filled with the Holy Spirit.' Immediately it was as if scales had fallen from his eyes, and he regained his sight. He got up and was baptized, and when he had eaten his strength returned.

He stayed some time with the disciples in Damascus. Without delay he proclaimed Jesus publicly in the synagogues, declaring him to be the Son of God. All who heard were astounded. 'Is not this the man,' they said, 'who was in Jerusalem hunting down those who invoke this name? Did he not come here for the sole purpose of arresting them and taking them before the chief priests?' But Saul went from strength to strength, and confounded the Jews of Damacus with his congent proofs that Jesus was the Messiah.

When some time had passed, the Jews hatched a plot against his life; but their plans became known to Saul. They kept watch on the city gates day and night so that they might murder him; but one night some disciples took him and, lowering him in a basket, let him down over the wall.

On reaching Jerusalem he tried to join the disciples, but they were all afraid of him, because they did not believe that he really was a disciple. Barnabas, however, took him and introduced him to the apostles; he described to them how on his journey Saul had seen the Lord and heard his voice, and how at Damascus he had spoken out boldly in the name of Jesus. Saul now stayed with them, moving about freely in Jerusalem. He spoke out boldly and openly in the name of the Lord, talking and debating with the Greek-speaking Jews. But they planned to murder him, and when the brethren discovered this they escorted him down to Caesarea and sent him away to Tarsus.

Comments on the Story

Conversion of a ready listener is one thing; savage opponents will present more of a challenge. Joy quickly yields to the rage of a monster, Saul, who, after cleansing Jerusalem of this noxious menace, seeks permission to widen his mission field. Permission granted, he sets out for Damascus, only to be struck by a bolt from heaven, the light of the risen Christ, who states his identity and commands Saul to finish his journey and await further instructions. So far this is a typical tale of the punishment of God's enemies. Of all the punishment stories in Acts this is the most vivid and, no doubt, the most apposite. Saul, who had intended to drag his opponents from Damascus, is himself led into the city by hand. He lingers without nourishment, blind and vanquished. The spiteful hearer, aware of his depredations, will see death by slow starvation as a suitable end to the story of Saul.

After three days in that spiritual tomb the story takes a surprising turn. Pious Ananias has a vision that corresponds with a simultaneous revelation to Saul. ("Double Dreams" or visions, another of which occurs in chapter 10, demonstrate beyond doubt that they come from a God who is in control of the story.) The vision is not welcome to Ananias. In case God has overlooked Saul's atrocities, he takes occasion to issue a brief reminder. Ananias is not the last believer who has seen fit to keep God up to date. Unpersuaded, the Almighty repeats the command, together with the prophecy that Saul will engage a vast audience, including high and low, gentile and Jew. In this dramatic setting the hearer receives the first explicit announcement of a gentile ("the nations") mission.

Promptly baptized, with the scales of error swept from his eyes, nourished

74

by new and spiritual food, the persecutor changes his outfit. The astonishing and immediate success of this turncoat sparks opposition. Saul, it appears, is caught in a box. Whatever harm he can do will be limited to Damascus, and another martyr will presently be added to the list. The believers, however, thwart these nefarious plans with their own clever scheme: Saul eludes his assassins by a surreptitious escape. Storytellers will have no difficulty in developing this adventure.

Where shall one go to evade a Jewish plot? *Jerusalem?* Only the bravest and most determined travel in a basket from the frying pan to the fire. What has Jerusalem in common with Damascus? Profound skepticism about this alleged change. Only through the agency of Barnabas does Saul gain entrance to the fold. This, it will transpire, is the beginning of an important friendship. The former holder of coats now dons the mantle of Stephen, whose fate he would surely have shared, had not the plot been exposed in time to send him to Tarsus and safety.

Within this brief passage come a number of vivid episodes, each gripping. There are several stories tellers can relate. The structure is not simply episodic, however. Verses 1-25 exhibit perfect symmetry, from Jerusalem to Jerusalem, a full circle: plot, blindness, conversion, initiation, commission, sight restored, and plot. Narrative structure and personal transformation coincide. Observe how many times the story could end: with Saul's death as punishment, with his conversion to the tranquil life of a disciple, with his assassination by enemies in Damascus, or, like Stephen, in Jerusalem. For all one knows, his story, like that of Philip, is essentially finished. Acts has many stories, some of which include more than one story. It also strives to be a story that never ends.

Retelling the Story

Immediately it was as if scales had fallen from his eyes, and he regained his sight. (Acts 9:18*a*)

My old neighbor Charlie Bonns used to sing hymns out loud as he worked on his farm, and I would often hear the strains of "Amazing Grace! How sweet the sound . . . " as he walked back

> It was a popular motif in ancient storytelling to relate incidents in which blindness is brought on by impiety and cured by repentance: "For those who have sinned in matters of mythology there is an ancient purification, unknown to Homer, but known to Stesichorus. For when he was stricken with blindness for speaking ill of Helen, he was not, like Homer, ignorant of the reason, but since he was educated, he knew it and straightway he writes the poem . . . and when he had written all the poem, which is called the recantation, he saw again at once." (Plato, *Phaedrus* 243A [fourth-century B.C.E.])

toward the house at mealtime. As he aged, his eyesight weakened, but Mr. Bonns never stopped singing the songs he knew by heart, including "Amazing Grace."

Once when visiting him he was singing and I was listening. "I once was lost, but now am found; was blind, but now I see," he sang. Suddenly he stopped singing and laughed out loud. "That's not me," Mr. Bonns stated. "I used to see and now I'm getting blind, but the feller who wrote this must have been just the opposite!"

Much later I learned that the "feller" who wrote "Amazing Grace" was a prolific hymn-writer named John Newton. Newton was an Anglican clergyman born in London in 1725. In the year 1779 he joined with William Cowper to produce a book of hymns. It was to be called *Olney Hymns* since Newton was at that time minister in the village of Olney. John Newton was so prolific that when the hymnal was finished he had written two hundred eighty-one of the hymns and his poet-partner William Cowper had written only sixty-seven.

Newton, who also wrote such hymns as "Glorious Things of Thee Are Spoken," and "How Sweet the Name of Jesus Sounds" went on to serve as rector of Saint Mary's Parish in London until he was eighty years old.

So, what does "Amazing Grace," written by a prolific and long-lived English clergyman, have to do with the story of Paul's conversion? They are really, in many ways, the same story.

This same John Newton, later hymn-writing clergyman, went to sea with his father when he was eleven years old. After falling into rough experiences, including imprisonment and personal enslavement, young Newton escaped and joined the crew of a slave-trading ship. Before much time had passed, he became master of his own slave ship and for some years was very active in the trade of human lives.

While he was an active worker in the slave trade Newton heard the preaching

When Paul himself describes his conversion in his letter to the Galatians, he relates it according to the model of a prophetic call, in which God "calls" one whom he had "set apart" from his "birth" (Gal. 1:15), much like the biblical call of Jeremiah: "Before I formed you in the womb I chose you, and before you were born I consecrated you" (Jer. 1:5). The story Luke tells, however, would probably remind gentile readers of experiences of the divine in Greek and Roman mystery religions. Apuleius, for example, in his novel *The Golden Ass,* describes in vivid detail the religious experience of a suppliant of the goddess Isis: "Then, little by little, I seemed to see the whole figure of her body, bright and mounting out of the sea and standing before me. . . . 'Behold, Lucius, I am come; thy weeping and prayer hath moved me to succour thee.' " (11.3-4 [second-century C.E.])

76

of George Whitefield and the Wesleys in England. At age thirty "scales fell from his eyes" and he left the slave trade and began to prepare for ordination. Not only did Newton become a priest in the Church of England, he, along with his coworker William Wilberforce, were mainstay leaders in ending the slave trade in England many years before it was outlawed in America.

When he died after forty-three years in the service of God's kingdom, John Newton was buried with this self-penned epitaph:

> John Newton, clerk
> Once an infidel and libertine, a servant of slaves in Africa: Was by the rich
> mercy of our Lord and Saviour, Jesus Christ, preserved, restored, and pardoned,
> and appointed to preach the faith . . .

Now, when I hear the words of "Amazing Grace," I no longer hear Mr. Charlie Bonns singing them. Instead I hear an imaginary duet made up of the apostle Paul and the Reverend John Newton (formerly Saul of Tarsus and John Newton the slave trader) as they sing "Amazing grace! How sweet the sound that saved a wretch like me! I once was lost, but now am found; was blind, but now I see."

(Donald Davis)

The Conversion of Peter—and Others

Peter, under divine guidance, converts the entire household of a prominent and sympathetic gentile.

The Story

At Caesarea there was a man named Cornelius, a centurion in the Italian Cohort, as it was called. He was a devout man, and he and his whole family joined in the worship of God; he gave generously to help the Jewish people, and was regular in his prayers to God. One day about three in the afternoon he had a vision in which he clearly saw an angel of God come into his room and say, 'Cornelius!' Cornelius stared at him in terror. 'What is it, my lord?' he asked. The angel said, 'Your prayers and acts of charity have gone up to heaven to speak for you before God. Now send to Joppa for a man named Simon, also called Peter: he is lodging with another Simon, a tanner, whose house is by the sea.' When the angel who spoke to him had gone, he summoned two of his servants and a military orderly who was a religious man, told them the whole story, and ordered them to Joppa.

Next day about noon, while they were still on their way and approaching the city, Peter went up on the roof to pray. He grew hungry and wanted something to eat, but while they were getting it ready, he fell into a trance. He saw heaven opened, and something coming down that looked like a great sheet of sailcloth; it was slung by the four corners and was being lowered to the earth, and in it he saw creatures of every kind, four-footed beasts, reptiles, and birds. There came a voice which said to him, 'Get up, Peter, kill and eat.' But Peter answered, 'No, Lord! I have never eaten anything profane or unclean.' The voice came again, a second time: 'It is not for you to call profane what God counts clean.' This happened three times, and then the thing was taken up into heaven.

While Peter was still puzzling over the meaning of the vision he had seen, the messengers from Cornelius had been asking the way to Simon's house, and now arrived at the entrance. They called out and asked if Simon Peter was lodging there. Peter was thinking over the vision, when the Spirit said to him, 'Some men are here looking for you; get up and go downstairs. You may go with them without any misgivings, for it was I who sent them.' Peter came down to the men and said, 'You are looking for me? Here I am. What brings you here?' 'We are from the centurion Cornelius,' they replied, 'a good and religious man, acknowledged as such by the whole Jewish nation. He was directed by a holy angel to send for you to his house and hear what you have to say.' So Peter asked them in and gave them a night's lodging.

Next day he set out with them, accompanied by some members of the congregation at Joppa, and on the following day arrived at Caesarea. Cornelius was expecting them and had called together his relatives and close friends. When Peter arrived, Cornelius came to meet him, and bowed to the ground in deep reverence. But Peter raised him to his feet and said, 'Stand up; I am only a man like you.' Still talking with him he went in and found a large gathering. He said to them, 'I need not tell you that a Jew is forbidden by his religion to visit or associate with anyone of another race. Yet God has shown me clearly that I must not call anyone profane or unclean; that is why I came here without demur when you sent for me. May I ask what was your reason for doing so?'

Cornelius said, 'Three days ago, just about this time, I was in the house here saying the afternoon prayers, when suddenly a man in shining robes stood before me. He said: "Cornelius, your prayer has been heard and your acts of charity have spoken for you before God. Send to Simon Peter at Joppa, and ask him to come; he is lodging in the house of Simon the tanner, by the sea." I sent to you there and then, and you have been good enough to come. So now we are all met here before God, to listen to everything that the Lord has instructed you to say.'

Peter began: 'I now understand how true it is that God has no favourites, but that in every nation those who are god-fearing and do what is right are acceptable to him. He sent his word to the Israelites and gave the good news of peace through Jesus Christ, who is Lord of all. I need not tell you what has happened lately all over the land of the Jews, starting from Galilee after the baptism proclaimed by John. You know how God anointed Jesus of Nazareth with the Holy Spirit and with power. Because God was with him he went about doing good and healing all were oppressed by the devil. And we can bear witness to all that he did in the Jewish countryside and in Jerusalem. They put him to death, hanging him on a gibbet; but God raised him to life on the third day, and allowed him to be clearly seen, not by the whole people, but by witnesses whom God had chosen in advance—by us, who ate and drank with him after he rose from the dead. He commanded us to proclaim him to the people, and affirm that he is the one designated by God as judge of the living and the dead. It is to him that all the prophets testify, declaring that everyone who trusts in him receives forgiveness of sins through his name.'

Peter was still speaking when the Holy Spirit came upon all who were listening to the message. The believers who had come with Peter, men of Jewish birth, were amazed that the gift of the Holy Spirit should have been poured out even on Gentiles, for they could hear them speaking in tongues of ecstasy and acclaiming the greatness of God. Then Peter spoke: 'Is anyone prepared to withhold the water of baptism from these persons who have received the Holy Spirit just as we did?' Then he ordered them to be baptized in the name of Jesus Christ. After that they asked him to stay on with them for a time.

News came to the apostles and the members of the church in Judaea that

Gentiles too had accepted the word of God; and when Peter came up to Jerusalem those who were of Jewish birth took issue with him. 'You have been visiting men who are uncircumcised,' they said, 'and sitting at the table with them!' Peter began by laying before them the facts as they had happened.

'I was at prayer in the city of Joppa,' he said, 'and while in a trance I had a vision: I saw something coming down that looked like a great sheet of sailcloth, slung by the four corners and lowered from heaven till it reached me. I looked intently to make out what was in it and I saw four-footed beasts, wild animals, reptiles, and birds. Then I heard a voice saying to me, "Get up, Peter, kill and eat." But I said, "No, Lord! Nothing profane or unclean has ever entered my mouth." A voice from heaven came a second time: "It is not for you to call profane what God counts clean." This happened three times, and then they were all drawn up again into heaven. At that very moment three men who had been sent to me from Caesarea arrived at the house where I was staying; and the Spirit told me to go with them. My six companions here came with me and we went into the man's house. He told us how he had seen an angel standing in his house who said, "Send to Joppa for Simon Peter. He will speak words that will bring salvation to you and all your household." Hardly had I begun speaking, when the Holy Spirit came upon them, just as upon us at the beginning, and I recalled what the Lord had said: "John baptized with water, but you will be baptized with the Holy Spirit." God gave them no less a gift than he gave us when we came to believe in the Lord Jesus Christ. How could I stand in God's way?'

When they heard this their doubts were silenced, and they gave praise to God. 'This means,' they said, 'that God has granted life-giving repentance to the Gentiles also.'

Comments on the Story

[SCENE ONE (10:1-8)]

Peter, once more following the footsteps of Philip, has come to the (largely gentile) coastal cities. At Lydda and Joppa he works miracles that enhance a broader mission. The narrator then turns to Caesarea, a prosperous port that served as the Roman capital of Judea. The focus is an officer with the fine Roman name of Cornelius. In status centurions resembled modern-day officers of field grade, for instance, colonels. Cornelius, then, is no yokel. He is also a generous man, noted for devotion and putting his money where his mouth is. Still, this officer, who dwells on the fringes of Palestine, is also at the margins of Judaism, conversion to which would probably cost him his position and entail many social difficulties. His religious quest is, like that of the Ethiopian, on hold. Jesus had also encountered a sympathetic centurion (Luke 7:2-10). If the story remains true to form, Cornelius will receive a pat on his spiritual back.

The skies hang low in this instance, however, for, at the peak of day, an angel appears. The scene has much in common with the angelophany that opened the Gospel of Luke. So what? This is also a portentous beginning. After bestowing suitable and well-deserved compliments, the angel directs the attention of Cornelius to Peter, who is at no great distance, with instructions that he send for this man, complete with directions to his house. All of this naturally baffles Cornelius. Hearers can enjoy the suspense this bafflement provokes, not least because we suspect what will happen. The angel preserves social proprieties. It would be beneath the dignity of Cornelius to dash off and visit Peter. Superiors send for their inferiors. There is, of course, more to this than that.

[SCENE TWO (10:9-16)]

So the delegation of three—Peter is not so inferior as to merit but a single messenger—sets out for Joppa. Exactly twenty-four hours later, at the time of Cornelius's visit from an angel, the delegation is about to arrive. Peter is at prayer, and hungry. Had his prayer been preceded by a fast, as in the case of other worthies (cf. Daniel 10)? Jesus' hunger from fasting preceded a visit from Satan (Luke 4:2). Will Satan now appear to Peter, in his guise as the armed forces of the evil empire?

The narrator reflects about none of this, but reports a vision: entranced, Peter sees an object descending from the open heaven. Heavens open for important revelations (cf. Luke 3:21-22). This vision is both elaborate and fascinating. Spread about something like a linen sheet are the various animals of the earth. Evocation of Gen 1:24-25 suggests the goodness of all creation, which, for some, was in tension with food regulations. Will Peter be left to interpret this vision on his own? No, for, as in Luke 3:21-22, there is a voice directing him to prepare and consume these creatures. Like Ananias (9:13), Peter objects, reminding the heavens of his piety. The voice contrasts Peter's views with those of God, who counts all clean. Have all of those elaborate regulations about what may be eaten been swept aside by this linen sheet? Has God acted anew to purify all foods? Peter is not the only one perplexed by all of this. Three times the command comes forth; three times does Peter demur. The possible allusion to Jesus' wilderness temptation may be a hint that Peter, like his master, has thrice said "no" to Satan. Another possibility is that his threefold denial of Jesus has just been repeated.

[SCENE THREE (10:17-23*a*)]

As in the story of Saul and Ananias (chap. 9), two persons have received divine visitations. There matters were clear; here the connection is less direct. While Peter wrestles with this perplexity, the emissaries from Cornelius make their opportune appearance. The Spirit tells Peter to accompany them "without any misgiving." The phrase is no less ambiguous than the vision. It may mean "without reservations," "without distinctions," or "without discrimination." Given his recent refusal, the advice is timely. So he meets the messengers, hears their report, and offers them lodgings. Hospitality is not just politeness, but the acceptance of a social bond. The chariot is moving, but only one of its wheels—the vision of Cornelius—functions.

[SCENE FOUR (10:23*b*-29)]

The next day the delegation sets forth, enlarged by some local believers. Cornelius had shrewdly estimated when they would arrive and assembled his family and some close friends for the occasion. As Peter entered Cornelius's abode, crossing the barrier that had separated gentile from Jew, the Roman officer prostrated himself. In this reversal of social roles the world was turned upside down. As the two quickly enter into friendly discourse, Peter explains his impropriety by reference to the vision (10:28). That interpretation is the moment of decision. The vision said nothing about accepting hospitality from gentiles. Peter came, through reflection, to view it as symbolic of a comprehensive breach of barriers. This is, in fact, the moment of his own "conversion," a change no less momentous than the about-face of Saul (cf. also Luke 24:45). Peter then inquires about the nature of Cornelius's business.

[SCENE FIVE (10:30-48)]

Thus invited, the centurion repeats the content of his vision. Such more or less *verbatim* repetitions are characteristics of oral narration. They provide different angles on the same material, as well as emphasis. Since his vision has been fulfilled, Cornelius could assure Peter that he had an audience of ready listeners.

One might expect that Peter would repeat his own vision and remark upon the startling coincidence. Instead, he delivered a brief missionary address. This is his one sermon to gentiles, a brief and symmetrical speech, predicated upon the conviction that Jesus' ministry is well-known. What he "need not tell" permits Luke from boring the audience with a long, familiar sermon. It also indicates that the word was out. The sermon contains the only "biography" of Jesus embedded within the book of Acts. The style is reminiscent of Stephen's portrayals of Joseph and Moses (chap. 7). The content is that of the creed. The cultural model is that of the "benefactor," an important social type at all levels of Greco-Roman society. Here, then, is the first reported instance of the "cultural adaptation" of the Christian message to particular circumstances, a precedent that has not always been followed.

Just at the point where Peter will begin to develop in more detail the message of death and resurrection, a subject with which the actual audience of Acts is familiar, his sermon is interrupted, not, in this case, by the police, as in

4:1, but by the Holy Spirit, who extends the benefits of Pentecost to this gentile household. This is a new beginning. Peter's Jewish colleagues express amazement. For him, only one conclusion was possible: these people are to be baptized. After the ceremony, Peter accepts Cornelius's kind invitation to remain for some time. Hospitality once again. By agreeing to stay, Peter affirmed that Cornelius and his household were full members of the body. (The Greco-Roman household included the nuclear family, other relatives, slaves, and dependents. In religious and other matters these persons were expected to follow the lead of the household head.) Doubtless this would also give opportunity for more extended instruction. Dramatically, it provides time for word of these events to make its way to Jerusalem.

[SCENE SIX (11:1-18)]

When, in due course, Peter returns to that city, he is taken to task by "those of Jewish birth." This anachronism—everyone was of "Jewish birth"—shows that Luke's major concern is with conflicts that arose in the mission of Paul. These objectors did not take issue with the baptism of gentiles but with Peter's willingness to associate and eat with them. "Table fellowship" was an essential mark of social solidarity, imposing obligations upon guests and hosts.

Only in the course of the story does it become clear that the setting is some kind of community assembly. Peter's defense is nothing other than a detailed summary of chapter 10. Once more, repetition serves the object of emphasis. This account, corroborated by the six witnesses whom Peter has had the foresight to bring with him, stifled all objections. The admission of gentiles is yet one more cause for gratitude to God. Peter, then, not Philip, nor Paul, began the gentile mission. In this pathbreaking act his ministry in Acts has come to an effective end.

This is the longest story in Acts. The careful scenic structure, those frequent repetitions, and the dense supernatural apparatus of vision and visitation are some of the means used to proclaim the importance of this event, which was in no sense an act of individual whimsy, but due to the Spirit's express direction in the face of substantial resistance. Nor, it might be noted, was this first gentile convert some anonymous member of the urban or rural work force, but a prominent soldier and citizen.

Retelling the Story

> God has shown me clearly that I must not call anyone profane or unclean. (Acts 10:27*b*)

After nearly a decade of precarious balance in European politics, 1914 was the year to see the world's first global conflict in human history break out.

After the assassination of Archduke Ferdinand in late June lit the flame, the actual fire of war broke out when Austria declared war on Serbia on the twenty-eighth of July of that same year.

Soon Germany joined the conflict by declaring war on both Russia and France, neutral Belgium was overrun, and by August of 1914 Great Britain had declared war on Germany. In the coming years Turkey, Bulgaria, Italy, Romania, Portugal, Greece, Japan, and finally the United States entered what was finally to be called "The First World War."

Never in the history of the world had so many different peoples been in a state of declared war with one another. Some of these peoples lived far around the globe from one another while most of the combatants in Central Europe were centuries-old neighbors.

And how were people convinced to mobilize to wage war on their neighbors? How do you interest the ordinary human in wanting to kill other humans who have for generations lived just across the border from your own ancient family home? Public service advertisements seen in newspapers of the day tell the story. "Send Kaiser Bill down the drain," and "Hang the Huns!" posters appeared on walls as well as in newspapers. These advertisements painted all those citizens who happened to live in Triple Alliance countries as some subhuman species, a dirty mistaken breed of animals that needed to be exterminated.

As winter came the front lines of war slashed a great crack down the center of Europe with Germans, Austrians, and Italians on one side and French and Britons down the other. Both sides blazed away at an enemy who had been defined as outside the pale of God's creation.

Then the Christmas season came and a very strange thing happened all along the front lines of war. No one knows quite where it started, but, once started it spread and spread for what was later reported to be hundreds of miles. Someone heard someone else singing Christmas carols and though the words were in different languages, the tunes

> The plot of the Cornelius story has some similarity to court legends in Greek and Jewish story-telling tradition. In such stories, the sage appears in the court of the foreign king, resolves a conflict or solves a riddle through the use of his divine wisdom, and is rewarded by the king. Among the stories of this type are those of Joseph (Genesis 40–41, *Joseph and Asenath* [first-century C.E.]) and Daniel (Daniel 5). Here in Acts Cornelius is pictured as a royal official rather than a king, but he is clearly a person of power and status in his world. He receives a vision from God, not unlike others in these types of stories, and is told to send for the sage (Peter) to interpret the vision. Peter provides the interpretation and Cornelius is led to praise God as a result.

were familiar. Then the singing was picked up on the other side of the line, in another language, and the singing grew.

Suddenly, those who had been being fired upon were no longer animals but had to be heard and then visualized as humans.

Shooting stopped until it was all quiet. Someone, no one knows where it started, ventured across the line.

Soon the front was filled with different sounds from the sounds of war. Christmas day was spent as enemy soldiers shared carols, shared food, soccer games, and celebrations of faith.

Then, when the day was over, the fighting started back. But, for one brief day, people who had been blinded by war had come to see one another as people. "The Christmas Truce of 1914" remains as one of the great enigmatic times in human history when a day of light penetrated through the years of darkness.

(Note: For a version of this story in another artistic medium, see John McCutcheon's song "Christmas in the Trenches.")   *(Donald Davis)*

In Peter's speech, Jesus' life is summarized in this way: "Because God was with him he [Jesus] went about doing good and healing all who were oppressed by the devil" (10:38*b*). This style fits a format often used by ancient storytellers to characterize the divinely chosen hero. Epictetus speaks of Heracles in a similar way: "Come, how many acquaintances and friends did he have with him as he went up and down through the whole world? Nay, he had no dearer friend than God. That is why he was believed to be a son of God (Zeus), and was. It was therefore in obedience to His will that he went about clearing away wickedness and lawlessness." (Epictetus 2.16.44 [early-second-century C.E.]; Conzelmann, 83)

Peter Escapes from Prison

An angel frees Peter; his would-be killer is struck down by an angel.

The Story

MEANWHILE those who had been scattered after the persecution that arose over Stephen made their way to Phoenicia, Cyprus, and Antioch, bringing the message to Jews only and to no others. But there were some natives of Cyprus and Cyrene among them, and these, when they arrived at Antioch, began to speak to Gentiles as well, telling them the good news of the Lord Jesus. The power of the Lord was with them, and a great many became believers and turned to the Lord.

The news reached the ears of the church in Jerusalem; and they sent Barnabas to Antioch. When he arrived and saw the divine grace at work, he rejoiced and encouraged them all to hold fast to the Lord with resolute hearts, for he was a good man, full of the Holy Spirit and of faith. And large numbers were won over to the Lord.

He then went off to Tarsus to look for Saul; and when he had found him, he brought him to Antioch. For a whole year the two of them lived in fellowship with the church there, and gave instruction to large numbers. It was in Antioch that the disciples first got the name of Christians.

During this period some prophets came down from Jerusalem to Antioch, and one of them, Agabus by name, was inspired to stand up and predict a severe and world-wide famine, which in fact occurred in the reign of Claudius. So the disciples agreed to make a contribution, each according to his means, for the relief of their fellow-Christians in Judaea. This they did, and sent it off to the elders, entrusting it to Barnabas and Saul.

IT was about this time that King Herod launched an attack on certain members of the church. He beheaded James, the brother of John, and, when he saw that the Jews approved, proceeded to arrest Peter also. This happened during the festival of Unleavened Bread. Having secured him, he put him in prison under a military guard, four squads of four men each, meaning to produce him in public after Passover. So, while Peter was held in prison, the church kept praying fervently to God for him.

On the very night before Herod had planned to produce him, Peter was asleep between two soldiers, secured by two chains, while outside the doors sentries kept guard over the prison. All at once an angel of the Lord stood there, and the cell was ablaze with light. He tapped Peter on the shoulder to wake him. 'Quick! Get up!' he said, and the chains fell away from Peter's wrists. The angel said, 'Do up your belt and put on your sandals.' He did so. 'Now wrap your cloak round you and follow me.' Peter followed him out, with no idea that the angel's intervention was real: he thought it was just a vision. They passed the first guard-post, then the second, and reached the iron gate leading out into the city. This opened for them of its own accord; they came out and had walked the length of one street when suddenly the angel left him.

Then Peter came to himself. 'Now I know it is true,' he said: 'the Lord has sent his angel and rescued me from Herod's clutches and from all that the Jewish people were expecting.' Once he had realized this, he made for the house of Mary, the mother of John Mark, where a large company was at prayer. He knocked at the outer door and a maidservant called Rhoda came to answer it. She recognized Peter's voice and was so overjoyed that instead of opening the door she ran in and announced that Peter was standing outside. 'You are crazy,' they told her; but she insisted that it was so. Then they said, 'It must be his angel.'

Peter went on knocking, and when they opened the door and saw him, they were astounded. He motioned to them with his hand to keep quiet, and described to them how the Lord had brought him out of prison. 'Tell James

and the nembers of the church,' he said. Then he left the house and went off elsewhere.

When morning came, there was consternation among the soldiers: what could have become of Peter? Herod made careful search, but failed to find him, so he interrogated the guards and ordered their execution.

Afterwards Herod left Judaea to reside for a while at Caesarea. He had for some time been very angry with the people of Tyre and Sidon, who now by common agreement presented themselves at this court. There they won over Blastus the royal chamberlain, and sued for peace, because their country drew its supplies from the kings territory. On an appointed day Herod, attired in his royal robes and seated on the rostrum, addressed the populace; they responded, 'It is a god speaking, not a man!' Instantly an angel of the Lord struck him down, because he had usurped the honour due to God; he was eaten up with worms and so died.

Meanwhile the word of God continued to grow and spread; and Barnabas and Saul, their task fulfilled, returned from Jerusalem, taking John Mark with them.

Comments on the Story

Luke wishes to show that the beginning of a mission to gentiles (Greeks) was marked by very close cooperation between Antioch and Jerusalem. In response to a prophesied famine the believers do not don white sheets and head for the mountains, but engage in practical ministry to their fellow believers.

The story about Peter (and others) is one of three accounts of deliverance from prison (5:17-23; 16:19-40). Appreciation of each of these stories will be enhanced by reflection upon all of them. They appear at crucial junctures in the narrative. The "parallelism" between Peter and Paul (16:19-40) is oft noted.

For both the smaller and larger story of Acts, however, the more important parallel may be Acts 27:1–28:10, Paul's deliverance from the sea. Acts 12 has many appealing features, including humor, drama, suspense, and balanced instances of "poetic justice." Storytellers need but evoke these to succeed in their enterprise.

Historians identify the villain as Agrippa I, King of Judea 41–44. At the story level it is more important to observe that "King Herod" in the New Testament is a label for wicked tyrants, monarchs who murder babies, the Baptizer, and apostles. The narrator communicates much in his brief introduction. The execution of James establishes that Herod plays for keeps. Attuned to the fickle winds of public opinion, the king decides to raise his standing in the polls by lowering Peter to the grave. There is, however, a retarding factor: the holidays. Earlier experience (5:17-25) demands elaborate security: not only sturdy chains but also four soldiers in four shifts, with two in immediate attendance. Let us see if the apostle can wiggle his way out of this predicament! When Passover has passed away, so will Peter. These "days of unleavened bread" add suspense. They also evoke the death of Jesus at Passover: disciples are to follow the master's footsteps. These words further establish the Exodus theme, and not without irony. The very festival of freedom from bondage and social death is the moment selected for chains and pending execution.

Given the monarch's proven ardor and the stringent conditions of confinement, there is little room for hope. However, the faithful continue in prayer without, it will soon become apparent, much credence. God nonetheless acted, for, at the last possible moment, when all seemed lost, an angel of the Lord erupted upon the scene in a blaze of light. Light is, of course, a standard feature of such manifestations (epiphanies), and angels are God's customary agents. At another level, Luke and Acts are about light to the nations (Luke 2:9; Acts 13:47), light that blinds those who will not see and illumines dark paths for those who look with open eyes.

The scene unfolds with excruciating tension. Peter does not fly on angels' wings from the horror of imminent death. Indeed, he has been facing death with such equanimity that the light does not rouse him. It took a prod of the angelic sandal and words used to restore the dead (cf. 9:40-41) to bring him to his feet, awake, but scarcely alert. As the guards remain inert (for how long?), the angel must, like a parent, supervise his dress. First comes the tunic. Then the sandals are to be laced up. Don't forget the cloak! Early spring nights are chilly.

By this point the hearers are about to go crazy. Of all the times to dispatch an angel with the mentality of a conscientious parent! This is a prison break, not a papal reception! Will he next be admonished to wash his hands? When the angel is finally satisfied that Peter is shipshape and wrinkle-free, the exodus may begin.

To Peter comes the invitation for discipleship: "follow me." That he does, not understanding what he did, for it seemed to him no more than a death's-edge dream. Not just one, but two guard posts must be passed before reaching the most awesome barrier of all, an iron door. How will they get through it? Easily enough; it opens before them. The angel guides Peter for another block, then vanishes. Where are mothers when we really need them? Bereft of an escort, the apostle finally realizes that he has been delivered. It will not do to loiter about the streets of a hostile city. He must slink through dark alleys to find a refuge. One such is at Mary's, known to a later generation as John Mark's mother.

In that place believers had assembled to pray (for Peter, presumably). Their prayers have been answered; he is standing at the door. Because of the persecution, the house is secured and watched. This is one more door through which Peter will have to pass. He must risk unwanted attention by pounding upon it. Nosy neighbors can in this case pride themselves upon doing their religious and patriotic duty. To the door came a slave named Rose (Rhoda). She was so excited by the appearance of one returned from the grave (cf. Luke 24:41) that she imprudently left the well-known apostle out in the cold and dashed within to share the good news. This should be the happy end. It is not.

Scores are being evened up. Peter has some debts to pay, one incurred in a courtyard encounter with another female slave (Luke 22:56), another in the general response to the message of the women who had visited Jesus' tomb. Rose is greeted with the same disbelief they had experienced (Luke 24:11). She does not give up. Accusations of insanity will not deter her. Those assembled for prayer now show their theological insight: she has seen the "guardian angel" of a departed soul. From this, one may conclude that their angelology was defective. They accepted guardian angels, but not liberating angels. As for faith in prayer, it is good to go through the motions, but one must, after all, be realistic.

They are fiddling while Rome burns, for Peter must continue to knock. Every moment raises the danger that neighbors will investigate. In due course a solution is found: try the door. To their astonishment it is Peter in the flesh (cf. Luke 24:36-43)! The sequel does not follow the logical course of Peter's entry and a general celebration. Silencing them with an oratorical gesture, the apostle delivered a report and asked that the message be conveyed to James and others, before he left for an undisclosed location. Hearers are left filled with curiosity.

The narrator gives no time for such questions, but cuts to the next day at the jail, where the disappearance is a cause célèbre. Executions do take place, not of Peter, but of the obviously negligent guards. Herod then retires to another place. Unknowingly following the footsteps of Peter, he goes to Caesarea, only to find himself embroiled in another quarrel, this with the citizens of the biblically notorious Tyre and Sidon. They sue for peace, well aware that their food comes from Herod's lands. In a corrupt court, bribery of officials is one effective means of action. With the chamberlain Blastus, their seed finds fertile soil ("Blastus" means "shoot," "sprig"). Givers of food are benefactors; benefactors require adulation. Such Herod will receive at the resultant celebration. He, too, gets dressed, in far from ordinary clothes, without an angelic valet. The effect of his appearance and oratory is hailed as an epiphany. The crowd dreams that divinity is in their midst. It soon will be, for Herod's turn for an angelic prod has come. He will expire from this blow, with the illness characteristic of tyrants, an infestation of worms.

The two stories are not unrelated. They run in reverse, *(ABBA)* order, mirroring each other. In contrast to the contrived "famine" threatening Tyre and Sidon and its corrupt solution stands the Christian response to an actual famine. Then there are the closely contrasted fates of Herod and Peter, each prompted by an angelic buffet.

This is more, however, than a tale about the apostle Peter. Themes of Exodus and of baptism permeate and universalize the text. In this paschal play Herod takes the role of wicked Pharaoh, from whose hand (Exod. 14:30) Peter, the prisoner in bonds, is rescued by divine agency, playing the part of the liberated people. His very act of getting dressed brings to mind the rubrics for eating the Passover feast (Exod 12:11).

Peter's passover is also ours, for the motifs of his rescue are those of initiation: the movement from sleep (death) to light (salvation), rising, behaving like a newborn babe, clothing oneself in the garments of salvation, crossing the portals separating slavery from freedom, Egypt from promised land, old from new. Through these symbols the story recapitulates and evokes the rebirth and redemption of every Christian in the paschal mystery of baptism. We too have passed from the prison of death to the household of faith and life.

Retelling the Story

> And one of them, Agabus by name, was inspired to stand up and predict a severe and world-wide famine. . . . So the disciples agreed to make a contribution, each according to his means, for the relief of their fellow-Christians in Judaea. (Acts 11:28-29)

During all of the years that I served in local parishes we took dozens and dozens of special offerings for disaster relief. As a United Methodist I presided and promoted as we took offerings for flood victims, for hurricane victims, for famine victims, for tornado victims, all initiated by various denominational and local disaster relief agencies and organizations. The one consistent thing about all of these special offerings was that they were all taken after the fact. Never in a single church that I served did we ever establish a fund for "Coming Trouble," though everyone surely knew that next year there would be more floods, fires, hurricanes, hunger, and other troubles not even invented yet.

This thought reminded me of something very different that my Uncle Moody did for me when I was born, something that I never even knew about for years and years, and something that I came to appreciate only after more years had passed since I first heard the story.

Uncle Moody was my father's older brother, a veteran of the First World War, and a wholesale grocer. As a young man he married Aunt Rebekah and as things turned out the two of them never had any children. I loved my Uncle Moody. He was tall and bald and loved to play and dance and sing when he and Aunt Rebekah came to visit. But of all of my uncles and aunts, Uncle Moody and Aunt Rebekah were the only ones who never remembered either my birthday or Christmas. I was sure that it was because they had no children to train them in the things that ought to be done to make children happy!

My father, Uncle Moody's younger brother, did not marry as a young man. In fact, he was in his forties when he and my mother met and was forty-three before he married the twenty-five-year-old bride who would, when he was forty-four, become my mother and the mother of my younger brother.

By the time I was ready to graduate from high school and think about going to college, my father was fast approaching his retirement years and my brother was still on his way to grad-

The story of Peter's miraculous release from prison has numerous elements of classic storytelling of the day. The theme is clearly that the hero, Peter, has the protection of divine power so that even chains cannot hold him. Similar stories occur in heroic sagas of the day, since it was commonly held that a hero would come under special care of a god or goddess and be guided, often miraculously, to the outcome planned by the deity. This motif is as old as the stories of Homer, where the gods intervene when necessary in human events. In Luke's day, many stories were circulating about the ability of a divine hero to break through any chains that might try to bind him. The Roman writer Ovid describes a scene in which "of their own accord the doors flew open wide; of their own accord, with no one loosing them, the chains fell from the prisoner's arms" (*Metamorphoses* 3.699-700 [early-first-century C.E.]). The Jewish writer Artapanus (first-century B.C.E.) presents a similar legend about Moses: "When night came the doors of the prison opened of their own accord and some of the guards died, while some were beset with sleep and their weapons were broken" (from Eusebius, *Praep. ev.* 9.27.23). (Conzelmann, 94)

uation two years later. Financing a college education for my brother and me would not have been an easy task in the beginning of our father's retirement years.

But I was lucky. Uncle Moody had seen "trouble coming" when I was born and had sought to do something about it before the fact instead of after. All of a sudden I realized that this one uncle whom I had thought had simply ignored Christmas and birthdays, the one whom I was sure did not know how to take care of children, this very one had gone a long way toward providing more for me than birthday presents.

Suddenly I learned that every year, starting with the year of my birth, childless Uncle Moody had bought my brother and me two one-hundred-dollar U.S. savings bonds, one for each of our birthdays and the other for Christmas. By the time eighteen years of this practice passed, he had gradually upped the amounts and these silent "before trouble came" gifts, with the interest they had earned, helped ease two boys through college.

> Herod Agrippa here dies the painful death of a tyrant, a formula often found in popular literature. Josephus has a similar story of his death, recounting how while he was at Caesarea, he was acclaimed by the crowds as a god. Immediately he was taken ill and died of an acute abdominal distress, but without the reference to worms (*Antiquities* 19.343-50 [late-first-century C.E.]). Death by worms occurs elsewhere, however. It is also the fate of the evil tyrant Antiochus (2 Macc. 9:9) and is a form of death attributed to divine punishment (Jdt. 16:17).

Uncle Moody and Agabus were two of a kind. And they were spiritual heirs of Joseph and his Pharaoh of the Genesis story. Remember there that it took seven years of planning ahead to avert the disaster of famine.

No, I don't want to stop taking special offerings for disasters after they come, but, once in a while I want to have the foresight of Agabus, of Joseph, of Uncle Moody, and realize that small plans made early just may have more power for good than big plans made too late.   *(Donald Davis)*

Making Straight the Path

In Antioch the Holy Spirit commissions Saul and Barnabas to begin a new phase of mission work.

The Story

THERE were in the church at Antioch certain prophets and teachers: Barnabas, Simeon called Niger, Lucius of Cyrene, Manaen, a close friend of Prince Herod, and Saul. While they were offering worship to the Lord and fasting, the Holy Spirit said, 'Set Barnabas and Saul apart for me, to do the work to which I have called them.' Then, after further fasting and prayer, they laid their hands on them and sent them on their way.

These two, sent out on their mission by the Holy Spirit, came down to Seleucia, and from there sailed to Cyprus. Arriving at Salamis, they declared the word of God in the Jewish synagogues; they had John with them as their assistant. They went through the whole island as far as Paphos, and there they came upon a sorcerer, a Jew who posed as a prophet, Barjesus by name. He was in the retinue of the governor Sergius Paulus, a learned man, who had sent for Barnabas and Saul and wanted to hear the word of God. This Elymas the sorcerer (so his name may be translated) opposed them, trying to turn the governor away from the faith. But Saul, also known as Paul, filled with the Holy Spirit, fixed his eyes on him and said, 'You are a swindler, an out-and-out fraud! You son of the devil and enemy of all goodness, will you never stop perverting the straight ways of the Lord? Look now, the hand of the Lord strikes: you shall be blind, and for a time you shall not see the light of the sun.' At once mist and darkness came over his eyes, and he groped about for someone to lead him by the hand. When the governor saw what had happened he became a believer, deeply impressed by what he learnt about the Lord.

Comments on the Story

The popular notion that Acts describes three missionary journeys of Paul derives from the Protestant overseas missions of the nineteenth century. Nonetheless, 13:1–14:28 is an enclosed unit, based upon a new axis: Antioch. Built as the capital of the Syrian empire founded by one of the successors of Alexander the Great, Antioch was a cosmopolitan mix of Greeks, Semites, and others, well situated for communication with the west by water and, through overland connections, with Palestine, Anatolia, and places further east.

93

That cosmopolitan character is symbolized in the leadership of the mixed Jewish-gentile Christian community, which includes a Black, evidently, from what is now Libya, a Cypriot of Levitic descent, a former associate of the Tetrarch Herod, and a man from Tarsus. This brief list signals, like others (1:13; 6:5; 20:3-4) a transition. In the midst of prayer and fasting, the Spirit breaks forth. Since the Spirit does not say "Send Barnabas and Saul to Cyprus and southern Asia Minor," the message creates suspense. The commission proper comes from the community, through a ceremony that Luke's first readers would have viewed as something like an ordination (cf. 2 Tim. 1:6). Accompanied by John (Mark; cf. 12:12, 25), Barnabas and Saul set out.

Their first destination is Cyprus. The narrator does not speak of results, but does note that they focused upon synagogues. The hierarchy of salvation history ("the Jew first" Rom. 1:16 and others) has not changed. Luke illustrates this mission with a single story, a kind of synecdoche. Parallelism is important. As Jesus had begun his work by encountering the devil (Luke 4:1-11), and Peter's first missionary journey climaxed in a confrontation with Simon, so will Saul also meet a diabolic agent. This creature goes by two names: "Son of Joshua" (Barjesus) and "false prophet" (Elymas). Now this fine Elymas had reached the pinnacle of his chosen profession, serving as domestic chaplain to the Roman governor, Sergius Paulus. That discerning fellow extended an invitation to the newcomers. The locale is Paphos. The narrator omits any details, so storytellers will have to supply them. First, I suggest, picture a gubernatorial palace, since Roman governors did not hold important audiences on street corners. To this add a very effective sermon, since the envy of deceiving Barjesus indicates that he envisioned an abrupt end to his comfortable livelihood. In defense of that position and whatever faith he may have cherished, he attempts a rebuttal. Of this we learn nothing, for *Paul,* as he is now called, brings him to a screeching halt with an eloquent curse, revealing in one burst his rhetorical and spiritual powers. With these words the sorcerer finds himself in that state Paul had once enjoyed (9:8). Blinding was a normal form of divine punishment. The irony is patent: Elymas's spiritual and physical conditions fully coincide. The redolent expression of verse 10 to "perverting the straight ways of the Lord," evokes the beginnings of another ministry aimed at the salvation of all (Luke 3:5-6). The learned proconsul had seen enough. He converted.

The outset of this new venture is thus marked by a victory over Satan and the conversion of one of the crème de la crème, a member of the small senatorial class that rested atop a vast social pyramid. Since senators were not noted for affiliating with revolutionary sects or lower-class cults, hearers may conclude that this movement deserved respect. For the earliest audience of Acts such a story was positively thrilling. Observe how the narrator works: not by saying, "at this time Paul emerged as the actual leader of the mission," but through showing the missionary vanquishing a fraud and garnering a prime convert. The new name Paul is no less apt for the Greek world than it is myste-rious for the reader.

Retelling the Story

"You son of the devil and enemy of all goodness, will you never stop perverting the straight ways of the Lord?" (Acts 13:10*b*).

My mother's father was not an out-going and sociable man. Yes, he was my grandfather, but when I went there to visit as a young child I always thought of the visit as going to "Grand-ma's house."

This set of grandparents lived on a subsistence homesteading farm located back in the north end of an Appalachi-an county, which pushed North Caroli-na smack against the border of East Tennessee and created a good chunk of the Great Smoky Mountains National Park. The farm had been in the family for generations, and since Grandfather was the baby of the family, it was he who inherited it in his generation after his older brothers and sisters had made their own way into the world and established homes of their own.

At one time the unpaved county road that ran to the back end of the moun-tainous north end of the county had run right past the house that he inherited from his own parents and grandparents. All of the traveling public came by his doorway, and he had but to step into the road to go anywhere he wished to go. But, as times changed, the county road was straightened and relocated, later even macadamized against all condi-tions of weather, and now it ran some full mile from Grandfather's house and directly down the bottom of the valley.

The narrator of Acts chooses at this point to change how he will refer to Paul—from his Jewish name "Saul" to his Greek name "Paul." Evidently this is to alert the reader that a new phase in the story is taking place in which Paul will now emerge as a preeminent missionary among the gentiles. Roman citizens normally had three names, a *praenomen* (such as Lucius), a *nomen* (such as Sergius), and a *cognomen* (such as Paulus). The name "Saul" could have Paul's *signum,* a kind of nickname, and "Paulus" his *cognomen.* But this is not definite since it was not common for people from Paul's part of the Mediter-ranean world to follow the strict rules of naming found at Rome. For the storyteller, however, indicating the apostle by the name "Paulus" in connection with the occurrence in the story of a noble Roman named "Sergius Paulus" puts Paul in good company, consistent with the point that will be made later that Paul is a Roman citizen. (adapted from Conzelmann, 100; Haenchen, 399)

When the new straightened and paved road came, a boon to the farming residents all around, the old and unpaved road simply became a part of Grandfather's farm. It was his own private road both across the farm and to his house.

And did he take care of it? Not at all. Grandfather didn't own a car or truck and had never learned to drive and now that this was his own private road he didn't think that anyone else should travel on it. So, he not only didn't take care of it, he even put up a gate and fenced it off.

That was not enough. In those days there were many fenced roads in rural areas because cattle were pastured all over those mountains. Rules of common courtesy simply dictated that travelers close any gates that were opened. Besides this, if anyone happened to be deliberately going for a visit or to do business at my grandparents' house, the only way to get there was to go on Grandfather's road.

Grandfather did not like that, so he took to "damaging" the road. He would take a mattock or a pick and start small gullies in the road bank that would wash out deeper when the rains came, thus making the road difficult to cross. He would roll rocks from the pasture down into the road itself and leave them there as barriers to anyone's travel.

Before long even the family could not come to visit. If we wanted to visit we either had to risk damaging our car (which we once did with the result that the entire exhaust pipe was left in the rocky road) or park a mile below in the field and walk up to the house. Grandpa took what was a good and straight road and crooked it all out of usable shape.

So what?

When I was young and all of this was happening, my grandfather worked the farm with horses and oxen and never traveled anywhere except by his own sled to the nearby community store. He didn't drive and didn't see any reason to provide a road for anyone else.

But, when my grandmother suffered a premature and unexpected heart attack in her fifties, the ambulance could not get down the road to take her to the county hospital.

I still remember that pitiful day when they tried, got all hung up, and finally parked down in the field at the bottom of the farm while the doctor, my father, and two attendants manually wrestled my poor and inert grandmother nearly a mile on a homemade stretcher to get her to the ambulance. I also remember the fits my mother and her brothers and sisters pitched at Grandfather, but to no avail.

True to his stubborn nature, even this did not change Grandfather. He did not try to straighten up the road until he himself later decided that he wanted to learn to drive.

It was the mid-fifties and Grandpa (in his sixties by now) had suddenly taken on a desire to be mobile and see the world. When he bought his own pickup truck (after learning to drive on a tractor) he was suddenly shocked to learn that he could not even get the truck home! And, God's gravity being what it is, it was a whole lot harder to move the big rocks back out of the road than it had been to roll them down into it from the hill to begin with. It also took more work to refill the gullies than when he had helped them to wash out on their own.

In our biblical story, Paul looked at Elymas and, as punishment, said, "You shall be blind, and for a time you shall not see the light of the sun." In my memory of Grandfather's struggle with his own selfishness, the entire family saw that he had already been blind and unable to see more than just the sun for quite some time. Perhaps both he and Elymas eventually learned that "the road you crook may be your own."

(Donald Davis)

Jewish magicians were widely known in the ancient world, despite the fact that magical practices were not allowed in the Jewish law. Josephus (late-first-century C.E.) refers to another Jew of Cyprus named Atomus "who pretended to be a magician" (*Antiquities* 20.142). In another context, he relates a cure wrought by another Jewish magician who, like Elymas in this story, was retained by a Roman official: "I have seen a certain Eleazar, a countryman of mine, in the presence of Vespasian, his sons, tribunes and a number of other soldiers, free a man possessed by demons, and this was the manner of his cure: he put to the nose of the possessed man a ring which had under its seal one of the roots prescribed by Solomon, and then, as the man smelled it, drew out the demon through his nostrils, and, when the man at once fell down, adjured the demon never to come back into him, speaking Solomon's name and reciting the incantations which he had composed" (*Antiquities* 8.46-47). (Foakes Jackson and Lake, 4,143)

97

ACTS 13:13-52

Sowing the Seed

A rousing sermon in Pisidia leads to opposition, the decision to preach to gentiles, and expulsion.

The Story

Sailing from Paphos, Paul and his companions went to Perga in Pamphylia; John, however, left them and returned to Jerusalem. From Perga they continued their journey as far as Pisidian Antioch. On the sabbath they went to synagogue and took their seats; and after the readings from the law and the prophets, the officials of the synagogue sent this message to them: 'Friends, if you have anything to say to the people by way of exhortation, let us hear it.' Paul stood up, raised his hand for silence, and began.

'Listen, men of Israel and you others who worship God! The God of this people, Israel, chose our forefathers. When they were still living as aliens in Egypt, he made them into a great people and, with arm outstretched, brought them out of that country. For some forty years he bore with their conduct in the desert. Then in the Canaanite country, after overthrowing seven nations, whose lands he gave them to be their heritage for some four hundred and fifty years, he appointed judges for them until the time of the prophet Samuel.

'It was then that they asked for a king, and God gave them Saul son of Kish, a man of the tribe of Benjamin. He reigned for forty years before God removed him and appointed David as their king, with this commendation: "I have found David the son of Jesse to be a man after my own heart; he will carry out all my purposes." This is the man from whose descendants God, as he promised, has brought Israel a saviour, Jesus. John had made ready for his coming by proclaiming a baptism in token of repentance to the whole people of Israel; and, nearing the end of his earthly course, John said, "I am not the one you think I am. No, after me comes one whose sandals I am not worthy to unfasten."

'My brothers, who come of Abraham's stock, and others among you who worship God, we are the people to whom this message of salvation has been sent. The people of Jerusalem and their rulers did not recognize Jesus, or understand the words of the prophets which are read sabbath by sabbath; indeed, they fulfilled them by condemning him. Though they failed to find grounds for the sentence of death, they asked Pilate to have him executed. When they had carried out all that the scriptures said about him, they took him down from the gibbet and laid him in a tomb. But God raised him from the dead; and over a period of many days he appeared to those who had come up with him from Galilee to Jerusalem, and they are now his witnesses before our people.

98

'We are here to give you the good news that God, who made the promise to the fathers, has fulfilled it for the children by raising Jesus from the dead, as indeed it stands written in the second Psalm: "You are my son; this day I have begotten you." Again, that he raised him from the dead, never to be subjected to corruption, he declares in these words: "I will give you the blessings promised to David, holy and sure." This is borne out by another passage: "You will not let your faithful servant suffer corruption." As for David, when he had served the purpose of God in his own generation, he died and was gathered to his fathers, and suffered corruption; but the one whom God raised up did not suffer corruption. You must understand, my brothers, it is through him that forgiveness of sins is now being proclaimed to you. It is through him that everyone who has faith is acquitted of everything for which there was no acquittal under the law of Moses. Beware, then, lest you bring down upon yourselves the doom proclaimed by the prophets: "See this, you scoffers, marvel, and begone; for I am doing a deed in your days, a deed which you will never believe when you are told of it." '

As they were leaving the synagogue they were asked to come again and speak on these subjects next sabbath; and after the congregation had dispersed, many Jews and gentile worshippers went with Paul and Barnabas, who spoke to them and urged them to hold fast to the grace of God.

On the following sabbath almost the whole city gathered to hear the word of God. When the Jews saw the crowds, they were filled with jealous resentment, and contradicted what Paul had said with violent abuse. But Paul and Barnabas were outspoken in their reply. 'It was necessary,' they said, 'that the word of God should be declared to you first. But since you reject it and judge yourselves unworthy of eternal life, we now turn to the Gentiles. For these are our instructions from the Lord: "I have appointed you to be a light for the Gentiles, and a means of salvation to earth's farthest bounds.' " When the Gentiles heard this, they were overjoyed and thankfully acclaimed the word of the Lord, and those who were marked out for eternal life became believers. Thus the word of the Lord spread throughout the region. But the Jews stirred up feeling among those worshippers who were women of standing, and among the leading men of the city; a campaign of persecution was started against Paul and Barnabas, and they were expelled from the district. They shook the dust off their feet in protest against them and went to Iconium. And the disciples were filled with joy and with the Holy Spirit.

Comments on the Story

Paul's mission replicates that of the Jerusalem apostles. In the beginning there is untroubled success. Subsequent success ignites hostility, the result of which is an expansion of the mission. Under Paul's guidance (Barnabas is not mentioned in verse 13 and John Mark drops out of the group a verse later) the mission leaps forward, over vast and formidable obstacles, landing in one bound in the heart of what is now Turkey, at Antioch, a Roman colony in Pisidia. (Many ancient cities were named Antioch.)

As in the case of Jesus' opening sermon (Luke 4:16-30), the passage begins by describing a synagogue service. The officials wonder if their visitors have a few words to say. Paul does. Standing like a professional orator, he delivers a full-scale homily. The message has much in common with Peter's address in chapter 2. Through this means, the author indicates that the great leaders of the early days shared the same faith. Paul reviews the promises of salvation history, announces that they have been fulfilled, and invites the audience to respond. His opening survey conveniently takes up where Stephen had stopped (chap. 7). Here, also, there is more than a hint of criticism of the Israelites for their hard-hearted ways. His final warning will not be heeded. Among those assembled are "others . . . who worship God" (v. 26). Acts envisions these "God-fearers" as gentiles like Cornelius and the official from Ethiopia—persons attracted to Judaism but unable or unwilling to become full members. Paul includes them in his remarks. His sermon had an immense impact. Stimulated worshipers asked for more. In the course of the next seven days, as suspense mounts and anticipation rises to its peak, a host of Jews and others aligned themselves with the missionaries. The whole town was in an uproar. With the arrival of the Sabbath came an audience nearly coextensive with the population. "The Jews" (who can now be identified as "the other") did not see this turnout as good news. On the contrary, overcome with jealousy, they attempted, like Barjesus, to repudiate the message. "Violent abuse" indicates that they were not minding their manners while so employed.

This intimidates Paul and Barnabas no more than it had Peter and John (chap. 3). They deliver a judgment. The chosen people have not deigned to see the fulfillment of their fondest hopes. Very well, the gentiles will be invited. Preaching to gentiles may seem to be a startling innovation. Isaiah 49:6 (cf. also Luke 2:32) is adduced to prove that this is not so. The bottom line is that the phrase "farthest corners of the earth" is intended both geographically and metaphorically, for God's ends embrace all humanity.

One result of this was an explosion of saving light—rapid acceptance by happy gentiles. Another was more dire. Not lacking in political acumen, Jewish emissaries make overtures to some of their better-placed women sympathizers, who, one may presume, are to influence their powerful husbands. From this pillow talk persecution is conceived. The troublesome pair are shown to the city gates (cf. Luke 4:28-30). Carefully detaching the last vestige of the hostile soil from their evangelizing feet (cf. Luke 10:10-12), the two move on to Iconium, while the narrator offers a final comforting glimpse of the joyous believers, whose faith refuses to flag.

Retelling the Story

Thus the word of the Lord spread throughout the region. But the Jews stirred up feelings among those worshipers who were women of standing, and among the leading men of the city; a campaign of persecution was started against Paul and Barnabas, and they were expelled from the district (Acts 13:49-50).

Again and again in this section of Acts we find conflict between the early Christians and some of the leaders of the Jews. Once again this trouble arises as the travelers arrive in Antioch of Pisidia. What in the world is the trouble about this time?

It's just another version of the same old thing. No, it is not an honest theological or doctrinal or even ethical disagreement, but a particular version of jealousy under which the Jews of Paul's day are infuriated that God's privileges could be offered to the uncircumcised gentiles.

Under this version of jealousy, the problem is not that we want what someone else already has, rather it is that we want to keep others from getting what we think should be reserved only for us.

When I was in high school I drove a school bus. At that time school buses in North Carolina and many other rural states were driven by student drivers. In the summer before my junior year in high school, I went to school to earn my bus driver's license.

In a normal synagogue service, such as what is described in Luke 4, the speaker stands to read the scripture and sits to expound upon it (Luke 4:16, 20). Therefore we would expect Paul to sit rather than stand when he speaks here. Philo, however, refers to a speaker in a Jewish assembly standing to speak if he is "of special experience" (*De Specialibus legibus* 2.62 [early-first-century C.E.]). Here, Luke wants us to picture Paul in such a tradition, as an orator of prominence (he stands to speak) and skill (he begins with a rhetorical gesture). (Conzelmann, 103)

Schools were segregated in those days, but integration was coming. One of the first steps toward integration was "administrative desegregation," which for me meant that bus drivers' school was integrated even though the children we would be driving were still kept in separate schools.

It was during that integrated bus driving school that I met Stanley Easter.

Stanley Easter was the first Black person my age I had ever even talked to, let alone come to know.

During the three-week bus driving course, Stanley and I became great friends. No, we did not get together outside of class and we didn't visit each other at home, but we did talk and laugh and joke and gradually exchanged even some real secrets about ourselves before it was all over.

Stanley and I admitted to each other that we were both afraid of the same two things: girls and our mamas! Finally Stanley even told me that his mama's pet nickname for him was "The Easter Bunny."

Near the end of our three-week friendship Stanley and I talked about our own future hopes and plans. I told him that I wanted to go to college and that I probably would. Stanley told me that more than anything else he would love to go to college, but that he didn't see how he could ever get the money to do that. Still, college was his greatest hope. So, we thought, even if we go to separate segregated high schools, maybe we just might end up back together in college some day.

When school started I got a bus route, and, each morning and afternoon, I met and waved to Stanley as our buses passed en route to our separate segregated schools.

In the fall, high school football season started. My daddy loved football and he always read aloud the football game reports at Saturday breakfast after the Friday night games.

Once in a while he would read about the Pigeon Eagles, the small one-A football team at the school where Stanley was a student. That year the Eagles had a good team and finally won every game. As my daddy read, it was always the same thing: somehow it was Stanley Easter who won the game. He rushed for the most yardage or scored the most points or caught a pass at just the right time.

I remembered what Stanley had said about wanting to go to college and not having enough money. I suggested in a conversation with Daddy, "Maybe he can get a football scholarship. Maybe Stanley and I might end up in college together after all."

"Oompf!" my daddy grunted. "Maybe one of those little colored schools will snap him up, but a real college wouldn't even take a chance on something like that!" I couldn't quite figure that out, but I did wonder how Stanley drove his school bus each day, worked on the farm the way he always told us he did, and still got to practice football enough to win all the games? And, I wondered why my daddy seemed to laugh at Stanley's hope instead being proud of it?

I did get to go to Davidson College. Going to college was the plan and dream all of my friends' parents had for

The gesture of shaking the dust from one's feet is also referred to in Luke 9:4 and 10:11. It is not entirely clear to us today how strong a gesture it was meant to be. It is an act done against an entire city, and seems to have symbolized something like "washing one's hands" of them. They had their chance to repent; now their fate is in their own hands as the missionaries move on. It may even indicate a curse, much like we find in the practices of magicians of the day. (Foakes Jackson and Lake, 5.270-71) their children. Everyone I knew went to college. My best friend Davy Martin had even gone to Harvard (which I secretly thought was a very stupid thing for a North Carolina mountain boy to do).

During my freshman year of college, I got to go to Washington, D.C., as part of a political science elective course I had signed up for. It was a wonderful trip and made me feel like I was grown up and on top of the world.

While on the trip, my Davidson roommate and I met two students in the same program who were both in the freshman class at Harvard. We all went out one night to tour the city and then get pizza.

While we were waiting for the pizza we fell into conversation. "Where are you from?" one of the Harvard students asked.

"Oh, a little town called Waynesville, North Carolina," I answered.

"Really? There's a guy in our class from Waynesville. He's the smartest boy in our class . . . on a full academic scholarship!"

"Davy Martin?" I questioned. "Davy Martin on an academic scholarship? I think somebody's pulling your leg!"

"Who's Davy Martin?" the other Harvard student replied, "The guy we're talking about is named Stanley Easter. He's smart, but he says that his mama still calls him "The Easter Bunny."

I never told my daddy about Stanley Easter. Maybe he found out about it on his own, but I didn't want to see his face when he found out. I guess I loved him too much to want to see the embarrassment of his disappointed jealousy.

(Donald Davis)

ACTS 14:1-28

Common Grounds with the Other

After meeting the same fate in Iconium as at Antioch, Paul moves on to Lystra and Derbe, where old superstitions and recently made enemies provide new challenges.

The Story

At Iconium they went together into the Jewish synagogue and spoke to such purpose that Jews and Greeks in large numbers became believers. But the unconverted Jews stirred up the Gentiles and poisoned their minds against the Christians. So Paul and Barnabas stayed on for some time, and spoke boldly and openly in reliance on the Lord, who confirmed the message of his grace by enabling them to work signs and miracles. The populace was divided, some siding with the Jews, others with the apostles. A move was made by Gentiles and Jews together, with the connivance of the city authorities, to maltreat them and stone them, and when they became aware of this, they made their escape to the Lycaonian cities of Lystra and Derbe and the surrounding country. There they continued to spread the good news.

At Lystra a cripple, lame from birth, who had never walked in his life, sat listening to Paul as he spoke. Paul fixed his eyes on him and, seeing that he had the faith to be cured, said in a loud voice, 'Stand up straight on your feet'; and he sprang up and began to walk. When the crowds saw what Paul had done, they shouted, in their native Lycaonian, 'The gods have come down to us in human form!' They called Barnabas Zeus, and Paul they called Hermes, because he was the spokesman. The priest of Zeus, whose temple was just outside the city, brought oxen and garlands to the gates, and he and the people were about to offer sacrifice.

But when the apostles Barnabas and Paul heard of it, they tore their clothes and rushed into the crowd shouting, 'Men, why are you doing this? We are human beings, just like you. The good news we bring tells you to turn from these follies to the living God, who made heaven and earth and sea and everything in them. In past ages he has allowed all nations to go their own way; and yet he has not left you without some clue to his nature, in the benefits he bestows: he sends you rain from heaven and the crops in their seasons, and gives you food in plenty and keeps you in good heart.' Even with these words they barely managed to prevent the crowd from offering sacrifice to them.

Then Jews from Antioch and Iconium came on the scene and won over the crowds. They stoned Paul, and dragged him out of the city, thinking him dead. The disciples formed a ring round him, and he got to his feet and

104

went into the city. Next day he left with Barnabas for Derbe.

After bringing the good news to that town and gaining many converts, they returned to Lystra, then to Iconium, and then to Antioch, strengthening the disciples and encouraging them to be true to the faith. They warned them that to enter the kingdom of God we must undergo many hardships. They also appointed for them elders in each congregation, and with prayer and fasting committed them to the Lord in whom they had put their trust.

They passed through Pisidia and came into Pamphylia. When they had delivered the message at Perga, they went down to Attalia, and from there sailed to Antioch, where they had originally been commended to the grace of God for the task which they had now completed. On arrival there, they called the congregation together and reported all that God had accomplished through them, and how he had thrown open the gates of faith to the Gentiles. And they stayed for some time with the disciples there.

Comments on the Story

Following the fulsome description of events at Antioch, Iconium needs but a summary. Verses 1-7 could provide the skeleton for a full-fledged story. Priority belongs to the synagogue, with substantial success among both Jews and gentiles. Opposition by unconvinced representatives of the former group leads the missionaries to prolong their stay. Like many Greek cities, Iconium suffered from factionalism. More or less everyone had to take one side or the other in the debate.

The anti-Pauline faction was unfettered by conventions of open debate and fair play, not least because they could not win by these rules. They therefore connived with leaders from among both gentiles and Jews to assure that the former would overlook a small breach of law and order. The latter would supply a posse charged with the task of stoning the loathsome pair. (The medical prognosis for stoning is not favorable.) This plot could not remain hidden, so Paul and Barnabas were able to evade their adversaries and escape to the region centered upon Lystra and Derbe. A happy end, but ominous.

The foes grow more determined and angry with each failure. How long will the missionaries be able to elude the arms of stone-throwing Iconians? Just when too much danger might become cloying, there is an interlude.

Lystra brings Paul face-to-face with a man unable to walk. Like Jesus and Peter (Luke 5:18-26; Acts 3:1-9), he heals this unfortunate. In the case of Peter, the healing brought a crowd, who received a sermon. Here the sermon has already been delivered and the crowd is to hand. Now Lystra was a bit off the beaten path and far from the heart of culture and sophistication. The inhabitants, who did not even speak Greek—at least when excited—leaped to the conclusion that the ones who had made the formerly disabled man leap were,

105

in fact, two of the leading gods, Zeus and Hermes, gods honored in one of their local temples. Gods demand sacrifices. These were promptly prepared. The narrator explains what these Lyconians were saying, but the dramatic characters, Paul and Barnabas, remained in the dark until it became unmistakably clear that these rustic types were about to perform a blasphemous action, "pagan" sacrifice, offered to mortals at that.

Luke is, in fact, playing with an old story. Many educated readers of his era were familiar with an ancient legend that described a visit by none other than Zeus and Hermes, in human disguise, to this very region. Strangers they were, and not well received by suspicious locals, until, at long last, they happened upon a very aged and impoverished couple, Baucis and Philemon, who had almost nothing, but happily shared what they had. Their reward was prompt: the lowly cottage was transformed into a temple of Zeus and Hermes, over which they were to preside until death. Quite aware of this monumental error, their descendants wanted to be absolutely certain not to repeat an old and oft-mentioned mistake. If Zeus and Hermes were at it once more, they were going to be ready. (Even those who do not know the old legend may, of course, appreciate this story.)

None of this was in the least amusing to Paul and Barnabas, who dashed in to extinguish this blaze with an emergency dose of natural theology. Their sermonette serves as a critique of the common view of miracle as something that "violates laws of nature." For Luke, creation, with its seasons and rhythms, is a miracle. Small things, like a healing, are the tip of an iceberg. This is an elegant little piece, and rightly so, for every ounce of rhetoric and wit was required to fend off disaster. This funny story does more than poke fun at rustic pagans. Beneath its amusing surface one can gain a glimpse of the obstacles faced by those like Paul who tried to make polytheists into Christians. Still and all, it is better to be offered oxen than rocks.

Barbarians are not only a superstitious lot; they are also fickle. Within a single verse they moved from deification to assassination. The agents of this rapid change of heart were a mob of Jews from Iconium. These good zealots had paused to pick up reinforcements from Antioch and had then undertaken a long and rigorous journey that finally brought Paul to bay. They burst upon the scene at the very moment when the danger of sacrifice was over. In the twinkling of an eye the crowd of worshipers became a mob of executioners. After battering Paul with showers of rocks, they hauled his polluting carcass out of town. Thereupon, it would seem, they left the field of honor, at which the believers can gather to mourn their departed hero and plan suitable obsequies. Paul, like Stephen, has paid the price for his eloquent convictions. And then . . . there rises before their very eyes an unbelievable sight: Paul! Though undoubtedly severely injured, he was in no way cowed. Rather than find a secure shelter, he marched back into the very lions' den! Rather than take a week or so to recover, he set out for Derbe the next day.

Those who spent portions of their younger days watching cowboy or gangster movies recognize the type of scene and its meaning. Like many heroes of popular fiction, the stalwart apostle could walk away from a severe beating and continue his quest. On this climactic note, marked by sophisticated theology and glittering rhetoric, a moving miracle story, and the closest call yet, the tension may reside. Things go well at Derbe, followed by courageous visits to the mission sites. After making a circle back to their home base, they deliver to the entire community a full report of their labors.

Retelling the Story

When the crowds saw what Paul had done, they shouted, in their native Lycaonian, 'The gods have come down to us in human form!' (Acts 14:11)

While traveling through Lystra, Paul healed a man who had been disabled since birth. None of the people in that town had ever seen anything like this! Instead of listening to Paul as he proclaimed the source of this healing, they pronounced him and his partner Barnabas gods and began trying to offer them worship and tribute.

There was no serious problematic outcome to this misunderstanding because Paul and Barnabas did not allow themselves to be deified. But everyone who is flattered by being thought godlike does not come off so well.

The story of Baucis and Philemon was the popular account of a visit to earth by Zeus and Hermes, disguised as mortals. This is the story that Luke alludes to here. In this story, the two deities appear as strangers seeking hospitality. They are turned away by all of the wealthy in the village, but the poor old couple Baucis and Philemon take them in and feed them with the last of their food. To the couple's amazement, the meager food they place on the table miraculously multiplies so that there is plenty for all, and more to spare. They immediately recognize that these are gods they have been entertaining and fall to their knees. The gods inform them that they alone have been hospitable, so they will be spared while the entire village perishes in a flood. Their hut is made into a temple and they are made to be priest and priestess within it. When at last they die, they are granted their wish that they die together. As a memorial to their great piety and a symbol of their intertwined lives, the gods cause two trees to grow together at the spot where the old couple was buried. (Ovid, *Metamorphoses* 8.610-700 [early-first-century C.E.]; Boring, no. 510)

My father and three of his brothers were sent away from home around 1915 to attend boarding school in Cullowhee, North Carolina. They were not sent to boarding school because this was a special thing to do, but because there was no public high school in the small farming community where the family lived and this was the only way their higher education could be attended to.

The four were not very well prepared for life in such a sophisticated and modern environment. One story is told of their vain struggle to blow out the electric lightbulb that was hanging in the center of their room on their first night there. Having seen nothing but oil lamps in their lives, they could not master the bulb and finally, so the story goes, Uncle Frank put his sock over it so they could sleep. (There was no later report about what this did to the sock.) But the boys learned fast. One at a time they graduated until at last, Uncle Frank, the youngest one, was approaching the proud day of his graduation.

Having the advantage of three older brothers and a longer number of years than anyone else at the boarding school, the family was very proud to know that Uncle Frank was finishing at the top of the class. He was even making a speech at the graduation ceremonies and he had worked on it and practiced it until everyone around him was looking forward to the day's finally being over.

On the night before graduation a big and fairly formal (for that time and place) dinner was given for all visiting families by the president of the academy. All of Uncle Frank's family had traveled to be there, including the three brothers who had preceded him in their own matriculation.

When the great dinner began, Frank Madison Davis, senior honor student and graduation speaker for the class, was seated at the head table with the president of the school and other honored guests.

One of the honored guests at the head table was the Reverend Davis, a local minister from the nearby town of Sylva, who would be called upon to deliver an invocation at the graduation ceremonies and who would be asked to bless the upcoming meal.

As things settled into place and the president began his role as master of ceremonies, Uncle Frank had no thoughts about anything except his own self-imagined greatness. He seemed to listen and smile through the introductions of special guests, but a close look would have revealed his smile to be the veneered look of one whose thoughts were somewhere else.

Suddenly the president finished all of his introductions and said, "Now, friends, if Mr. Davis will lead us by asking the blessing, we will all be ready to eat."

Suddenly Uncle Frank was on his feet praying! Of course for a split second he realized that he had not been asked in advance if he would do this, but, of course, he was surely the logical choice for such an honor and the president had just assumed that he would do it!

Uncle Frank prayed about the food, he prayed about the graduating class and its singular achievements, he prayed about the faculty and all of the members of their families, he prayed about the history of the school, he prayed his way all the way back to the very creation of the world itself. Then he finally said his "amen" and sat down, victorious with his smile.

The school president never missed a beat. He simply said, "Thank you Frank. Now if our special guest, Reverend Davis from Sylva, will ask our official blessing, we will be well prepared to eat."

The family never stopped laughing about and remembering Uncle Frank's assumption of greatness!   *(Donald Davis)*

The tearing of one's garments, which was undertaken in response to blasphemy, was a symbolic act in Judaism. For example, it is specified as the action members of the Sanhedrin were to take when hearing testimony about blasphemy, a custom that the Gospels allude to at the trial of Jesus (Mark 14:63; Matt. 26:65). It was also used as an act of sorrow (especially at funerals), as an act of protestation (as in Numbers 14:6), and, in the Greek tradition, as an act of entreaty. (Foakes Jackson and Lake, 5.271-72)

Managing Conflict

Paul and Barnabas lead a delegation from Antioch to resolve a conflict with the Jerusalem church over requirements of the law for Gentiles.

The Story

SOME people who had come down from Judaea began to teach the brotherhood that those who were not circumcised in accordance with Mosaic practice could not be saved. That brought them into fierce dissension and controversy with Paul and Barnabas, and it was arranged that these two and some others from Antioch should go up to Jerusalem to see the apostles and elders about this question.

They were sent on their way by the church, and travelled through Phoenicia and Samaria, telling the full story of the conversion of the Gentiles, and causing great rejoicing among all the Christians.

When they reached Jerusalem they were welcomed by the church and the apostles and elders, and they reported all that God had accomplished through them. But some of the Pharisaic party who had become believers came forward and declared, 'Those Gentiles must be circumcised and told to keep the law of Moses.'

The apostles and elders met to look into this matter, and, after a long debate, Peter rose to address them. 'My friends,' he said, 'in the early days, as you yourselves know, God made his choice among you: from my lips the Gentiles were to hear and believe the message of the gospel. And God, who can read human hearts, showed his approval by giving the Holy Spirit to them as he did to us. He made no difference between them and us; for he purified their hearts by faith. Then why do you now try God's patience by laying on the shoulders of these converts a yoke which neither we nor our forefathers were able to bear? For our belief is that we were saved in the same way as they are: by the grace of the Lord Jesus.'

At that the whole company fell silent and listened to Barnabas and Paul as they described all the signs and portents that God had worked among the Gentiles through them.

When they had finished speaking, James summed up: 'My friends,' he said, 'listen to me. Simon has described how it first happened that God, in his providence, chose from among the Gentiles a people to bear his name. This agrees with the words of the prophets: as scripture has it,

Thereafter I will return and
   rebuild the fallen house of
   David;
I will rebuild its ruins and set it
   up again,
that the rest of mankind may
   seek the Lord,
all the Gentiles whom I have
   claimed for my own.
Thus says the Lord, who is
   doing this as he made known
   long ago.

'In my judgment, therefore, we should impose no irksome restrictions on those of the Gentiles who are turning to God; instead we should instruct them by letter to abstain from things polluted by contact with idols, from fornication, from anything that has been strangled, and from blood. Moses, after all, has never lacked spokesmen in every town for generations past; he is read in the synagogues sabbath by sabbath.

Then, with the agreement of the whole church, the apostles and elders resolved to choose representatives and send them to Antioch with Paul and Barnabas. They chose two leading men in the community, Judas Barsabbas and Silas, and gave them this letter to deliver:

From the apostles and elders to our brothers of gentile origin in Antioch, Syria, and Cilicia. Greetings!

We have heard that some of our number, without any instructions from us, have disturbed you with their talk and unsettled your minds. In consequence, we have resolved unanimously to send to you our chosen representatives with our well-beloved Barnabas and Paul, who have given up their lives to the cause of our Lord Jesus Christ; so we are sending Judas and Silas, who will, by word of mouth, confirm what is written in this letter. It is the decision of the Holy Spirit, and our decision, to lay no further burden upon you beyond these essentials: you are to abstain from meat that has been offered to idols, from blood, from anything that has been strangled, and from fornication. If you keep yourselves free from these things you will be doing well. Farewell.

So they took their leave and travelled down to Antioch, where they called the congregation together and delivered the letter. When it was read, all rejoiced at the encouragement it brought, and Judas and Silas, who were themselves prophets, said much to encourage and strengthen the members. After spending some time there, they took their leave with the good wishes of the brethren, to return to those who had sent them. But Paul and Barnabas stayed on at Antioch, where, along with many others, they taught and preached the word of the Lord.

Comments on the Story

While Paul and Barnabas are basking in the success of their mission, a cloud appears on the horizon. To Antioch there come some unnamed Judeans. The narrator does not in any way suggest that these persons acted under the auspices of the apostles at Jerusalem. They were certainly willing to share their views: circumcision is necessary for *salvation*. The androcentric character of early Christian literature is quite clear in the language of this debate. Only males were to be circumcised, although the texts treat the issue as universal. (For Greeks and Romans male circumcision was about as repugnant as is female "circumcision" to westerners today.)

This demand sharply raises the question of continuity by requiring that all (males) must, in effect, become Jews. The language does not, however, speak of covenant but of salvation, or *soteriology,* to use the technical term. Such language was not unheard of among first-century Jews, but it does represent a shift into different categories of thought, categories Christians would develop. This is the first of several instances indicating that Luke casts the entire debate in Christian terms.

The proposal does not please Paul and Barnabas. Of the subsequent sharp debate the narrator says no more than that it took place. In developing this story one might wish, possibly with assistance from Jewish sources and Pauline letters, to flesh out that debate, providing strong arguments for each side. To readers who know neither the end of this story nor the letters of Paul, this quarrel comes as a complete surprise. Had not the question been disposed of with the conversion of Cornelius? Faced once more with internal dissension (cf. Acts 6 and 11), the community resolves to send an emissary to Jerusalem to meet with "the apostles and elders."

The delegation, led, naturally, by Paul and Barnabas, made a leisurely progress, stopping in Phoenicia (the coastal cities) and Samaria, missions to which occupied much of chapters 8–10. Reports of success among gentiles elicited considerable jubilation. The quest was off to a very good start. They were also warmly, if not joyously, received at Jerusalem. Some believers, identified as members of the Pharisaic party, did not hesitate to present forthright objections to their practice: circumcision *and* observance of Torah are obligatory. Thus far the debate had been informal. Moreover, these objectors are identified as Pharisees, their demands include keeping the entire Torah, and, most important, they do not speak of what is necessary to *salvation.* This is a small opening, but wide enough to include all the nations of earth.

The matter calls for a meeting of apostles and elders (v. 6), although at some point the entire assembly of believers is included (v. 22). Luke envisions the assembled church as rather like the government of a Greek city with several "houses" and the full body of citizens. Early readers would have been impressed at the official and orderly nature of these proceedings, including high-toned debate, crisp resolutions, and official letters. Aristocratic Romans did not admire the fabled "democracy" of Greek cities, which they saw as little more than mob rule (for an example see Acts 19). Luke paints the Sanhedrin in colors taken from the same polemical palette. Christian assemblies, to the contrary, are orderly, that is, subordinate, and decorous.

The meeting includes a lively debate, of which the narrator shares not a word. (Again, storytellers may wish to fill in this gap if they have not done so elsewhere.) Such condensation throws the limelight upon the decisive words. It is characteristic of Peter to allow others to speak first (cf. Luke 9:18-21). He reminds the audience of the precedent set with Cornelius, a case in which he had acted under divine direction. This whole business is nothing new. Moreover, the Torah is an impossible burden. Only through grace can salvation come to both Jews and gentiles. (This is, in fact, a gentile view of Torah; for Jews, obedience is a source of joy.) Taking, as it were, a leaf from the book of Gamaliel, Peter warns them against trying the patience of God.

That times have changed becomes apparent when Peter's word is not the last. This role belongs to James, who has become the leader at Jerusalem. Before he plays his part, however, opportunity is given to Paul and Barnabas. They appeal to proof based upon the wonders exhibited in their gentile ministries.

After the "foreign" missionaries have been given a respectful hearing, the new leader takes the floor to give his *Nihil obstat* (nothing objectionable) to the words of Peter, followed by the first explicit *theological* justification for a gentile mission. Scripture confirms the experience of the Spirit, as a substantial citation from Amos demonstrates. James thus joins Peter in viewing the gentile mission as the result of a hermeneutical breakthrough, the new understanding of Scripture brought to minds opened by Easter (Luke 24:45). Fulfillment of the promises to David takes place in the proclamation of a messianic salvation offered to all.

James exhibits his authority by delivering the conclusion to be reached. Gentile believers are not to be harassed. They are, however, to observe four customs known through the public reading of Scripture. These are more or less the regulations imposed upon gentile residents of the promised land. Maintenance of these principles (which to us appear to commingle "moral" and "ritual" matters) will make fellowship possible. ("Fornication" probably refers not only to sexual misconduct but also to marriage within certain degrees of consanguinity.) The vitality of these questions for early believers is visible in 1 Corinthians 8–10 and Galatians 2. At stake is not which restaurant we shall choose or who serves the most nutritionally correct meals, but sacramental life. Those who could not eat together could not share in a common eucharist. To make an effective story one may wish to find some analogous controversial boundaries from contemporary life. In vital conflicts, discerning the voice of the Spirit is central. That includes listening to various sides and playing by the rules.

The result is all that could be expected. Without a further word of debate, the entire body concurred with their leaders and voted to communicate the decision in the form of an official decree, issued as a letter to be conveyed by a delegation that will include Judas Barsabbas and Silas. This is all quite stately and dignified. Verses 30-35 nicely reverse the itinerary of verses 1-5, indicating that the situation has also been turned around. In place of conflict there is consolation; peace reigns where turmoil had boiled. Chapter 15 could have been an unpleasant interlude. By its end Paul and Barnabas are back where they were at the conclusion of chapter 14. Well-managed conflict leads to growth.

Retelling the Story

SOME people who had come down from Judaea began to teach the brotherhood that those who were not circumcised in accordance with Mosaic practice could not be saved. That brought them into fierce dissension and controversy with Paul and Barnabas. (Acts 15:1-2*b*)

Just what is all this business about circumcision after all?

According to Cicero, Greek assemblies were notorious for being unruly affairs: "Thus he extorted those 'elegant' decrees read to you—decrees passed neither by formal vote nor proper authority, nor even hallowed by oath, but carried by the upraised hands and loud shouts of an excited mob" (*Pro Flacco* 15-16 [first-century B.C.E.]). In contrast, the Christian assembly is presented here as a model of decorum. (Pervo, *Profit*, 39)

Charles Lloyd was one of the finest classroom teachers I ever met or knew in my life. As an undergraduate I sat in his freshman English class and came to know Steinbeck, Hemingway, Emily Dickinson, Robert Frost, Wallace Stevens and a whole host of others whom, through his bright teaching genius, we came to know as real people and not just dead producers of dusty books. My lifelong love of reading and literature started with Charlie Lloyd.

I earned spending money in college by working in the processing room at the college library. My job there consisted of getting new books and rebound books numbered, stamped, bug-proofed, and generally ready for shelving and circulation. One day a number of old college catalogues returned from the bindery where they had been put in hardback covers for archival preservation. As I prepped them, I glanced through some from years gone by. Suddenly a familiar name popped out into my vision: Charles Lloyd. I was looking at the catalogue and wondering how long this man had been teaching when suddenly I realized that he was not listed in the English department, but in the mathematics department. Was this the same person who was my English teacher?

When I asked about him, I was fascinated by what I learned. Yes, it was the same Charles Lloyd, and, yes, he had in the past also taught math. In fact, he had also taught Latin and filled in for short terms in other departments. The man was not only a brilliant teacher, he was a brilliant scholar.

One story that I heard about him was that he had come to the college as an instructor as a very young man. When, after a few years in this role, the college

114

insisted that he return to school and pursue a graduate degree, his question was: "What do you want me to get it in? English, or physics or, perhaps, mathematics?" The final choice had been English.

He was a great bushy-headed bear of a man who often wore tattered clothing, usually needed a haircut, sported bow ties and always wore an overgrown moustache. He was, for me, the perfect model of a gentleman scholar.

In those days faculty members held open house for students after vespers on Sunday evening. Each professor's home was open on one Sunday evening every month. Often such visitation was done as some sort of obligatory attempt at getting enough recognition by a teacher to hope that one's grade improved. Not so at the Lloyd house. It was always filled with students who came for the conversation. Instead of an hour, we often stayed there late into the night debating, questioning, and being questioned with the knowledge that in this place we were fully alive and respected and that naive stupidity would never be held against us.

In class we answered the roll with quotations from literature. The real contest was to see whether we could be so obscure as to trick Professor Lloyd, a quest that had us searching in tomes we would never have looked at otherwise. Once in a while someone fooled him, and when that happened, he was the most delighted of all. The man was a great director of learning.

Some time ago a notice came in the alumni magazine that Charlie Lloyd had died. When this a notice prompted me to think about him again, I went back to my old college annuals and looked him up. There he was, his very photograph professorial, though he looked much younger in the picture than I remembered him in life. There was his academic listing: Assistant Professor of English.

After all those years of teaching, with all of the brilliance he had in the classroom, given the inspiration he gave to all who learned under him, why was he not a full professor or even an associate? I remembered the story. The answer was very simple: He did not have a Ph.D.

Yes, Charles Lloyd was not academically circumcised!

What was the big deal about circumcision with those in Judea with whom Paul and Barnabas tangled? Was it that circumcision made them better Christians? Was it that circumcision increased their faith? Was it that circumcision assured a higher level of morality?

Or could it have been that a "since we had to do it, you can't get in unless you do it too" mentality existed even then? Could it even be that sometimes in the jealousies of human life, different versions of circumcision, just like some academic degrees, are used to keep people out instead of being used to bring people in?

Read all of the fifteenth chapter of Acts and see whether you think Charlie Lloyd would have made full professor at the university in Jerusalem.

(Donald Davis)

The rules to be imposed on Gentiles by the decision of the council are the rules listed in Leviticus for Gentiles to follow when they reside in a Jewish land (Leviticus 17–18). They primarily concern a version of Jewish dietary laws, thus making it possible for Gentiles and Jews to share a common table. In this way, the council is represented as reaching a compromise, not requiring the Gentiles to become Jews through circumcision, but requiring them to obey the law nevertheless, that is, the law as specified for Gentiles in a Jewish land. This is one of many instances in which Luke has merged the saga of the beginnings of the church with the saga of the people of Israel.

Off to a Slow Start

Paul, with a new team, visits some earlier cities, then strikes out for new ground, but is thwarted until a vision summons him to the other side of the Aegean.

The Story

A FTER a while Paul said to Barnabas, 'Let us go back and see how our brothers are getting on in the various towns where we proclaimed the word of the Lord.' Barnabas wanted to take John Mark with them; but Paul insisted that the man who had deserted them in Pamphylia and had not gone on to share in their work was not the man to take with them now. The dispute was so sharp that they parted company. Barnabas took Mark with him and sailed for Cyprus. Paul chose Silas and started on his journey, commended by the brothers to the grace of the Lord. He travelled through Syria and Cilicia bringing new strength to the churches.

He went on to Derbe and then to Lystra, where he found a disciple name Timothy, the son of a Jewish Christian mother and a gentile father, well spoken of by the Christians at Lystra and Iconium. Paul wanted to take him with him when he left, so he had him circumcised out of consideration for the Jews who lived in those parts, for they all knew that his father was a Gentile. As they made their way from town to town they handed on the decisions taken by the apostles and elders in Jerusalem and enjoined their observance. So, day by day, the churches grew stronger in faith and increased in numbers.

They travelled through the Phrygian and Galatian region, prevented by the Holy Spirit from delivering the message in the province of Asia. When they approached the Mysian border they tried to enter Bithynia, but, as the Spirit of Jesus would not allow them, they passed through Mysia and reached the coast at Troas. During the night a vision came to Paul: a Macedonian stood there appealing to him, 'Cross over to Macedonia and help us.' As soon as he had seen this vision, we set about getting a passage to Macedonia, convinced that God had called us to take the good news there.

Comments on the Story

At first this venture appears to be anything but auspicious, merely a pastoral visit to earlier cites. Conflict erupts when Barnabas proposes that they once more utilize the services of John Mark. As far as Paul was concerned, Mark did not have what it took. Unable to resolve this issue, they parted ways. In the end this was good, for it led to a widened mission, with Barnabas and Mark setting out for Cyprus, while Paul selected a new colleague, Silas, who had come from Jerusalem. For ancient readers this ability to choose his own team demonstrated that Paul was now an authority in his own right. He is on his own, "commended" by the faithful. (In historical fact, Paul's quarrel with Barnabas and Antioch was theological.) Having played his part as a bridge between Jerusalem and Antioch, the apostles and Paul, Barnabas travels away from the pages of Acts. His story is over.

The course of this routine pastoral visit leads in due time to Lystra. There Paul learns that a potential new member of his missionary team, one Timothy, is of mixed parentage. (The matriarchal principle—those born of a Jewish mother are Jews—had not yet been established.) Paul has this well-recommended (young?) man circumcised. In light of chapter 15 this seems a surprising action. The narrator presents it as a missionary tactic, in conformity with Paul's commitment to preach to Jews first. Reference to this decision, as well as to the decree (which 15:23 limits to specific areas), shows Paul as a liberal and flexible person, pursuing a course of moderation and accommodation. Stories about heroes tend to acquire such colors as a means of expressing harmony. Luke's story of Paul is like the stories told about Civil War figures in later decades as a means to heal the breach. So Lincoln became the great moderate, foe of radical and reactionary alike, and Lee an opponent of slavery. In fact, Lincoln differed from the radicals in tactics, not goals, while Lee fought long and ably in defense of the right to hold slaves. The object of such "revisionist" legends is the promotion of unity. The Paul of Acts is such a figure.

Our new team slings its knapsacks for fresh fields, but the Spirit blocks any endeavor to preach in Asia Minor. Not until they reach the coast does this prohibition subside. One can trace their movements quickly on a map without appreciating the ardors involved. Land travel in the ancient world was a dangerous and racking business. Behind all these summaries lie many stories not told. What is told is enough to create suspense. Why has the Spirit issued this gag order? Curiosity mounts.

Finally they come to Troas, on the Aegean coast, a place redolent with legend, regarded as the location of Troy, around which much epic poetry revolved. In that fateful place Paul receives a vision. The first is suitably epochal, a nocturnal appearance of a Macedonian summoning him to "help us." Visions of personified provinces or nations were not routine. These came to such greats as Alexander or Caesar at crucial junctures in their careers. So it will be here. Brief as it is, the vision intimates something no less momentous than the conversion of Cornelius. Paul is destined for "Europe." Luke's images fit their circumstances. In chapter 10 the gentile Cornelius was visited, like Abraham and Gideon, by an angel, all in good biblical fashion. As Paul crosses the boundary between "Asia" and "Europe" to begin his independent career, the vehicle of revelation is not biblical, but Greco-Roman. Here is a powerful model and formidable challenge for storytellers: the selection of images that are not only vivid but also in themselves expressive of the desired theme.

At this crucial moment there also appears the first-person "we," which will return from time to time. What does it mean? Whom does "we" include? The narrator now emerges as a part of the story. One can hypothesize first-person plural sources, note that "we" is common in travel accounts, or suspect that the author of Acts was with Paul on some occasions. Each of these proposals has strengths and weaknesses. Without prejudice to them, "we" is, at the narrative level, a mystery provoking and enticing the reader, while embracing all who hear or read the story, transforming it from a story about "them" into a story about "us." With this intimacy comes a wealth of detail and color lacking in most of the earlier stories. For the first readers, "we" reflects the story of their own origins, the fruit of Paul's "missionary journeys." To a large degree this is true of all subsequent Christians, for the church that emerged in the Roman Empire was largely the fruit of the early Greek-speaking urban missions.

Retelling the Story

> AFTER a while Paul said to Barnabas, 'Let us go back and see how our brothers are getting on in the various towns where we proclaimed the word of the Lord.' . . . [But] the dispute [between them] was so sharp that they parted company. (Acts 15:36, 39a)

I have a friend who is living somewhere between his fifth and sixth marriages. Not only has he been married five times to date, but each of the five weddings was more elaborate than the one before, with number five being a memorably lavish affair that could never have been managed by anyone with less experience at planning such events.

At the last wedding someone commented to the very person in question about the size and grandeur of this, his fifth wedding. His reply was simple and straightforward: "Well, like I always said, there's nothing like getting off to a good start!"

We may laugh, but all of us are sometimes victims of our own belief that the way we start something has everything to do with how it comes out in the end.

Let me share with you another wedding story. It is, in fact, the story of the first wedding I was ever called on to perform in my twenty-three years of ministry in the local church.

The engaged couple was very young. I knew they were going to be young because when the bride's mother came to see me to talk about the wedding plans (I had not yet met the bride and groom), she was very young. And, I thought, so disorganized that this daughter's wedding might never be put together enough to happen at the appointed time.

Finally I got to meet John and Mary. (Their names are, of course, changed to protect the guilty!) They were both eighteen years old, just graduated from high school, and just starting new jobs in the local furniture industry. But, their wedding was to be the most special wedding anyone in the world had ever had. Mary's mother had told me so.

Since family funds were limited, Mary's mother was making both the wedding dress and the wedding cake for the reception to follow. Mother's sister was in charge of flowers and decorations, with the flowers to be wildflowers freshly picked on the day of the wedding itself.

I got to the church fairly early on the morning of the wedding and found that the two sisters, mother and aunt of the bride had really taken over the entire church, kitchen to sanctuary, as their pre-wedding command center. The kitchen was headquarters. In the church kitchen oven the wedding cake was still baking. There were masses of wildflowers and greenery stuffed in every big sink as pots were washed and polished and arrangements were being put together.

Then there was the sewing machine. Yes, the bride's dress was not quite finished and the bride's mother was going back and forth between the oven and the sewing machine, monitoring the cake and working on the dress. Once in a while the aunt in charge of flowers added her two cents' worth.

This was a frightening scene to me, so I wished them good luck, feebly offered my help if it were needed, and retreated to my office to hide out!

Miracles do happen. When there was exactly one hour left before the wedding, the last wildflower arrangement was placed in the sanctuary, a ceramic bride and groom were placed on the still-warm and just iced cake, and the wedding dress was pronounced finished.

With only thirty minutes left, I began to doubt the last statement. When I went to the bride's room to check on the party there, I found the nervous eighteen-year-old bride being sewn into the new dress by her mother.

"There just wasn't time to put in the zipper or work the buttonholes," she said. "So, I just sewed the buttons right on where they belong and we'll sew her in instead of zipping her up! We'll just cut her out of it after the reception."

The wedding started exactly on time.

As I saw the bride coming down the aisle, I was filled with relief and a sense that this was really going to work after all.

The first part of the traditional ceremony was held on the main floor of the sanctuary, just where the aisle bumped into the steps that led up to the altar. Promises were made, the bride was given away by a proud father, and, now helped along by the groom, we began to ascend the three steps that took us on up to the altar for the exchange of vows.

Those three steps were carpeted with fitted carpet. That's where all the trouble started.

The night before, at the rehearsal, everyone had been very informally dressed. Besides that, the bride had watched the rehearsal as her sister stood in for her. She had, herself, never taken these three carpeted steps up to the altar.

With one hand filled with wildflowers and the other hand linked through her husband-to-be's elbow, there was no hand left to lift the hem of her long lace-edged wedding dress. The lace caught on the rough carpet, the bride stepped up to the first step, stepping on the hem of her own dress, and the groom kept pulling her along. As she took the second step, something happened that I will never forget. She stepped again on the dress and all of the slack of the full skirt ran out. The sewn-together dress simply came apart at the waist! The waist failure, luckily, did not go all the way around; it only came apart in the front!

Actually, the bride did a great job at recovery and maintenance of control. She simply bunched up the front of the split dress and held her flowers over it. The bouquet of gathered wildflowers was so big that they camouflaged the accident not only through the wedding but all the way through the reception as well.

When it was all over, it didn't take as much work to cut her out of the dress as her mother had thought it would!

That all happened twenty-seven years ago! And, guess what? In spite of that bad start, that couple today is still married, happy, and well! A good start isn't everything. *(Donald Davis)*

Ancient storytellers often referred to the receiving of supernatural instructions by way of dreams. Several such stories are found in the Old Testament (as in Gen. 31:10-13) as well as in Greek and Roman popular legend and literature. The Greek historian Herodotus, for example, refers to a dream of Xerxes: "It seemed to Xerxes that a tall and goodly man stood over him and said . . ." (7.12 [fifth-century B.C.E.]). (Conzelmann, 127)

Dreams were the favorite form for healing messages. Aelius Aristides, who spent his entire life in search of healing for various ills, wrote copiously in the 140s of the divine instructions he received in dreams, ranging from instructions on healing to commands to continue his studies in rhetoric to "marvelous symbolic dreams, which pertained not only to my body, but also to many, many other things." (*Sacred Discourses* 2.15, 4.15 [second-century C.E.])

121

Dreams were often invoked as the authority for missionary activities of a religious cult. The Sarapis cult was especially famous for dream messages of this sort. In the third-century B.C.E., the image of Sarapis was said to have been brought to Alexandria from Sinope on command of the god in a dream, thus establishing the Greek form of the cult there. Later in the same century, a certain Zoilus of Aspendus reported receiving a dream in which Sarapis urged him to sail to Alexandria and solicit help from the court of Ptolemy II to build a temple of Sarapis in Greece. Also in the third-century B.C.E., the temple of Sarapis on Delos was built by command of the god received in a dream. A column erected at the site told of this event and functioned as propaganda for the cult: "When I inherited the sacred things and devoted myself busily to the observances of piety, the god gave me an oracle in my sleep. He said that he must have a Sarapeum of his own dedicated to him and that he must not be in hired quarters as before, and that he would himself find a place where he should be set and would show us the place. And so it was." (Nock, 49-51)

First in Philippi

After winning the household of a woman entrepreneur, Paul runs into
legal trouble in Philippi, but is ultimately vindicated.

The Story

We sailed from Troas and made a straight run to Samothrace, the next day to Neapolis, and from there to Philippi, a leading city in that district of Macedonia and a Roman colony. Here we stayed for some days, and on the sabbath we went outside the city gate by the riverside, where we thought there would be a place of prayer; we sat down and talked to the women who had gathered there. One of those listening was called Lydia, a dealer in purple fabric, who came from the city of Thyatira; she was a worshipper of God, and the Lord opened her heart to respond to what Paul said. She was baptized, and her household with her, and then she urged us, 'Now that you have accepted me as a believer in the Lord, come and stay at my house.' And she insisted on our going.

Once, on our way to the place of prayer, we met a slave-girl who was possessed by a spirit of divination and brought large profits to her owners by telling fortunes. She followed Paul and the rest of us, shouting, 'These men are servants of the Most High God, and are declaring to you a way of salvation.' She did this day after day, until, in exasperation, Paul rounded on the spirit. 'I command you in the name of Jesus Christ to come out of her,' he said, and it came out instantly.

When the girl's owners saw that their hope of profit had gone, they seized Paul and Silas and dragged them to the city authorities in the main square; bringing them before the magistrates, they alleged, 'These men are causing a disturbance in our city; they are Jews, and they are advocating practices which it is illegal for us Romans to adopt and follow.' The mob joined in the attack; and the magistrates had the prisoners stripped and gave orders for them to be flogged. After a severe beating they were flung into prison and the jailer was ordered to keep them under close guard. In view of these orders, he put them into the inner prison and secured their feet in the stocks.

About midnight Paul and Silas, at their prayers, were singing praises to God, and the other prisoners were listening, when suddenly there was such a violent earthquake that the foundations of the jail were shaken; the doors burst open and all the prisoners found their fetters unfastened. The jailer woke up to see the prison doors wide open and, assuming that the prisoners had escaped, drew his sword intending to kill himself. But Paul shouted, 'Do yourself no harm; we are all here.' The jailer called for lights, rushed in, and threw himself down before Paul and Silas, trembling with fear. He then escorted them out and said, 'Sirs, what must I do to be saved?' They answered, 'Put your trust in the Lord Jesus, and you will be saved, you and your household,' and they imparted the word of the Lord to him and to everyone in his house. At that late hour of the night the jailer took them and washed their wounds, and there and then he and his whole family were baptized. He brought them up into his house, set out a meal, and rejoiced with his whole household in his new-found faith in God.

When daylight came, the magistrates sent their officers with the order, 'Release those men.' The jailer reported these instructions to Paul:

'The magistrates have sent an order for your release. Now you are free to go in peace.' But Paul said to the officers: 'We are Roman citizens! They gave us a public flogging and threw us into prison without trial. Are they now going to smuggle us out by stealth? No indeed! Let them come in person and escort us out.' The officers reported his words to the magistrates. Alarmed to hear that they were Roman citizens, they came and apologized to them, and then escorted them out and requested them to go away from the city. On leaving the prison, they went to Lydia's house, where they met their fellow-Christians and spoke words of encouragement to them, and then they took their departure.

Comments on the Story

Acts 16:11-40 is a narrative composed of several stories, each of which could stand alone, and all of which stand together, although not without some difficulty. For this premier mission on European soil Luke has provided a showcase. At the conclusion there are two "house churches," one led by a woman of Jewish sympathies, the other by a man of polytheist background.

The narrative of 16:6-7 glibly chronicled the passing of entire provinces. At 16:11-12 the pace slows dramatically, with details about each day's experience. This change of pace is a narrative signal. The European mission will dawn at Philippi, which is the beneficiary of a flattering introduction. Well-situated at the juncture of east and west, land and sea, surrounded by arable land and mineral deposits, Philippi also gained from its location as the battleground where the future Augustus and Marc Antony defeated the assassins of Caesar and formed a Roman colony. "Colony" in Roman constitutional practice did not have the connotation associated with modern European colonialism. Colonies were pieces of Rome, as it were, seeds scattered on strategic sites. Those who held this title were proud of it. The political status of Philippi will be important for both the outcome of this particular story and the place of the church in the Roman Empire.

Once in place, the missionaries must wait, patiently or otherwise, for sabbath to come. There were not sufficient Jews or resources to provide a synagogue building, so the faithful met outside near a river. The narrator implies that only women were present, or, at any rate, receptive. One of these was engaged in the (manufacture and) sale of purple goods. Her name suggests that she was once a slave. Lydia was a "God-fearer" rather than a full convert. Persuaded by Paul and baptized, together with her household, she pressed Paul to accept her hospitality. This is no more than proper, but it portends something new, for the narrator has not said that Paul has lived with gentiles. The one who opened her heart (v. 14) opened Paul's as well. Lydia is the Cornelius of this mission, proof that barriers between Jew and gentile, female and male, are passing away.

One guardian of these boundaries was Satan. Verse 16 introduces an unfortunate woman whose prophetic capacity (internal noises interpreted as oracles) had made her a valuable commodity. This last word is no metaphor. The anonymous woman was a piece of property, a "slave-girl." (Peter also had difficulties with female slaves. See 11:19–12:25.) The power that possessed her, like the demons of Gospel accounts, recognized the enemy. She attached herself to Paul and his entourage, blaring out endless advertisements for their message. This might seem like a good thing, but Paul had absolutely no use for this kind of vulgar religion, which resembled the superstitions hawked in public squares by unscrupulous quacks. Nonetheless, he somehow put up with her for several days, until he could stand it no more. Intoning an exorcism, the irritated missionary pulled the plug on his free advertising. The real source of her gifts was, as he had discerned, a demon. In this humorous account, the narrator draws a close parallel between Paul and Jesus. Just as the latter began his Galilean ministry with an exorcism (Luke 4:31-37), so the former opened his mission to Europe with an exorcism symbolizing the inbreaking of God's rule and the downfall of Satan.

With that downfall came a sharp downturn in her owner's fortunes. Exorcism was for them very bad news. Instead of admiring crowds, the exorcism results in an angry mob. The owners were shrewd enough to veil their own callous greed. They masked their avarice with a heady cocktail composed of four jiggers of the last refuge of scoundrels, an ounce of old-time religion, and a dash of racism. The recipe was a hit. In practically less time than it takes to tell, they arraigned the missionaries on these base charges, supported by an even more base and vile mob. Stampeded by this outburst of civic unrest, the helpless magistrates sought to cast oil on the waters by having the alleged perpetrators viciously whipped and then put in firm custody. In obedience to the demand for security, the jailer chained them in the farthest corners of his facility.

These were the farthest corners of the earth for Paul and Silas. Far from the groans and laments such injustice and abuse would justify, they gave themselves to prayer and hymns of praise, devotions that moved even the hearts of calloused criminals to silence. Although chained for loosing a demon, they worshiped with souls unfettered. One could dwell for some time on this wondrous conduct, but the narrator has more in immediate store. The earth rever-berates (cf. 4:31), followed by an open door and shattered chains. Paul has come to share in the miracle worked for Peter and others (chaps. 4 and 12); he is now free to escape from wrongful arrest.

Before describing this expected escape, the narrator turns to the jailer, whom the disturbance had aroused from sound sleep. Spying the open doors, he drew the obvious inference. His charges have fled. Rather than stand trial on the charge of dereliction, he decided to do away with himself. At the last possible moment, with the blade poised to descend, he was halted by reassuring words from Paul. After summoning slaves equipped with torches, he rushed into the cell and threw himself at his rescuers feet. Fully aware that this is a divine visi-tation, the jailer then removed the two and laid before them the essential ques-tion: "What must I do to be saved?"

That is a question for which the two prisoners have an answer, delivered not just to him, but to the entire household. The injuries of Paul and Silas were washed; for the jailer and his people there came in turn the bath of regenera-tion. Thereafter the two were introduced into the jailer's private quarters for a family meal. So much for a remarkable night.

Daylight comes, as do a number of questions for hearers. What will the pub-lic in general and the magistrates in particular think of that earthquake? Will the jailer now place before his superiors his revised opinion of his two most recent convicts? Will there now ensue a trial at which the insidious manipula-tions of the unscrupulous oracle-mongers will be exposed to the full light of truth? Each of these sequels is quite plausible. In fact, the magistrates had determined on their own to throw in the towel. There presently arrived at the prison the official police escort of the ruling magistrates, with instructions to release the pair. No grounds for this change of mind are provided. Quite natu-rally delighted with this good news, the jailer rushed off to inform his charges. So the story has come to a happy end! Leave they must, but without imprison-ment or worse.

The deal sounds good, but Paul isn't buying. Confronting those same lictors, he checks off a list of official misdeeds, informing them (and us) that both he and Silas hold Roman citizenship (a privilege enjoyed by very few in the east-ern Mediterranean). What sort of self-denial is this? Since the punishments they had endured were illegal in the case of Roman citizens, we, in their shoes, would have raised this legal point much earlier in the game. Be that as it may, Paul is now prepared to assert his rights, to which he adds the demand for a formal escort. Appalled at their conduct, the officials wished to make amends and granted his request. So the mission to Philippi ends with a splendid tri-umphal procession, since, rights notwithstanding, the magistrates *do* think it best that the two depart, and depart they will, after making a pastoral call upon Lydia and those of her household.

Amidst some of the loose ends and improbable turns taken by this action-packed account are many symbols and cross-references. Paul, like Jesus, exorcises demons and suffers. Miraculous "release" from prison, when contrasted with the earlier accounts in chapters 5 and 12, suggests that more confidence may be placed in Roman justice than in the Sanhedrin. The earthquake and its attendant actions symbolize rather than accomplish their eventual release. Within the story of the earthquake the author places the experience of the jailer. In bringing light (cf. 12:7) to the prison he will be the one illumined. His literal rescue from death and disgrace symbolizes his spiritual deliverance. The open doors of the jail at Philippi were doors admitting gentiles to the faith.

Both conversions follow the same pattern: proclamation, initiation of the whole household, hospitality. A new community, based upon house churches, has been given birth. Its pioneers are a named woman and an anonymous man, reversing the more normal usage. Caught as he was in conflicts that could be life-threatening, the author had no interest in presenting ancient polytheism in a sympathetic light or showing Judaism to its advantage. Encased in this popular, sometimes vulgar, frame is the story of Satan's defeat. That story, please note, does not include the conversion or emancipation of the slave. Luke was less interested in freed slaves than in relating that the first colony of the renewed people of God in Europe took root within a leading city and Roman colony.

Retelling the Story

When the girl's owners saw that their hope of profit had gone, they seized Paul and Silas and dragged them to the city authorities in the main square. (Acts 16:19)

Sometimes staying sick has so many rewards it is more profitable to remain that way instead of getting well.

In this section, Paul meets and heals a woman who is possessed by a spirit of fortunetelling. She is a slave woman and her owners have used her possession by this spirit as a way to make

The storyteller sets up a circumstance in which Paul is actually treated illegally, since it is now revealed that he is a Roman citizen. Roman law on this point is mentioned by the Roman historian Livy who refers to "a heavy penalty if anyone should scourge or put to death a Roman citizen" (10.9.4 [59 B.C.E.–17 C.E.]). Another Roman jurist states: "By the Julian law on public violence he is condemned who, endowed with some power, will have killed, or ordered to be killed, should torture, scourge, condemn by law or order to be incarcerated in the state prison a Roman citizen appealing previously to the people and now to the emperor" (Paulus, *Sententiae*, 5.26.1 [third-century C.E.]). (Conzelmann, 133) money. Paul meets her and makes her whole, and, instead of being grateful that she is well, her owners complain because they can no longer use her ill state for profit.

This story reminds me of a friend whom I shall here call Anna Mitchell.

Anna had had a hard life. Her only son had died suddenly in high school when what looked like a very minor automobile accident turned out to have caused a blood clot in his brain. One moment he was being released from the hospital, and the next he was dead.

Her husband had developed lung cancer at the age of fifty and died at age fifty-three leaving her all alone.

Then Anna herself was found to have a deep skin cancer on her back, which required both surgery and extensive follow-up skin grafting and chemical therapies. She had had years of hard life and hard luck.

Yet through all this, Anna was the liveliest and happiest spirit anyone ever met. She sang in the church choir, entertained at picnics and parties, and was generally the comic delight of every event she was a part of. Everyone was sad when an event was held and Anna was not there. Her buoyancy and life picked everyone up.

In fact, Anna was on her way to entertain children at a birthday party when her big accident happened. All dressed up for the party, walking the short distance from her house to the neighbor's home where the party was to occur, Anna was struck by a hit-and-run driver who left her for dead.

The first report I received was that she was in the trauma room at the hospital and could not possibly live. Anna was unconscious, had lung punctures, a ruptured spleen, abrasions all over, and so many broken bones that there was not yet even an estimate of breaks and fractures.

Twenty-four hours passed and she had survived two trips to surgery. Now on a ventilator, she began to stabilize and gain strength. Soon there was more surgery for pinning broken and shattered bones. Still she grew stronger.

In all, Anna spent fourteen weeks in the hospital before there was even any discussion about being moved elsewhere. Then it was time for a move.

With no one living with her, how could she be moved home? She still could not walk at all and had no use yet of her right hand.

Neighbors planned, choir members got together, friends united and organized. Anna could come home! The whole community was organized to help. Food schedules were worked out, sitting arrangements were made, plans were put in order to have Anna, everyone's dear friend, cared for twenty-four hours each day so she could come back and finish recovery in her own home.

No one minded caring for Anna. She was such a character and such a positive force that everyone actually enjoyed the times when it was their turn to sit with her or drive or feed her. All seemed to be going well and Anna's brave story of survival and pluck was told again and again.

Then she began to really get well and that's when all the trouble started. Anna had become so accustomed to everyone's undivided attention that she didn't want to have to get well and thus give it up! It was hard to realize this at first. She just gradually shifted from being gracious to being more and more demanding and as the schedule of sitting and feeding began to properly drop back, she began to complain that her friends "weren't doing their duty to her anymore," "had all let her down," "had all gone off and left her," and other such complaints.

Finally, the friends and neighbors, who were hurt at first, realized what was happening. Healing this part of Anna turned out to be the hardest part of all. She had wanted to recover physically, but she didn't want to get well enough to go back to living on her own. It took confrontation, tears, love, determination, and hard-nosed patience on the part of friends and neighbors to finally push Anna through this part.

(Donald Davis)

Stories of imprisoned heroes are frequent in popular literature of the time. One motif is for the hero to face imprisonment with courage and faith, as exemplified by the singing of hymns to the deity. In the hellenistic Jewish elaboration on the Joseph saga, the hero refers to his imprisonment in this way: "When I was in fetters, the Egyptian woman was overtaken with grief. She came and heard the report how I gave thanks to the Lord and sang praise in the house of darkness" (*Testament of Joseph* 8.5 [second-century B.C.E.]). Similarly in the Greek tradition, Epictetus refers to the example of the imprisoned Socrates: "And then we shall be emulating Socrates, when we are able to write paeans in prison" (2.6.26 [early-second-century C.E.]). (Conzelmann, 132)

Miraculous escapes from prison are also frequent in ancient literature and folklore. For example, in Euripides' Bacchae, when the followers of Bacchus, the god of wine, are wrongfully imprisoned, they find that the god has not deserted them: "The bonds loosed themselves from their feet and the bolted doors opened themselves without mortal hands" (455 [fifth-century B.C.E.]). The motif was so common that in later Christian literature it had become a folk belief that magicians could loosen bonds and open prison doors through the use of magical incantations (Origen, Contra Celsum, 2.34 [third-century C.E.]). (Haenchen, 497)

Marching Through Macedonia

Although riots stirred up by unscrupulous opponents require Paul to leave both Thessalonica and Beroea, the mission flourishes.

The Story

THEY now travelled by way of Amphipolis and Apollonia and came to Thessalonica, where there was a Jewish synagogue. Following his usual practice Paul went to their meetings; and for the next three sabbaths he argued with them, quoting texts of scripture which he expounded and applied to show that the Messiah had to suffer and rise from the dead. 'And this Jesus,' he said, 'whom I am proclaiming to you is the Messiah.' Some of them were convinced and joined Paul and Silas, as did a great number of godfearing Gentiles and a good many influential women.

The Jews in their jealousy recruited some ruffians from the dregs of society to gather a mob. They put the city in an uproar, and made for Jason's house with the intention of bringing Paul and Silas before the town assembly. Failing to find them, they dragged Jason himself and some members of the congregation before the magistrates, shouting, 'The men who have made trouble the whole world over have now come here, and Jason has harboured them. All of them flout the emperor's laws, and assert there is a rival king, Jesus.' These words alarmed the mob and the magistrates also, who took security from Jason and the others before letting them go.

As soon as darkness fell, the members of the congregation sent Paul and Silas off to Beroea; and, on arrival, they made their way to the synagogue. The Jews here were more fair-minded than those at Thessalonica: they received the message with great eagerness, studying the scriptures every day to see whether it was true. Many of them therefore became believers, and so did a fair number of Gentiles, women of standing as well as men. But when the Thessalonian Jews learnt that the word of God had now been proclaimed by Paul in Beroea, they followed them there to stir up trouble and rouse the rabble. At once the members of the congregation sent Paul down to the coast, while Silas and Timothy both stayed behind. Paul's escort brought him as far as Athens, and came away with instructions for Silas and Timothy to rejoin him with all speed.

Comments on the Story

One venerable model of composition is the A-B-A pattern, susceptible of infinite variation. In music, for example, composers often follow a fast movement with a slow one, then return to a more vigorous exposition. Between the famous stories about Paul's work at Philippi and Athens come two relatively short summaries. Having established a pattern, the author can indicate through summation that the experiences narrated at some length are typical. Fifteen verses will dispose of the rest of the province of Macedonia. Storytellers of today, like their forebears in the early Church, may choose to expand these summaries into more vibrant and circumstantial accounts.

The road leads first to Thessalonica, which has a synagogue. Following his accustomed practice, Paul started there, and was able to offer a short course of three weekly exegetical lectures, followed by discussion. The full-fledged Jews were not particularly receptive. Among God-fearers, including a number of well-connected and prosperous women, the results were different. Jealousy over the loss of well-placed adherents provoked Jews to action, in this case the tried-and-true formula of stirring up an urban riot. Underemployment was chronic in the ancient world. Those without adequate employment had little better to do than loiter about the agora (town square). It was assumed that such "ruffians from the dregs of society," as Luke unflatteringly labels them (v. 5), were labile. Paul's Jewish opponents therefore had no difficulty piecing together a mob to rush upon the house of Jason. Even the narrative is rushing. Who is this Jason? Evidently, he is the missionaries' host. Their plan was to extract Paul and Silas from this domicile and subject them to a citizens' arrest. When the missionaries were nowhere to be found, they settled for second prize: Jason and some others. These persons were brought to court on the charge of sheltering Paul and Silas, well-known fomenters of un-Roman activity. Hyperbole can boomerang, as it will in this case.

The very notion of such base sacrilege inflames this good patriotic posse. For their part, the officials are deeply concerned. The charges are grave, and mobs can be dangerous. Dismissal of these charges might lead to inquiries by the Roman governor. Their solution is to require Jason to post a peace bond, presumably a sum that would be forfeited in the event of recurrent disorder. In any case, there is one sure and certain recipe for disorder: the activity of Paul. He will therefore leave, and, just to be on the safe side, will do so surreptitiously, by night.

If the object of such experiences was to teach Paul that he should find a new career, he proves to be a very slow learner. Within a verse the narrator places him in a new town and another synagogue. The Jews of Beroea proved more fair-minded. A program of daily Bible study yielded the expected results. As one has come to expect, converts included many from the highly placed members of local society, as many gentiles as Jews. In the absence of local opposition all went swimmingly. Can such tranquility endure? A cloud soon appeared on the horizon. In shades of Lystra (14:19-20), the alert Jews of Thessalonica caught word of events and undertook some itinerant missionary work of their own. Arriving in Beroea, they attempted to see if the old game of troublemaking might be played once more. It could. These experienced rabble-rousers found the local rabble rousable. Concern for Paul's safety motivated members of the community to escort him out of town. Silas (and Timothy) were not major targets, although Paul would have them join him as soon as possible. The next stop is Athens.

Acts 9:15 promised that the life of the former persecutor of believers would be no bed of roses. Events have confirmed the sagacity of this prediction. Paul has begun missions in three stations of Macedonia. Three times these have led to civic unrest and his prompt departure. Three strikes and you should be out. What his enemies fail to see is that, whenever they strike, Paul lights out for a new mission while the communities he has founded do not wither, but grow. Nor, it might be added, are readers of Acts likely to think that there is the slightest grain of truth in the accusations made against Paul. His opponents, motivated by such noble virtues as jealousy and greed, will promote every fabrication and shrink from no iniquity in pursuit of their oafish goals.

The narrator tells us that the crowd was "recruited . . . from the dregs of society" (17:5). This sets the scene as one in which we as hearers of the story will not expect that justice will take place. Plutarch uses a similar device in telling the story of Aemilius Paullus: "Appius saw Scipio rushing into the forum attended by men who were of low birth and had lately been slaves, but who were frequenters of the forum and able to gather a mob and force all issues by means of solicitations and shouting" (*Aemilius Paullus* 38 [late-first–early-second-century C.E.]). (adapted from Conzelmann, 135)

Retelling the Story

Following his usual practice Paul went to their meetings [in the synagogue]; and for the next three sabbaths he argued with them, quoting texts of scripture. (Acts 17:2)

Over and over again in this section of Acts we read that the travelers reach a town and then Paul goes straight to the synagogue! When we think back to Paul's personal history—his birth and early life as a strong Jew, his early persecution of the Christians, his own conversion and subsequent work at proclaiming and spreading the very message he had once opposed—we might wonder at his choice of the synagogue as a starting place. After all, he is now at more enmity with the Jews than with anyone else! He left them and now works for a competing company! Why would he not want to get as far away from the synagogue as possible to do his work?

When I was in the eighth grade, I weighed seventy-nine pounds and no one ever wanted to choose me to be on their softball team at recess. With an odd number of students in the class, I was the leftover one. Some other students suggested that I just play catcher for both sides and not bat at all.

One day my teacher, Mr. Haupt, came up with another idea. He created for me a position he called "base coach." My job was to stand out near first base, watch out whenever anyone hit a ball, then yell, "Hold your base . . . hold your base . . ." over and over again as the runner came wildly running and not looking at all at where their ball had gone or much less whether or not it had been fielded.

Mr. Haupt's observation was that many kids who got good hits ended up making an out because they tried to run farther than they were ready to run. It worked! Everyone did better for the whole game!

There are times when everyone needs a base. When we face new challenges, are caught by new foes, or simply run out of energy, we all end up in a bind. We all need to have a familiar base to start from and to run to in order to keep our sense and wits about us.

The synagogue is Paul's base. Even in the middle of the strongest opposition, at the synagogue he knows who and what he is fighting with. It is a familiar base and he knows all of the rules of the game and even most of the players. In the foreign worlds of Macedonia, in the midst of foreign religions and cultures of every kind, at the synagogue Paul is in a predictable battlefield.

Uncle Frank's old neighbor Phyleete Jolly had a hard life. He was poor as dirt, tenant farmed on land he would never own, had more children than he could feed, and a spouse he could never please. Uncle Frank thought that surely Phyleete would like a break from his normal life.

"Phyleete," he said to him one day, "did you know that we could go to Asheville and catch the train and be in Atlanta, Georgia, by midnight?"

Phyleete didn't even think before he replied, "What would I do in Atlanta, Georgia, at midnight?" Even an uncomfortable base is preferable to the unknown.

In one of my former congregations the church organist, Joy, was a single mother with one troubled teenage son. She was a fine musician and very loyal to her position as director of all music programs at the church. When this one son was seventeen years old, he was killed in a car wreck on his way home late on a Saturday night.

The next morning I arrived at church after making early calls to secure a substitute organist for the worship services only to find Joy at church already practicing for the service. I blurted out, "What are you doing here? Don't you want to go back home?"

"This is my base," she answered. "I need to spend as much time as I can right here before I can make it at home." Paul and Joy both knew that your base doesn't have to be comfortable in order for it to work for you.

My "base coach" job, that I mentioned earlier, lasted almost the entire year before it occurred to me to ask Mr. Haupt, "What if somebody really ought to keep on running?"

"Oh, you don't need to worry about that. If they see that they really ought to run, they won't pay any attention to you anyway."

While "base" rests and restores us, "home plate" is always our goal. As we keep reading on through the book of Acts, we see that while Paul starts again and again with the synagogue base, he never just stays there. He heads out again and again for home plate, journey after journey, even on to prison and death in Rome. But even then he holds his base as we read that "From dawn to dusk he put his case to them; he spoke urgently of the kingdom of God and sought to convince them about Jesus by appealing to the law of Moses and the prophets" (28:23). His old Jewish base served him on his way to the plate right to the very end. *(Donald Davis)*

The accusation of "the Jews" that Paul and his party have "made trouble the whole world over" (17:6) is full of irony, since the same accusation had been used by Roman officials to persecute the Jewish nation. It is the Jews who had been accused by the emperor Claudius "as fomenting a general plague for the whole world" (from a letter to the Alexandrian Jews preserved in *Papyrus London* 1912.96-100 [41 C.E.]). A similar charge is weighed against Jews by their pagan detractors in the *Acts of Isidore:* "I accuse them [the Jews] of wishing to stir up the entire world" (late-second–early-third century C.E.). (adapted from Conzelmann, 135)

A Jerusalemite in Athens

While in Athens, Paul shows how to reach those unfamiliar with the faith.

The Story

While Paul was waiting for them at Athens, he was outraged to see the city so full of idols. He argued in the synagogue with the Jews and gentile worshippers, and also in the city square every day with casual passers-by. Moreover, some of the Epicurean and Stoic philosophers joined issue with him. Some said, 'What can this charlatan be trying to say?' and others, 'He would appear to be a propagandist for foreign deities'—this because he was preaching about Jesus and the Resurrection. They brought him to the Council of the Areopagus and asked, 'May we know what this new doctrine is that you propound? You are introducing ideas that sound strange to us, and we should like to know what they mean.' Now, all the Athenians and the resident foreigners had time for nothing except talking or hearing about the latest novelty.

Paul stood up before the Council of the Areopagus and began: 'Men of Athens, I see that in everything that concerns religion you are uncommonly scrupulous. As I was going round looking at the objects of your worship, I noticed among other things an altar bearing the inscription "To an Unknown God". What you worship but do not know—this is what I now proclaim.

'The God who created the world and everything in it, and who is Lord of heaven and earth, does not live in shrines made by human hands. It is not because he lacks anything that he accepts service at our hands, for he is himself the universal giver of life and breath—indeed of everything. He created from one stock every nation of men to inhabit the whole earth's surface. He determined their eras in history and the limits of their territory. They were to seek God in the hope that, groping after him, they might find him; though indeed he is not far from each one of us, for in him we live and move, in him we exist; as some of your own poets have said, "We are also his offspring." Being God's offspring, then, we ought not to suppose that the deity is like an image in gold or silver or stone, shaped by human craftsmanship and design. God has overlooked the age of ignorance; but now he commands men and women everywhere to repent, because he has fixed the day on which he will have the world judged, and justly judged, by a man whom he has designated; of this he has given assurance to all by raising him from the dead.'

When they heard about the raising of the dead, some scoffed; others said, 'We will hear you on this subject

135

some other time.' So Paul left the assembly. Some men joined him and became believers, including Diony-sius, a member of the Council of the Areopagus; and also a woman named Damaris, with others besides.

Comments on the Story

As far as the narrator is concerned, Paul planned no mission at Athens. He was merely at loose ends, awaiting his assistants. Athens was then, as later, a prime site for tourists, the very navel of what was even in Paul's day regarded as the "golden age" of Greek culture and the location of unnumbered artistic marvels. The narrator begins by observing that Paul, like Jesus (Luke 21:5-6), is no gawking tourist. All that he can see is the effluvia of idolatry. Idols or no, Paul will not be idle. As a kind of bicultural philosopher, he engages in dialogues in both synagogue and the famous agora. Among his predecessors in the latter activity was one Socrates, who, come to think of it, did not live happily ever after.

To show that this movement is no gross superstition, but a manifestation of Greek wisdom, Paul entered into discussion with representatives of the two leading philosophical sects, Stoics and Epicureans. Their reactions, like those of an earlier crowd at Jerusalem (2:12), were mixed. For some, he is a mere philosophical dilettante. Others suspect that he is proclaiming new gods. This latter charge was a capital offense in classical Athens, the very one for which Socrates had been executed. Things are beginning to look ominous. That sense does not lessen when he is brought before the ancient and venerable Council of the Areopagus, named for the place where it met ("Mars' Hill"), where he is requested to provide an explanation.

The narrator is being a bit cagey just now. Are readers to imagine this a trial proper (with the fate of Socrates dangling overhead), a kind of "grand jury" investigation, or something like a seminar? The narrator also takes a hit at the Athenians, who were renowned for wasting their time on whatever was trendy. This may explain why someone like Paul could get much attention but few results. Still and all, the setting is thrilling: the leading representative of this young movement poised to share his faith before the traditional arbiters of culture. Imagine a spokesperson for the Branch Davidians invited to address the French Academy.

Whether his hearers were serious inquirers or mere captives to the latest idol of fifteen seconds' admiration, Paul will give them his best: an apposite, witty, erudite, and well-crafted address. His opening words "Men of Athens" duplicate those of the orations of Demosthenes and others studied in school. Orators are well advised to win the good will of the audience. Paul does so by complimenting their piety, a nice touch for the readers, who are well aware of what he actually thought of this nonsense. In the course of his tourist explorations, he says, he came upon an inscription erected "To an Unknown God." There's a sermon in that, object lesson and text as well. Paul meets his audience where they are, rather than impose his own presuppositions. His own conversion began with an encounter by an "unknown god" (see 9:5). From this Athenian stone God can raise up children for Abraham (cf. Luke 3:8). Paul will squeeze three ideas from it: there is a religious longing that polytheism cannot meet, polytheist practice tacitly confesses ignorance of the true God, and Paul's message contains nothing novel.

In Jewish contexts Paul can take Scripture as a given. With these polytheists he must first establish that there is a single God who has created all. Nature and history alike reveal divine providence and human longing for the ultimate. His second text is taken from pagan poetry, which acknowledges that all people are descendants of God (cf. Luke 3:38). From this claim he can adduce not only the oneness of God but also the fundamental unity of the human race, without which a world mission could not succeed.

For various reasons, pagans had remained ignorant of God. This will no longer be overlooked. By exploiting this theme of ignorance, Luke is able to place Jews (3:17) and gentiles (17:30) on a level playing field. The one God who made all from one will judge all upon a single criterion, through one agent, so designated by rising from the dead.

This business of resurrection proves to be an obstacle, as it has been earlier and will be later, for Jews no less than gentiles. Even so, there were at least a few whose minds remained open. Converts included an actual member of the distinguished Areopagus and a woman of undisclosed status. Frugal as its harvest may have been, the mission to Athens was most heartening for those who did not care to hear their faith characterized as intellectually worthless. By small but deft touches of local color, the narrator has produced an enduring portrait, a silver-tongued oration in a golden old setting. This is also a story of how to evangelize people of a different culture. For a long time, Christians, bristling with cultural and political superiority, began their missions by literally or figuratively burning the idols and bringing Bibles, brassieres, and bullets. In a post-Constantinian age the story of Paul at Athens might provide some constructive reading.

Retelling the Story

"Paul stood up before the Council of the Areopagus and began: 'Men of Athens, I see that in everything that concerns religion you are uncommonly scrupulous.' " (Acts 17:22)

Paul took a deep breath and let it out slowly. He thought to himself, "I can do this. If I can do it so well when Timothy and Barnabas and Silas are around,

For the ancient storyteller, Athens represented Greek civilization at its highest, or most pretentious, depending on the viewpoint taken in the story. The second-century C.E. novelist Chariton typified Athens much as Luke did: "So they all [the pirates] thought it best to sail down to Athens. But Theron did not care for the peculiar officiousness of that town. 'Is it possible,' he said, 'that you have not heard of the meddlesome curiosity of the Athenians? They are a talkative people and fond of lawsuits. . . . The Areopagus is near at hand.' " (*Chaereas and Callirhoe,* 1.11.6-7 [second-century C.E.]; from Conzelmann, 139)

I can do it solo. Just wait until they hear what I can accomplish when I really have the chance. And in Athens! I told them they should have come with me! I'll have a whole church started when they catch up, and then maybe some of this bickering will calm down. They'll see!"

The sun was glaring in his eyes, and he frowned as he began internally berating himself even as he started to speak to the small but curious crowd. "Compliments. Give them compliments. Come on now Paul, get a hold of yourself from the very beginning this time. At least don't insult them as you run out of the starting gate again. Breathe. You can do this."

His words took off slowly and began to soar. "Excuse me . . . Excuse me! My dear friends of Athens! I just want to tell you how impressed I am by your beautiful city. I can see that you are extremely religious in every way.

"As I explored your city, I found an altar with the inscription, 'To an Unknown God.' Are you so afraid of offending a god that you might have missed, that you don't even know, that you worship an altar Just-In-Case? And this unknown god is then satisfied with whatever worship you do? This stranger-god must also be extremely religious in every way. But what you worship, you don't even know about! Let me tell you about the God that you can know about in every way!

The Athenians, like other Greeks, often set up dedications to foreign deities whose specific appellations were unknown to them. Pausanias, for example, refers to altars in Athens in this way: "altars of the gods named Unknown and of heroes, and of the children of Theseus and Phalerus" (1.1.4 [second-century C.E.]). This was not directed at a single unknown deity, but rather was an attempt to honor deities of foreigners. (Conzelmann, 140)

"The God who made heaven and earth and everything in them doesn't live in houses made by human hands. He doesn't need us to create him and keep him alive, but he gives himself to all living things. Beginning with one ancestor and spreading to all nations, we search for God, perhaps groping, perhaps finding, yet this God is never far from us in any way."

Paul looked around, scrutinizing the faces of his listeners. He himself was groping for the words that would spread out over these people who were culturally so different from himself but who in their yearnings were not so far away from him.

"You, Stoics, are like us Pharisees back home. You say that since obeying God is our purpose, you are devoted to denying desire and to scrupulously following the Law in every way. But turn away from this sin! God is at work despite our human ignorance! Hey, wait a minute. Where are you going? Stoics, come back! Don't turn away from me! God comes to us; don't you see that you can't go to God by your own diligence? Not just you, I'm saying that ALL humans are ignorant . . . Well, yes, I'm including myself. . . ."

Paul quickly forced himself to push on with his message and try to capture the crowd again.

"You, Epicureans, are like our Sadducees back home. You say that since there is no life after this life, you are religiously devoted to the pursuit of pleasure in every way. I have good news! God has chosen a man who will indeed evaluate how we've lived our lives, and we know this because that

Historians and other ancient storytellers often presented speeches of their heroes at key points in the action. Thucydides, the Greek historian, explained how this was done: "As to the speeches that were made by different men, either when they were about to begin the war or when they were already engaged therein, it has been difficult to recall with strict accuracy the words actually spoken, both for me as regards that which I myself heard, and for those who from various other sources have brought me reports. Therefore the speeches are given in the language in which, as it seemed to me, the several speakers would express, on the subjects under consideration, the sentiments most befitting the occasion, though at the same time I have adhered as closely as possible to the general sense of what was actually said." (Thucydides 1.22 [fifth-century B.C.E.]; from Cadbury, 184)

very man was raised from the dead. Wait a minute! Why are you outraged? Resurrection? Yes, I know that in Greek it sounds like Anastasis, the name of one of your goddesses. No, this isn't a love story about a dalliance of two deities, Jesus and Anastasis. But it's still a good story! If you're convinced that this life is so pleasurable, why can't you believe that the love story continues on after death? Well, no, it's not that kind of juicy love story but it is about real love. . . ."

By now most of them had wandered away, but Paul took a few moments to himself as he watched the paltry few who remained arguing among themselves about some of the points he had made. He made a pretense of getting something to drink so that he could regroup his thoughts and his confidence.

He found it just as difficult to talk to himself. "Well, that's that. Off they all go. Again. So, Self . . . I see you, too, are extremely religious in every way. But not necessarily effective. Every time I preach solo, I have these problems. Remember Damascus, sneaking over the city wall in a basket at night to save my life? And right after that, in Jerusalem, where the reaction to my preaching was so bad they had to ship me home to Tarsus? So, Athens, you all just walked away. Well, at least there's not going to be any persecution of me here. But no new church either."

Talking to himself was not helping, so he turned to another who might help. "Jesus, those Stoics all walked away, but can you come to me now, please? I'm tired of trying to build a house for you in their hard hearts with my own human hands. They're insulted because I dared to suggest that they don't have to grit their teeth and clamp onto the Law and do it all by themselves. And Jesus, those Epicureans just want life to be a romance novel! Can't I trade in a little of my persecution for just a little of the pleasures that they worship?"

Paul lifted his head and looked around at this strange street in this foreign city. He smiled at the few folks who were still chattering away among themselves. "OK, Jesus, you are not my Unknown God. I do know you. But sometimes I sure don't recognize myself. You know those unknown parts of myself that I do, in fact, worship? I'm ready for you to proclaim them to me. I'm trying to be ready." *(Margie Brown)*

Pitching Tents in Corinth

At Corinth, Paul's mission leads to the usual conflict with local Jews,
who are again unsuccessful in their attempts to squelch him.

The Story

After this he left Athens and went to Corinth. There he met a Jew named Aquila, a native of Pontus, and his wife Priscilla; they had recently arrived from Italy because Claudius had issued an edict that all Jews should leave Rome. Paul approached them and, because he was of the same trade, he made his home with them; they were tentmakers and Paul worked with them. He also held discussions in the synagogue sabbath by sabbath, trying to convince both Jews and Gentiles.

Then Silas and Timothy came down from Macedonia, and Paul devoted himself entirely to preaching, maintaining before the Jews that the Messiah is Jesus. When, however, they opposed him and resorted to abuse, he shook out the folds of his cloak and declared, 'Your blood be on your own heads! My conscience is clear! From now on I shall go to the Gentiles.' With that he left, and went to the house of a worshipper of God named Titius Justus, who lived next door to the synagogue. Crispus, the president of the synagogue, became a believer in the Lord, as did all his household; and a number of Corinthians who heard him believed and were baptized. One night in a vision the Lord said to Paul, 'Have no fear: go on with your preaching and do not be silenced. I am with you, and no attack shall harm you, for I have many in this city who are my people.' So he settled there for eighteen months, teaching the word of God among them.

But when Gallio was proconsul of Achaia, the Jews made a concerted attack on Paul and brought him before the court. 'This man,' they said, 'is inducing people to worship God in ways that are against the law.' Paul was just about to speak when Gallio declared, 'If it has been a question of crime or grave misdemeanour, I should, of course, have given you Jews a patient hearing, but if it is some bickering about words and names and your Jewish law, you may settle it yourselves. I do not intend to be a judge of these matters.' And he dismissed them from the court. Then they all attacked Sosthenes, the president of the synagogue, and beat him up in full view of the tribunal. But all this left Gallio quite unconcerned.

Paul stayed on at Corinth for some time, and then took leave of the congregation. Accompanied by Priscilla and Aquila, he sailed for Syria, having had his hair cut off at Cenchreae in fulfilment of a vow. They put in at Ephesus, where he parted from his companions; he himself went into the synagogue and held a discussion with the Jews. He was asked to stay longer, but he declined and set sail from Eph-esus, promising, as he took leave of them, 'I shall come back to you if it is God's will.' On landing at Caesarea, he went up and greeted the church; and then went down to Antioch. After some time there he set out again on a journey through the Galatian country and then through Phrygia, bringing new strength to all the disciples. .

Comments on the Story

Paul moves from Athens, basking in antique splendor, to another old city that was actually new. Refounded around 50 B.C.E. as a Roman colony, Corinth was a rough and vigorous place, a natural hub of commerce by land and sea, brimming with immigrants from around the Mediterranean. There he meets other recent arrivals, Aquila and Priscilla, who had been forced to leave Rome when the Jews were expelled. (When religions proved troublesome at Rome, their adherents were sometimes punished by expulsion, never permanent and rarely complete.) The introduction suggests that this couple is important. One thing we should like to know about is their religious history: Were they followers of Christ, even missionaries? Did Paul convert them? These are questions the narrator does not answer. One is instead informed about their trade. Because Paul was in the same line of work, he lodged with them. This is a bit of a surprise, for no one reading Acts from the beginning would have imagined that Paul did not devote his whole life to religious work. Rather, his education and status suggest a gentleman of some means.

Leaving the pair aside for some verses, the narrator indicates that Paul's evangelistic efforts were restricted to the synagogue. The eventual arrival of Silas and Timothy (cf. 17:15) somehow freed Paul for full-time missionary work. The pace then quickens. With that appears the usual opposition, culmi-nating here in one of Paul's solemn declarations that he will concentrate on gentiles. Whether to symbolize this separation from the synagogue or for some other reason, Paul moved his base to the home of a God-fearer, Titius Justus. Paul may have left the synagogue, but his prime convert was none other than its one-time president, Crispus. There were others as well. In the midst of this triumphant progress, Paul received a vision that provided courage and the grounds for a long stay. So ordered, he labored for a year and a half.

A sojourn of such duration will bring many new believers. It will also give emergent enemies scope for concocting dire plots. Opportunity seemed to come with the arrival of the (new?) Roman governor, Gallio (a person known to history primarily as the brother of the famous Seneca). Not for the first time, his Jewish adversaries trundled Paul into court, claiming that "this man is inducing people to worship God in ways that are against the law." The charge contains a studied ambiguity, for it does not say just which or whose law is

142

being transgressed. Gallio was a shrewd enough lawyer to see through that loophole. Even before Paul can begin to mount his defense, Gallio dismissed the charge. From his quoted comments it is clear that he knew full well that no serious criminal issue was in question, but rather mere Jewish legal trivia, matters in which he had no interest. Following this rather curt dismissal, those present expressed their displeasure by administering a sound beating to the (new?) head of the synagogue, one Sosthenes, who could not save his skin, thus joining the growing list of would-be persecutors required to swallow the potion they had brewed for others. As for Gallio, he could not have cared less.

This is how the narrator portrays the beating Judaism took at Corinth. Subtle it is not. Hearers will also note that Paul has come face-to-face with two Roman governors. Sergius Paulus, at Cyprus, had religious interest and converted. Gallio appears to have lacked such interest, but he saw nothing unlawful. The message is that this movement is no threat to Roman law and order. How many variations can Luke play on the simple theme of proclamation, success, opposition, and vindication? There is only one story. And many.

In time Paul will leave of his own volition, not because of legal difficulties. After a formal farewell, he set out for Syria, accompanied by Priscilla and Aquila. His action at Cenchreae (the southern and eastern port of Corinth) suggests that his goal is a pilgrimage to Jerusalem. Paul is no apostate. Pressed for time, he must deposit his friends in Ephesus and do no more than whet the appetite of the synagogue congregation—and the appetites of those hearing the story. When he next comes to Ephesus it will be from the other direction, for, after sailing to Judea and visiting the Jerusalem community, he traveled north to Antioch, from which, after a suitable sojourn, he traversed the sites of earlier Asian missions, covering the ground of 15:41–16:7. Many stories underlie this terse summary, not least the message that, conflict notwithstanding, Paul was still welcome both at Jerusalem and at Antioch.

Retelling the Story

Because he was of the same trade, he [Paul] made his home with them [Aquila and Priscilla]; they were tentmakers and Paul worked with them. He also held discussions in the synagogue sabbath by sabbath, trying to convince both Jews and Gentiles. (Acts 18:3-4)

The needle poked him again between first finger and thumb. Paul squinted

The expulsion of the Jews by Claudius evidently took place in about 49 C.E. and is mentioned by the Roman historian Suetonius: "Since the Jews constantly made disturbances at the instigations of Chrestus, he [Claudius] expelled them from Rome" (*Claudius* 25 [early-second-century C.E.]). The name *Chrestus* is probably a misspelling of *Christos* or Christ.

into the sun and peered down the road before turning his attention again to the leather splayed across his lap. His mood couldn't get much lower as he thought, "Silas and Timothy better get here fast with some money."

Priscilla came out with a jug and a basket. She shielded her eyes against the sun and murmured, "What's taking Aquila so long? It wasn't that big of a delivery." She helped Paul with a cumbersome corner on the tent he was making, then picked up her own project of leather work.

They worked in silence with drifts of gossip from their time on the road. Paul had recently wandered alone from Athens into Corinth, while she and her husband had landed here from Italy after Claudius's decree came down kicking all the Jews out of Jerusalem. She spoke bitterly as she broke some thread with her teeth. "Poor emperor is getting a little headache from the occasional riot, so he has to uproot thousands of us. If he can't take ruling, he should retire and pass the baton on to someone else. No," she added as an afterthought, "whoever comes next would probably be worse."

The refugees were turning Corinth into a boomtown; the couple were doing well with their tent business. They could use Paul's extra set of hands until his friends caught up with him. They were glad to provide him with a place to stay and some work while he kept things lively with intriguing arguments about the present time and the fulfillment of prophecies. Not only did they get to hear him lecture every Sabbath at their synagogue, but at home they got to relish the freedom of a more boisterous debate without all the tension of the doubtful synagogue audiences.

A few weeks rushed by with an undertow of noise: tents thrown with a thud on piles of tents, unending bickering over prices, and the hopeful helplessness of new refugees pouring daily into Corinth. Silas and Timothy finally arrived from Macedonia with some donations from a number of small churches, so Paul quickly finished the tents he'd been working on, and went to the temple each morning for unending bickering while trying to prove that Jesus was really the Christ. Sometimes the truth swept new listeners into its undertow. Sometimes his words landed with a thud. At first the listeners only mocked Paul, but over time they grew more abusive until one day Paul lost his temper.

Paul stood on the corner in front of the synagogue door, shouting at a small group of men who had followed him out and were teasing him. The dusty wake of a wagon threw a billowing cloud behind him, while dirt was slung at him from his tormentors as they shouted, "Your words are just dirt and garbage, so here! We throw them right back at you!"

Paul shook out his clothes both in rage and in the ritual of protest. He brushed dirt from his arm, then he bent down to wipe the dust from his shoes as a further insult to them. Remembering suddenly that that might not be such a good idea to give his foes such an easy target, he quickly stood again and shouted, "Your blood be on your own heads! You had the chance, now have your own consequences! I did my job! From now on I'm only going to go to the gentiles!"

He stormed home to pick up his belongings from the house of Priscilla and Aquila. They tried to calm him down, but he was beside himself with anger and disappointment. Unable because of his rage to fold anything in an orderly fashion, he just carried his clothes by the armload and dumped them at the entrance of the house of Titius Justus next door.

Titius Justus received him warmly, but warily, since Paul's anger still showed in his face. That night after he had cooled off, Paul began to have second thoughts. Why couldn't he control his temper? Had he just thrown away the mandate that God had given him? Could he salvage it at all?

That first night in his new quarters, Paul tossed and turned on his guest mat on the roof. He slept fitfully, as his dreams poked him like needles. In his dream, he saw himself peering down a moonlit street. Through an open synagogue door, he could see scrolls of Torah thrown with a thud on piles of scrolls, and he heard unending bickering over politics. Refugees of all sorts stood in the shadows as unnoticed as dust.

A voice came to him above the din in this vision, and everything slowly quieted and calmed as the voice spoke with strength and reassurance. "Don't be afraid . . . keep on speaking . . . I have so many children in this city . . . ones whom you already know and others whom you don't yet . . . children who already know me, and children who don't know about me yet. . . ."

So Paul stayed on in Corinth for a year and a half. He taught everyone he could about the word of God, sometimes fitfully, sometimes peaceably. Once, a coalition of religious leaders conjured up charges against him in court, claiming that he was an outside instigator. But the Proconsul Gallio was bored and irritated by their wrangling over semantics, and had them all thrown out of the courtroom. When they took out their frustration on one of their own, Sosthenes, and beat him up on the courthouse steps, Gallio just ignored them, and the dirt and garbage of their words billowed back over them instead of tainting Paul.

> The story of Paul's appearance before Gallio provides the most important data we have for dating Paul and his missionary activity. This is because we have firm evidence for the period in which Gallio governed Corinth. An inscription has been found at Delphi, which mentions the proconsulship of Gallio in connection with the "twenty-sixth acclamation" of the Emperor Claudius, which took place during the years 51–52 C.E. Since a proconsul usually served for only one year, we can date the rule of Gallio somewhere between 51 and 53. Providing such specific historical data gives the story a greater aura of authority. (Conzelmann, 152-53)

Paul continued shaking off his past religious community and moving into new neighborhoods of strangers turned friends in the faith. Eventually the three colleagues, Paul and Priscilla and Aquila, pulled up stakes and set sail for new ports. Paul felt his own inner compass changing course, and he sealed his new commitment by cutting off his hair as a vow that he belonged solely to the Lord now. As his hair fell to the floor, he remembered the words he had spoken in his rage: "Your blood be on your own heads! You had the chance, now have your own consequences! I did my job!" The controversy of his entire life's work now stormed in his heart, until he heard a voice from the eye of that hurricane whispering to him, "I'll do my job, you do your job. From now on you're only going to go to the Gentiles!"

That night aboard ship, other passengers wondered about Paul's newly stark appearance, but only the moonlit water carried the ripples of the trio's soft conversation as they talked of close shaves, head shaves, and the beckoning of God.   *(Margie Brown)*

Tumultuous Success in Ephesus

In the metropolis of Asia, Paul achieves his climactic success, illustrated by numerous incidents.

The Story

While Apollos was at Corinth, Paul travelled through the inland regions till he came to Ephesus, where he found a number of disciples. When he asked them, 'Did you receive the Holy Spirit when you became believers?' they replied, 'No, we were not even told that there is a Holy Spirit.' He asked, 'Then what baptism were you given?' 'John's baptism,' they answered. Paul said, 'The baptism that John gave was a baptism in token of repentance, and he told the people to put their trust in one who was to come after him, that is, in Jesus.' On hearing this they were baptized into the name of the Lord Jesus; and when Paul had laid his hands on them, the Holy Spirit came upon them and they spoke in tongues of ecstasy and prophesied. There were about a dozen men in all.

During the next three months he attended the synagogue and with persuasive argument spoke boldly about the kingdom of God. When some proved obdurate and would not believe, speaking evil of the new way before the congregation, he withdrew from them, taking the disciples with him, and continued to hold discussions daily in the lecture hall of Tyrannus. This went on for two years, with the result that the whole population of the province of Asia, both Jews and Gentiles, heard the word of the Lord. God worked extraordinary miracles through Paul: when handkerchiefs and scarves which had been in contact with his skin were carried to the sick, they were cured of their diseases, and the evil spirits came out of them.

Some itinerant Jewish exorcists tried their hand at using the name of the Lord Jesus on those possessed by evil spirits; they would say, 'I adjure you by Jesus whom Paul proclaims.' There were seven sons of Sceva, a Jewish chief priest, who were doing this, when the evil spirit responded, 'Jesus I recognize, Paul I know, but who are you?' The man with the evil spirit flew at them, overpowered them all, and handled them with such violence that they ran out of the house battered and naked. Everybody in Ephesus, Jew and Gentile alike, got to know of it and all were awestruck, while the name of the Lord Jesus gained in honour. Moreover many of those who had become believers came and openly confessed that they had been using magical spells. A good many of those who formerly practised magic collected their books and burnt them publicly, and when the total value was reckoned up it came to fifty thousand pieces of silver. In such ways the word of the Lord showed its power, spreading more and more widely and effectively.

When matters had reached this stage, Paul made up his mind to visit Macedonia and Achaia and then go on to Jerusalem. 'After I have been there,' he said, 'I must see Rome also.' He sent two of his assistants, Timothy and Erastus, to Macedonia, while he himself stayed some time longer in the province of Asia.

It was about this time that the Christian movement gave rise to a serious disturbance. There was a man named Demetrius, a silversmith who made silver shrines of Artemis, and provided considerable employment for the craftsmen. He called a meeting of them and of the workers in allied trades, and addressed them: 'As you men know our prosperity depends on this industry. But this fellow Paul, as you can see and hear for yourselves, has perverted crowds of people with his propaganda, not only at Ephesus but also in practically the whole of the province of Asia; he tells them that gods made by human hands are not gods at all. There is danger for us here; it is not only that our line of business will be discredited, but also that the sanctuary of the great goddess Artemis will cease to command respect; and then it will not be long before she who is worshipped by all Asia and the civilized world is brought down from her divine pre-eminence.'

On hearing this, they were enraged, and began to shout, 'Great is Artemis of the Ephesians!' The whole city was in an uproar; they made a concerted rush into the theatre, hustling along with them Paul's travelling companions, the Macedonians Gaius and Aristarchus. Paul wanted to appear before the assembly but the other Christians would not let him. Even some of the dignitaries of the province, who were friendly towards him, sent a message urging him not to venture into the theatre. Meanwhile some were shouting one thing, some another, for the assembly was in an uproar and most of them did not know what they had all come for. Some of the crowd explained the trouble to Alexander, whom the Jews had pushed to the front, and he, motioning for silence, attempted to make a defence before the assembly. But when they recognized that he was a Jew, one shout arose from them all: 'Great is Artemis of the Ephesians!' and they kept it up for about two hours.

The town clerk, however, quietened the crowd. 'Citizens of Ephesus,' he said, 'all the world knows that our city of Ephesus is temple warden of the great Artemis and of that image of her which fell from heaven. Since these facts are beyond dispute, your proper course is to keep calm and do nothing rash. These men whom you have brought here as offenders have committed no sacrilege and uttered no blasphemy against our goddess. If, therefore, Demetrius and his craftsmen have a case against anyone, there are assizes and there are proconsuls; let the parties bring their charges and countercharges. But if it is a larger question you are raising, it will be dealt with in the statutory assembly. We certainly run the risk of being charged with riot for this day's work. There is no justification for it, and it would be impossible for us to give any explanation of this turmoil.' With that he dismissed the assembly.

Acts 19:1-41

Comments on the Story

While Paul was on his pilgrimage and round of pastoral visitations, an eloquent Alexandrian named Apollos, whose theology was defective, appeared in Ephesus, to great success. Priscilla and Aquila took it upon themselves to round off his education, after which he was sent, with appropriate credentials, to Corinth. (There are blanks here that readers of 1 Corinthians will fill in, but the narrator of Acts chooses not to do this.)

Credentials remain in the fore. When, after what must have been some time, Paul returned to Ephesus, he found believers, not Aquila and Priscilla, but individuals who had not so much as heard of the Holy Spirit! They knew of John's baptism. One is tempted to associate them with the mission of Apollos when less informed, but the narrator stresses their lack of a sacramentally mediated experiential gift (the Spirit). Paul, like Jesus and Peter, gives John his proper and honorable place in salvation history (1:5, 22), then perfected their initiation, with the expected consequences. Paul thereby did in Ephesus what Peter and John had done in Samaria (8:14-25). Once more, the statistics come at the end. Twelve is an entirely satisfactory number.

Having dealt with this aberration, Paul resumed his normal practice: mission in the synagogue. After about three months, the normal pattern emerged. Withdrawing his followers, he relocated to a lecture hall, where instruction occurred on a daily basis. In the course of the following two years the word radiated throughout the vast province. As in the case of Jerusalem, where the climax of the mission to the indigent population is characterized by extraordinary wonders (5:12-16), so at Ephesus the same illustration serves similar ends. What Peter's shadow had worked was matched by Paul's cast-off scarves. Satan, in short, is being wiped off the face of the earth.

Religion has economic dimensions. The Greco-Roman world included many who provided services to individuals (cf. 16:16-18). One by-product of the Ephesian mission was a severe depression in the exorcism trade. Free markets encourage competition, some of which amounts to jumping on bandwagons launched by others. Such pressures stimulated exorcists to begin using the potent names of Jesus and Paul. Among those seeking to avoid obsolescence were seven sons of one Sceva, alleged to be a Jewish high priest.

One example of their ministry will suffice. If no mortal can be fooled all the time, no demon can be fooled even once. So here, after acknowledging the names of Jesus and Paul, the demon demanded the names of the therapists. Possession of names is power. In this case the question is rhetorical. Through the medium of its unfortunate victim, the demon counterattacks, forcing the whole pack to retire in considerable disgrace, wounded and nude. Would-be exorcists who end up looking like the victims of demons (cf. Mark 5:1-20) have not made a successful house call. Luke certainly wished hearers to find this story hilarious.

149

Word of this reversal spread, moving many to take counsel of their spiritual life and conduct. Ephesus was rather notorious for the practice of magical arts. A vast number of those so engaged determined to avoid the fate of Sceva's sons and threw in the towel, represented in this instance by magical papyri heaped into a public bonfire. Burning Satan in effigy involved no small sacrifice. The closing statistical comment assigns these texts a market value of about one million dollars. Monetary value is one trope for power. Followers of Jesus are not to dabble in magic or the like. His name is power enough.

At this very moment, when his success had reached an almost unbelievable peak, a vision directs Paul toward the west. After visiting some of his earlier stations, he "must see Rome also" (v. 21). "Must" echoes the verb used by Jesus to predict his passion (Luke 9:22). Just as Jerusalem, the ambiguous center of revealed religion, was the city of Jesus' destiny, so there now looms on the horizon another fateful place. Dispatching two of his assistants to prepare the way (cf. Luke 9:51-52), Paul lingers for a while.

In the meantime, the devil will have a last hurrah. Exorcists and magicians were not the only people feeling an economic pinch. The narrator's camera turns away from Paul toward one Demetrius, who was involved in the manufacture of silver models of the great temple of Artemis of Ephesus, one of the world's wonders. Calling a meeting of the Brotherhood of Silver Craftsmen, so to speak, Demetrius exhibited considerable oratorical skill. Reminding his comrades that the bread on their tables came from their labor, he observed that this livelihood was in grave peril. Paul's denunciation of idolatry was having an adverse effect upon the tourist trade. Using the witness of an implacable opponent to demonstrate the protagonist's success is a good narrative technique. Demetrius and the slave owners at Philippi appear to have read the same "bartender's" manual. Into his basic ingredient of economic grievance he poured a measure of patriotism, topping the whole with the garnish of religion: "Hey, we'll lose our jobs. Bad enough. Even worse, Ephesus will lose face. If this goes on, Artemis herself will be neglected, to the great peril of not only this city but everyone. This may be the end of civilization as we know it."

Demetrius knew how to reach his audience. Goaded by personal, civic, and religious threats, the silversmiths tried to set things right with their ritual shout, "Great is Artemis of the Ephesians!" In no time the entire city was intoxicated by Demetrius's brew. Everyone flocked to the theater for a spontaneous town meeting, dragging two of Paul's colleagues, Gaius and Aristarchus, with them. It was incumbent upon Paul, not only as a missionary but also as an accomplished orator and good citizen, to attempt to quiet this unruly horde, come what may. Fear that this mob was beyond all reason prompted worried believers to restrain him. At this critical moment, some of the Asiarchs, civic leaders all, who numbered Paul among their friends, also took the time to deter him from action.

Meanwhile, the theater was in bedlam. Everyone was speaking, no one was listening, and no accurate information could be found. The frothy and confused narrative brings the reader into this very chaos. An attempt by Jews to have one Alexander deliver an address sparked a howl of anti-Semitic rage. The crowd can do no more than resume its ritual cultic chant. For two hours the place quaked with "Great is Artemis of the Ephesians!" Granted that paganism may speak with a single voice, its message is no more than the quacking of a benighted rabble stirred up by the ruthless machinations of greedy craftsmen.

Artemis, it transpired, never did respond. The government finally did. With either riot or vain frustration threatening, both injurious to the city and her patron goddess, the chief official gained the platform. He could have learned his speech at the feet of Gamaliel. After reminding the people that their city's status and place was not subject to challenge, he proceeded to give the Christians a most welcome acquittal and vindication. Should Demetrius and his splendid company have any legitimate grievances (which one may doubt), let them resort to the lawful courts. Moreover, "there are proconsuls." The reminder of who the genuine ruling power is may be unpleasant, but it is a fact. Roman governors were not inclined to admire this kind of participatory democracy. Those who doubted might remember that cities disturbed by unrest were liable to lose their treasured rights and privileges. On that note the assembly (*ekklesia* is also the word for "church") is, like the sons of Sceva, sent packing.

There can be no doubt about why Acts 19 is a famous piece. Through a series of compelling episodes, each gripping and vivid, a story in itself, yet all cohering into a well-developed plot, the narrator has depicted the climax of Paul's missionary labor. Lines there are between truth and falsehood, Christian miracles and pagan quackery, urban mobs and believing assemblies. The aggrieved partisans of the local deity, Artemis, can do no more than lash back with a hapless incantation, the net result of which is a timely warning of the iron fist beneath Rome's velvet glove.

The most remarkable thing about this depiction of Paul's missionary success in Asia is that, for three-fourths of the account, he is not personally active. A historical explanation of this odd phenomenon will not only take note of the desire to absolve him from personal involvement in the riot, but also, and more cogently, look to the Ephesian church of Luke's time, in which Paul was present by reputation and legend, message and memory. Even the absent Paul cares for his mission.

Retelling the Story

On hearing this [Demetrius's speech], they were enraged, and began to shout, "Great is Artemis of the Ephesians!" (Acts 19:28)

Demetrius sneered. The customer hesitantly smiled back, and hurried out with the silver casting of the goddess Artemis as a mouse scurries from the viper's lair. Demetrius dropped the coins into the basket, running his fingers quickly through the pile, and then returned to his cronies waiting for him behind the curtain.

It was not only the town's silversmiths who used his back room. Bankers and politicos, visiting dignitaries and entrenched racketeers operated from this hub of profit and power. Demetrius's reputation was cast in silver with this crowd.

There was a new rodent gnawing at their profits these days, and that rat's name was Paul. This upstart new preacher had the town dazzled about a god who didn't want their money or their idols, simply their whole lives and how they lived them! People would tire of that soon enough. Much easier to appease the universe with a silver-plated bribe than to struggle day after day with innocent hope thrown into the invisible face of a capricious cosmos. But business can't wait for emotional fads like this to wane, and business itself is a craft as much as any silversmithing.

In 98 C.E., the Roman governor of Bithynia, Pliny, wrote to the emperor Trajan about how he had solved a problem for the local religious establishment much like the one described here at Ephesus. After he had undertaken a program of persecution of the Christians, Pliny was able to file the following report: "Tis certain at least that the temples, which had been almost deserted, begin now to be frequented. And the sacred festivals, after a long intermission, are again revived; while there is a general demand for sacrificial animals, which for some time past have met with but few purchases." (*Letters,* 2.405; from Conzelmann, 165)

Wisps and straws of rumors of who this foreigner was were tucked into this nest of negotiators. Some had heard that he was a miracle worker. Others knew that he was an escapee from troubles in several other cities. Was he like themselves at heart? Was he so streetsmart that he had figured out how to earn money on invisible idols that he didn't even have to make? Or was he too stupid to know how to ingratiate himself with the leaders in this town so that there would be profit for everyone?

Paul's schtick apparently was invoking the name of some dead man named Jesus. Someone told a good story about a rumor they'd heard. Some charlatans had tried to copy Paul's style in their own miracle show, by driving out evil spirits in the name of Paul. A snarling voice came out of nowhere, bellowing, "I know for sure who Jesus is, and I've heard all I want to hear about Paul, but who are you?" Then the sick man turned crazy, beating everyone to a pulp. Everyone in the room laughed, but then Demetrius snorted and the side conversations ceased.

"I've certainly heard all I want to hear about Paul, and the question is, what are we going to do about it? You fools, are we going to be put out of business by this flash in the pan? You know there's not enough money in the tourist trade to make up for a sales collapse here in town! And this Paul is playing to the tourists too, saying that man-made gods are fakes! It's not just that our business is going down the tubes, but it's also a slap at the temple and even the goddess herself! That's the spin we have to put on it. Our city will lose its civic pride and its high reputation! And what is Artemis herself going to do then?"

The plan sounded workable. After a few drinks, they all got in the mood of feigned hysteria, running out of the establishment and into the street with yelling and whistles and catcalls. "Great is Artemis! Great is Ephesus! Long live Artemis! We're number one!"

Soon the whole city was in an uproar. People rushed two of Paul's helpers and dragged them down the street as the mob surged toward the the-

Whereas Artemis in Greek myth was a young huntress and sister of Apollo, in Ephesus she was worshiped in a distinctive form, as the fertility goddess, the great mother. The temple of Artemis at Ephesus was huge for its day, about two-thirds the size of Saint Peter's Basilica in Rome, and was known as one of the seven wonders of the ancient world. This made Ephesus something of a tourist center, and when the festival of the goddess was held in May, the crowd of worshipers could reach up to thirty thousand. The image of Ephesian Artemis was distinctive: it showed a stiff, erect female figure with a multitude of breasts in rows down the front of her body representing fertility. This well-known image is what the silversmiths would have been making for the tourist trade. (Ferguson, 21)

ater. Paul chafed to get to the front of the crowd to distract them, but the other disciples wouldn't let him.

"Great is Artemis! Great is Ephesus! Long live Artemis! We're number one!"

Even the few top officials with whom Paul had hobnobbed sent him a message begging him to please not go into the theater. The theater was in chaos. Different parts of the crowd were shouting one garbled slogan or another, but it was obvious that most of the people had no idea what the rally was even about.

"Great is Ephesus! We're number one!"

Even the leaders of the synagogue got caught up in the hysteria. They decided to take advantage of the situation and try to rid the city of this thorn in their side named Paul. They pushed their own Alexander to the front, and some in the crowd shouted for him to speak up and for the crowd to pipe down. He lifted his arms for silence and to make a dignified gesture in the hope of turning their wild sport into more of a legal proceeding. But when they realized he was a Jew, and not a lover of Artemis any more than the two captives huddled in the corner in terror, there was a tidal wave of shouting that went on unabated for about two hours.

"We're number one! We're number one!"

Demetrius was already beginning to tally up his imagined sales for the month. With the crowd stirred up into this kind of frenzy, he could sell out in no time! He sent his assistants back to the warehouse to bring back as much as they could carry. The crowd was in a carnival mood and with such "fan fever," he knew that they'd be ready to fork over money for whatever trinkets his idol cartel could provide.

Then the unexpected happened. The city clerk, of all people, stepped forward and took it upon himself to remind the crowd that they certainly didn't want the Roman legions coming to calm them down. That sobering thought quickly subdued the crowd and they dispersed as quickly as they'd come.

Demetrius ground his teeth and glowered at the clerk while his workers tried in vain to seduce the people back with souvenirs. He'd get even. He could pull a few strings and get this guy replaced by someone more congenial to the business community. As for himself, he'd bide his time. There would be another day to break sales records. He knew his craft.   *(Margie Brown)*

A Fateful Journey

Paul begins his final journey, a highlight of which occurs when he brings life to a dead youth in Troas.

The Story

WHEN the disturbance was over, Paul sent for the disciples and, after encouraging them, said goodbye and set out on his journey to Macedonia. He travelled through that region, constantly giving encouragement to the Christians, and finally reached Greece. When he had spent three months there and was on the point of embarking for Syria, a plot was laid against him by the Jews, so he decided to return by way of Macedonia. He was accompanied by Sopater son of Pyrrhus from Beroea, Aristarchus and Secundus from Thessalonica, Gaius of Derbe, and Timothy, and from Asia Tychicus and Trophimus. These went ahead and waited for us at Troas; we ourselves sailed from Philippi after the Passover season, and five days later rejoined them at Troas, where we spent a week.

On the Saturday night, when we gathered for the breaking of bread, Paul, who was to leave the next day, addressed the congregation and went on speaking until midnight. Now there were many lamps in the upstairs room where we were assembled, and a young man named Eutychus, who was sitting on the window-ledge, grew more and more drowsy as Paul went on talking, until, completely overcome by sleep, he fell from the third storey to the ground, and was picked up dead. Paul went down, threw himself upon him, and clasped him in his arms. 'Do not distress yourselves,' he said to them; 'he is alive.' He then went upstairs, broke bread and ate, and after much conversation, which lasted until dawn, he departed. And they took the boy home, greatly relieved that he was alive.

Comments on the Story

Paul will undertake no new missions. He is destined for Rome, after a visit to his foundations in Macedonia and Greece, followed by one more trip to Jerusalem. Terse summary is the narrator's mode. At 20:3 the specter of a plot against Paul's life succinctly reminds hearers of the circumstances in which he must labor. Paul's Jewish enemies, thwarted hitherto, have not given up. His plans must change. So, surrounded by an entourage of seven companions, samples also of his harvest, Paul set out for the holy city. This list is the last use of

155

the device as a kind of solemn punctuation (cf. 1:13; 6:5; 13:1-3). At Philippi the "we," last heard from in the same place (16:17), returns to perplex us. The rather prosaic details of stopping points create a drumbeat to pace the journey, ticking off steps on the road to destiny. Troas brings a seven-day hiatus and halt. It will provide the single illustrative example of Paul's pastoral activity among his converts.

On Sunday he offered the eucharist and preached to a community assembled in the third story of an urban tenement. This was no occasion for a few brief remarks by a visiting notable. Paul spoke on and on, even until midnight. Lamps were required. They bring light, as well as heat, smoke, and, perhaps, symbol. There was an unfortunate young man with the initially ironic name of "Lucky" (Eutychus), who was perched in a windowsill, possibly, as one might imagine, because of the dense crowd, or in order to hear and see all the better, or to catch a bit of fresh air. Because Paul continued speaking until midnight, Lucky grew drowsy and fell asleep. Anyone who has ever dozed during a long sermon will smile at this. Windowsills are not good places for sleeping, however: Lucky plummeted down to the street and death. Not even Paul would preach through that incident. Making the descent, he embraced the body (cf. 1 Kings 17:21-24; Luke 4:24-27) and spoke some reassuring words. Then, as if this were all in a night's work, he returned to the third floor and his sermon. The service went on until dawn. Hearers are glad that his sermon is not recorded, for we cannot take our minds from the body of that boy. As for Paul, when worship, meal, and conversation are finished, he leaves. Only at this moment and in what seems no more than an afterthought does the narrator inform us that Eutychus had been fortunate after all.

Understatement can be quite effective. As had Jesus (Luke 7:11-17), and Peter (Acts 9:38-41), Paul has brought someone back from the dead. Not by chance does this story take place in a section that is taking on the color and shape of a passion narrative. The Easter message proclaims the defeat of death. We, too, are fortunate that though we may drift off during some sermons, we have also, like Eutychus, been raised to new life and nourished with celestial food.

Retelling the Story

And they took the boy home, greatly relieved that he was alive. (Acts 20:12)

Eutychus ran down the street and careened around the corner, trying to catch up. Ducking the tree limb overhanging the town wall, he glanced at the graffiti he'd put up just two nights before and grinned, but then squinted to keep his sights steady on the six young men cresting the hill. He already had a headache from last night's tumble. He didn't need branches adding to it, or this morning sun, or this fear that maybe he was too late. His stomach spun with his head, and his vision wavered. Maybe he didn't really want to go with them. But his feet kept going.

It had only been two weeks since the gang had arrived in Troas to scout things out ahead of their boss's arrival—that preacher named Paul. But already it seemed like they'd been buddies for ages. Eutychus had met them at the inn and through all of his boasting and swaggering, he managed to talk them into letting him be their guide around the city. He got to show them around and let them see how everybody in town knew him. But secretly he was envious of their guts and their joking, and he felt honored to hang out with them.

How do you get on the inside track with Paul and his traveling show? he wondered. He wasn't that different from these boys. Bored of their hometowns, they were smart enough to pull up roots and hit the road setting up new churches rather than stick around with the same old people they'd known forever. Isn't it more fun to watch new people get excited about changing their lives? More believable, anyway. And they got to meet girls, see the world, ditch spies, duck riots and sneak out of town in the middle of the night, too! And since last week after Paul showed up and started preaching all over town, they included him even more in all their gofering chores, teasing him and his name by saying, "Eutychus, you take us here! Eutychus, you take us there!"

Last night was the going-away bash with Paul making his big finale by trying to get in everything he had to say. Eutychus had learned by now that Paul had a lot to say. Some of it was crystal clear, and some of it didn't make sense yet, but it was fine with Eutychus that the party ran into the early morning hours. Because Paul and his entourage were leaving first thing in the morning, Paul wanted all the more to burn the candle at both ends. And that was Eutychus's style exactly.

According to the Greek, the meeting of the Christians is held "on the first day of the week" or Sunday (Acts 20:7). But it is held at night. The REB translation used here understands it to be "Saturday night," which, according to the Jewish way of reckoning the calendar, would be the beginning of the next day, or Sunday. When following a Jewish calendar, therefore, the evening meal on Saturday would be the primary evening meal of the first day of the week, just as the evening meal on Friday would be the Sabbath meal for Jews. It seems to have been more common, however, for early Christians to meet early in the morning on Sunday. The Roman governor Pliny, for example, describes Christian practices as they had been related to him by those he interrogated: "they gathered regularly on a fixed day before sunrise . . . after which it was their custom to disperse and then reassemble to share food." (*Epistles* 10.96.7 [ca. 115 C.E.])

The room was crammed full, and and the guys hung out against the back wall while Eutychus sat on the windowsill. That way they had the best view of what was happening and who was coming and going. Paul told story after story, and Eutychus watched the birth of other stories happening right before his eyes, as everyone had such different reactions to what Paul was saying. He knew all of these people, and it was fun to see those who reacted predictably and the others who got as excited as he was. But the party kept on going until way after midnight, and it was getting to be hotter and hotter what with all the people in there and all the lamps going full blast.

The Christians in this story were meeting in a house containing at least three floors. The third-floor room where they were meeting was evidently a dining room since they were meeting there for "breaking of bread" (20:7). This is consistent with the meeting places otherwise identified by Luke as "upper rooms" where Christians gathered, lodged, and ate communal meals (Luke 22:12; Acts 1:13). The listener of the story would presumably have been able to picture a common architectural style of the day, in which houses often had multiple floors with the upper floors used for living quarters and lodging of guests. Dining rooms were not uncommon on upper levels. Ground floors, on the other hand, often were reserved for storage and for animals. (Donceel and Donceel-Voûte, 30-31)

Eutychus really had been listening on and off, daydreaming about leaving his folks and joining up. Paul's stories and Eutychus's daydreams and the warm room all just put him right to sleep. Next thing he knew, he was on the ground; he had fallen right out of the window! Every bone in his body knew that it had been the third-story window! People ran out and picked him up, and in Eutychus's pain he agreed with them that he must surely be dead!

Paul himself pushed his way through the crowd and grabbed Eutychus up with one arm, using the other to shield him from all the people who were jostling to get a look. Since it was the middle of the night and everyone was both exhausted and excited, it added a layer of hysteria on top of everything else. Some swore he was dead, and some were just scared that he would be dead, but Paul just kept shouting over and over, "Don't be afraid! He's alive!"

Some people were pretty surprised that after all that, Paul just went right back upstairs and kept on talking. But to calm everyone, he knew that it was past time for them all to break bread and have a little something to eat. That got things onto an even keel again, and Eutychus heard that Paul kept right on talking with them all the way until daylight!

Eutychus remembered seeing stars, and feeling Paul's arm around him, and then having his folks and their friends take him home. They were so relieved that he was OK that he decided that maybe now was not a good time to spring his intention of leaving on them. Why didn't he just sleep the whole day away? He certainly deserved it! Didn't he have enough on his plate now putting together this whole wild week?

Eutychus paused to rub his head and wipe the sweat from his eyes. He peered into the sun and thought, "I know their pattern by now! I bet they'll be coming back this way again!" He hesitated, wondering which direction his heart really wanted to take him. He looked at the writing on the wall. And then his feet kept moving.

(Margie Brown)

Justin Martyr describes an early Christian worship service in this way: "And on the day which is called the day of the sun there is an assembly of all those who live in the towns or in the country, and the memoirs of the apostles or the writings of the prophets are read for as long as time permits. Then the reader ceases, and the president speaks, admonishing and exhorting us to imitate these excellent examples. Then we all rise together and pray and, as we said before, when we have completed our prayer, bread is brought, and wine and water, and the president in like manner offers prayers and thanksgivings according to his ability and the people assent with Amen; and there is a distribution and partaking by all of that over which thanks have been given, and to those who are absent a portion is sent by the deacons." (*Apology* 1.67 [second-century C.E.])

God's Will and Paul's Testament

At Miletus, Paul delivers a farewell speech to leaders of the church at Ephesus.

The Story

Paul had decided to bypass Ephesus and so avoid having to spend time in the province of Asia; he was eager to be in Jerusalem on the day of Pentecost, if that were possible. He did, however, send from Miletus to Ephesus and summon the elders of the church. When they joined him, he spoke to them as follows.

'You know how, from the day that I first set foot in the province of Asia, I spent my whole time with you, serving the Lord in all humility amid the sorrows and trials that came upon me through the intrigues of the Jews. You know that I kept back nothing that was for your good: I delivered the message to you, and taught you, in public and in your homes; with Jews and Gentiles alike I insisted on repentance before God and faith in our Lord Jesus. Now, as you see, I am constrained by the Spirit to go to Jerusalem. I do not know what will befall me there, except that in city after city the Holy Spirit assures me that imprisonment and hardships await me. For myself, I set no store by life; all I want is to finish the race, and complete the task which the Lord Jesus assigned to me, that of bearing my testimony to the gospel of God's grace.

'One thing more: I have gone about among you proclaiming the kingdom, but now I know that none of you will ever see my face again. That being so, I here and now declare that no one's fate can be laid at my door; I have kept back nothing; I have disclosed to you the whole purpose of God. Keep guard over yourselves and over all the flock of which the Holy Spirit has given you charge, as shepherds of the church of the Lord, which he won for himself by his own blood. I know that when I am gone, savage wolves will come in among you and will not spare the flock. Even from your own number men will arise who will distort the truth in order to get the disciples to break away and follow them. So be on the alert; remember how with tears I never ceased to warn each one of you night and day for three years.

'And now I commend you to God and to the word of his grace, which has power to build you up and give you your heritage among all those whom God has made his own. I have not wanted anyone's money or clothes for myself; you all know that these hands of mine earned enough for the needs of myself and my companions. All along I showed you that it is our duty to help the weak in this way, by hard work, and that we should keep in mind the words of the Lord Jesus who himself said, "Happiness lies more in giving than in receiving." '

As he finished speaking, he knelt down with them all and prayed. There were loud cries of sorrow from them all, as they folded Paul in their arms and kissed him; what distressed them most was his saying that they would never see his face again. Then they escorted him to the ship.

Comments on the Story

With the departure from Troas the narrative reverts to a summarizing style. There is no halt at Ephesus. When the party does halt at Miletus, Paul summons the presbyters of Ephesus, to whom he has something to say.

Early, if not modern, readers of Acts would have recognized that this sermon takes the form of a farewell address, or testament, the final words of a dying worthy. A common setting for such speeches is the family or a circle of intimates. Prophecy about coming events and advice about behavior are normal components. With very few exceptions, such speeches were composed well after their dramatic date and refer to issues pertinent to the date of their composition. Through farewell speeches, the assuring and informed voices of tradition speak to the present time. Since Luke chose not to narrate the death of Paul, he presents the speech at Paul's last meeting with leaders of his most important community, a setting familiar to us today, since we expect leaders to make farewell addresses when they leave office.

There are a number of parallels here with the final message of Jesus to his disciples (Luke 22:14-38). By placing this speech in proximity to the celebration at Troas, the author has produced a kind of "last supper" for Paul. For those who have been following the larger story of Acts, these verses come as something of a surprise, for Paul's mission is characterized not by the rapid overthrow of opposition but as blood, sweat, and tears. Its rhetorical color makes full and moving use of pathos.

Paul presents himself as a model for Christian leaders, who are to care for themselves and the flocks they serve. "Shepherd" was a widespread metaphor for leaders in the ancient world. Pastors (identified here with titles later used for distinct offices, presbyters and bishops) are not to seek personal gain. Money was a matter for concern and contention even in the first decades of Christian life. The sheep are not alone. There are wolves out there. So long as heroic shepherds like Paul are on the scene, they will keep their distance. Once he is gone, these false teachers will strike. They are to be countered with the message he taught. This is well known, for it was always public.

In addition to addressing problems of a later day, the speech also sets forth a defense of Paul against charges made by those who were not numbered among his fondest admirers, as well as those whose speculative theologies allegedly derived from Paul's secret teaching. Readers of Paul's letters can see the genesis of much of this, but for the audience of Acts they are outrageous, bald-faced lies. Even so, it is surprising to learn that Paul supported not only himself but also his companions by his work (v. 34).

With its references to "intrigues of the Jews" and hints about difficulties in Jerusalem, the speech drips foreboding. Like Jesus, Paul predicts his own "passion." After an exhortation to generous giving and a final prayer, the scene collapses into unrelieved grief and sorrow, feelings that hearers have been led to share. Only now, at the end of his ministry among believers, does Acts depict Paul engaged in the work of pastoral exhortation and care. The picture is rather more grim than is much of the narrative. Instead of miracles and mass conversions, there is patient toil and much trouble. In the long run the Paul who counts is not the one whose soiled scarves could heal infirmities but the one who sweated to soil them.

This is a story, then, about "how it really was." How shall one say goodbye? One approach is to highlight all the good times, summarizing the stats and exclaiming about the scarves and that pile of burning magical books. The route taken here is different. It highlights the hard and dull moments of weariness and fear, while predicting that things will get worse instead of better. Such testaments may be unwelcome, but they can also be what is needed.

Retelling the Story

> There were loud cries of sorrow from them all, as they folded Paul in their arms and kissed him; what distressed them most was his saying that they would never see his face again. (Acts 20:37-38*a*)

The hotel staff was putting away the coffee and doughnuts in the lobby as the last stragglers hastened to grab something before checking out of their rooms. Other conventioneers lounged over breakfast in the adjoining coffee shop, or lingered poolside before the hot trip back to Ephesus. Conversations inevitably swerved back to quips, cuts, and retorts about last night's keynote speaker.

An argument erupted near the elevator. Cynical laughter burst out over by the fountain. A grim-faced old man stalked away from a small group in the lobby, angrily banging his luggage against the revolving door.

Being a church elder had its perks, and most of the gathering had been glad for this chance to get a little vacation out of town. Usually their apostle Paul came through pretty regularly to check on his foundlings, and it was an honor for them to be invited to where he was staying this time. They had excitedly caravanned together and had expected a party and a pep talk for their efforts. Sure, it would be educational, hearing the latest on the cutting edge of the new church movement, but it would be entertaining as well. Paul knew how to play the crowd and embellish the melodrama of his adventures!

But they were not going home on their usual uplifted cloud of goodwill. Paul had been terse and austere. He was going to go to Jerusalem. He just wanted to say good-bye, and that he would probably never see them again. Good luck on their church work.

Some of them were immobilized with hand-wringing. How could they convince Paul not to go off with this next cockeyed scheme? Others were seething with feelings of being manipulated and betrayed. Was this just another personal drama that Paul was enjoying at their expense?

Their daily grind back home was for political survival, both in a culture that hated them and also in the midst of their own religion, which detested the direction their spirituality was taking them. It seemed that the fundamentalists were in their face and behind the scenes at the same time, plotting every day. It was cloak-and-dagger stuff, sending spies to stir up dissent, fabricating rumors and news leaks. But Paul was always in their face right back, like a walking, talking bumper sticker for Jesus. How would they survive without him? And what good would it do for him to go right to headquarters itself? The power base doesn't invite the prophet for lunch; they eat him for lunch.

The elevator doors slid open onto an informal roast of Peter's address. A falsetto voice was claiming to be the Holy Spirit pushing Paul into this idea, while Paul's impersonator feigned complete surprise. While a few laughed, others slipped out quickly ahead of the revelers, muttering, "What does he think's going to happen to him there that makes it worth going?"

Paul's speech here takes the form of a farewell address, a motif widely used in ancient literature. It is the basis for the entire collection of Jewish writings known as the *Testaments of the Twelve Patriarchs* (second-century B.C.E.). Similarly, the *Phaedo* of Plato consists of an extended discourse that functions as the farewell address of Socrates before he commits suicide (fourth-century B.C.E.). Even the charlatan Peregrinus gets a farewell speech just before he commits suicide. He tells "of the life he had led and the risks that he had run, and of all the troubles that he had endured for philosophy's sake . . . [and that] one who had lived as Heracles should die like Heracles and be commingled with the ether. 'And I wish,' said he, 'to benefit mankind by showing them the way in which one should despise death' " (Lucian, *Peregrinus* 32-3 [second-century C.E.]). Since Paul's death is not recorded in Acts, this farewell speech in which he predicts his death functions like that of Peregrinus, as his last will and testament.

Across the lobby by the coffee shop's ferns, people shook it off. They'd either been through, or heard about, the unending saga of Paul's troubles and triumphs. But if he was unwilling to take their advice for his own good, he was on his own. One more level of competition had now unexpectedly disappeared, and there were certainly enough eager beavers to fill the leadership void.

Out in the parking lot, well-wishers had gathered around Paul's entourage for a final good-bye or autograph. Words gushed in the emotion of the moment. "Don't say that your life is worth nothing!" "Look at all the good you've accomplished!" "You do what you have to do."

Others stood watching the kowtowing from the atrium. The wolves were going to be at the door once they returned home, salivating over the tender little baby Christians. No doubt there were even some wolves in sheep's clothing right in their own pews who would be waiting to twist the truth into a lariat for their own sheep rustling.

A bellhop shook his head at the conversation around the baggage cart. Did Paul make his own way and pay his own bills, or didn't he? Did anyone know if Paul had ever been accused of siphoning off a person's jewels or furs? Wasn't this whole convention just a charade about more money? Paul's defenders retorted that nothing was going to come easy, and that it was up to them all to help out. The bellhop flexed his sore hands and waited. Some kind of similar money conversation happened whenever religious types were guests at the hotel. He waited for their answers not with his ears, but with his palm.

Car doors slammed. Words died down, those spoken and unspoken. Back in the offices, gossip about different guests played among the desks. Upstairs, women worked silently cleaning up the rooms and looking without anticipation for tips.

The grim face on the old man riding in the backseat fell into worry lines. He checked his borrowed bag for any dents he might have inflicted when he had tried unsuccessfully to walk out in a huff. Then he leaned back and thought about how the nearer he got to his home, the farther Paul would be to his opposite destination. Or destiny. Was it really God or guts that kept pulling words so fast and furiously out of Paul's mouth? As the man turned to watch the scenery rush by, he sighed a prayer both for Paul and for himself. Wherever this new turmoil tossed him, may he be set down wherever he was supposed to be.   *(Margie Brown)*

The saying attributed to Jesus, "Happiness lies more in giving than in receiving" (NRSV: "It is more blessed to give than to receive" [Acts 20:35]) is actually a Greek proverb. Thucydides stated that Persian rulers lived by the rule "to give rather than to receive" (2.97.4 [fifth-century B.C.E.]). Plutarch referred to a saying of Artaxerxes: "It is more kingly to give to one who has than to take away" (*Moralia* 173d [late-first–early-second-century C.E.]). It is not found in the Gospels or anywhere else as a saying of Jesus, nor is it found in any Jewish literature. Early Christian preachers often made use of this idea, however. *Didache* 1:5 has this version: "Blessed is he that gives according to the mandate" (ca. late-first-century C.E.). *First Clement* 2:1 reads: "giving more gladly than receiving" (late-first-century C.E.). The audience would presumably recognize it as a wise saying whose truth was apparent because it was so widely known. (adapted from Conzelmann, 176; Haenchen, 594)

Gentiles and Jerusalem

Amidst increasingly dire warnings, Paul arrives in Jerusalem, where he learns that some people are defaming him.

The Story

We tore ourselves away from them and, putting to sea, made a straight run and came to Cos; next day to Rhodes, and thence to Patara. There we found a ship bound for Phoenicia, so we went aboard and sailed in her. We came in sight of Cyprus and, leaving it to port, we continued our voyage to Syria and put in at Tyre, where the ship was to unload her cargo. We sought out the disciples and stayed there a week. Warned by the Spirit, they urged Paul to abandon his visit to Jerusalem. But when our time ashore was ended, we left and continued our journey; and they and their wives and children all escorted us out of the city. We knelt down on the beach and prayed, and then bade each other goodbye; we went on board, and they returned home.

We made the passage from Tyre and reached Ptolemais where we greeted the brotherhood and spent a day with them. Next day we left and came to Caesarea, where we went to the home of Philip the evangelist, who was one of the Seven, and stayed with him. He had four unmarried daughters, who possessed the gift of prophecy. When we had been there several days, a prophet named Agabus arrived from Judaea. He came to us, took Paul's belt, bound his own feet and hands with it, and said, 'These are the words of the Holy Spirit: Thus will the Jews in Jerusalem bind the man to whom this belt belongs, and hand him over to the Gentiles.' When we heard this, we and the local people begged and implored Paul to abandon his visit to Jerusalem. Then Paul gave his answer: 'Why all these tears? Why are you trying to weaken my resolution? I am ready, not merely to be bound, but even to die at Jerusalem for the name of the Lord Jesus.' So, as he would not be dissuaded, we gave up and said, 'The Lord's will be done.'

At the end of our stay we packed our baggage and took the road up to Jerusalem. Some of the disciples from Caesarea came along with us, to direct us to a Cypriot named Mnason, a Christian from the early days, with whom we were to spend the night. On our arrival at Jerusalem, the congregation welcomed us gladly.

Next day Paul paid a visit to James; we accompanied him, and all the elders were present. After greeting them, he described in detail all that God had done among the Gentiles by means of his ministry. When they heard this, they gave praise to God. Then they said to Paul: 'You observe, brother, how many thousands of converts we have among the Jews, all of them staunch upholders of the law. Now they have been given certain information about you: it is said that you teach all the Jews in the gentile world to turn their backs on Moses, and tell them not to circumcise their children or follow our way of life. What is to be done, then? They are sure to hear that you have arrived. Our proposal is this: we have four men here who are under a vow; take them with you and go through the ritual of purification together, and pay their expenses, so that they may have their heads shaved; then everyone will know that there is nothing in the reports they have heard about you, but that you are yourself a practising Jew and observe the law. As for the gentile converts, we sent them our decision that they should abstain from meat that has been offered to idols, from blood, from anything that has been strangled, and from fornication.' So Paul took the men, and next day, after going through the ritual of purification with them, he went into the temple to give notice of the date when the period of purification would end and the offering be made for each of them.

Comments on the Story

As the group draws nearer to Jerusalem, warnings become increasingly more dire and vivid. Throughout them all Paul remains staunch in his commitment. Not even the threat of martyrdom will dissuade him. One should contrast this with the stations visited in chapter 15. Why is it that Paul, who, since the end of chapter 9, has visited Jerusalem whenever he wished, is now in such great danger? That Jerusalem can be dangerous is beyond doubt, witness the fates of Jesus, Stephen, and James.

After a brief and moving summary of the visit to Tyre, from which a good story may be extracted, the party reached Caesarea, where Cornelius had been converted and where Philip, one of the Seven, had come to rest (8:40). His family includes four daughters endowed with the gift of prophecy. Pentecost (2:17) is not only a thing of the past. Nonetheless, the narrator does not make any use of these gifts. When prophecy comes, the source is Agabus of Jerusalem, who arrived to deliver a dramatic and detailed forecast of Paul's fate, demonstrating with a belt how he will be bound in Jerusalem. All, including "we," objected to Paul's plans. This is his "Gethsemane" (cf. Luke 22:33-42). He will not take flight, as had other disciples; like Jesus, he will march into the valley of the shadow of death. All then joined in words echoing Jesus' own prayer: "Your will be done." For readers the suspense has become all but unbearable.

There is plenty of suspense. Moreover, the narrator pulls together in this unhappy scene people and places who represent various elements of Acts: Philip, one of the Seven authorized by the apostles; Agabus, a prophet from the "mother city," whose ministry also included Antioch, where Paul worked with

Barnabas (11:27-30), and the site of the first explicitly gentile conversion. The narrator thus shows all of these elements coexisting in harmony. The question of unity is not abstract, as the following verses will firmly demonstrate. Agabus, with his good old Jerusalem credentials, is well-suited for this prophecy. One group not mentioned is the original apostles. They belong to the past.

Caesarea was not the only place connected to the gentile mission. At Jerusalem the party lodged with another believer of long standing, Mnason, who, like Barnabas, came from Cyprus. Others were equally receptive. The day after their arrival, Paul reported to James, who, surrounded by a group of presbyters, received him warmly. As in chapter 15, his report receives its due acclaim. The reply shows that Jerusalem has not been taking its ease, for "many thousands" of strict Torah observers had aligned themselves with the movement.

This laudable success has brought a slight problem. Observant Jewish Christians have been the recipients of the most unspeakable gossip and calumny about Paul, who, they hear, encourages Diaspora Jews to abandon their covenant with God and apostasize. Readers of Acts, remembering the circumcision of Timothy (16:1-3) and frequent references to Paul's piety, receive these allegations with anger and shock, but there they are. Paul is or has a problem. A solution, in their judgment (the group is represented as speaking in unison), lies to hand. Paul is directed to finance the vows of four (poor?) believers who have undertaken a vow and "go through the ritual of purification together" with them. This will silence any criticism. James and the elders also note that this recommendation does not affect gentile converts, who remain bound by no other requirements than those imposed in chapter 15. Gentile and Jewish converts can thus coexist. Only the latter are subject to Torah. Paul is, of course, one of the latter.

The narrator need not say that Paul, for whom vows are a part of his spiritual life (18:18), will happily oblige them in soothing this lesion. Within the ointment, however, there lurks an insect. Evidently Paul had planned a rather low-key and brief visit. The ritual procedure envisioned will extend over a week, granting ample time for the forces of malice to swing into action. Readers must wait out this week with growing anxiety. Still, things go fine on the first day, as on the subsequent, followed by the day thereafter, and so on, until, at long last, the seventh day comes. This has been harrowing, but it is nearly over. Paul is almost out of the woods.

In the Anglican tradition we speak of pursuing "not compromise for the sake of peace but comprehension for the sake of truth." Acts 21:1-25 is less about a compromise to make Paul look acceptable than finding a means for two quite different groups to find unity in their common faith. Paul did, in fact, give his life in a quest for unity, even if the details are not clear. Readers of Romans 15 are aware that the purpose of this visit was to present the collection Paul had raised. Controversies about that were evidently so bitter that Luke passes over it, although he was aware of the actual purpose (24:17). In the environment where Acts was written, believers of Jewish observance evidently found themselves an increasingly besieged minority.

Retelling the Story

So Paul took the men, and next day, after going through the ritual of purification with them, he went into the temple to give notice of the date when the period of purification would end and the offering be made for each of them. (Acts 21:26)

Paul fidgeted impatiently as he waited in line to make an appointment with the temple clerk. The sun was hot, and the babbling cries of vendors and crowds made him cranky. Was this the big deal? After all of his steeling himself for altercations with the powers that be in Jerusalem that hated his guts, and after all his incessant rehearsals in his own mind of the defense that he would inevitably have to make before those who were suspicious of his work among foreigners and of his liberal intentions, it came down to this? A little bureaucratic mumbo jumbo. Pay the fee for a few guys making a retreat. Money fixes everything, doesn't it? Make the retreat with them so everything looks good. Make an appointment to finish everything up at the temple, and voilà, you're forgiven for being a rabble-rouser. If you act like one of us, you must be one of us, and we'll give you a good-old-boy slap on the back as a secret warning to stay in line from now on.

> Dramatic departure scenes were effective devices for skilled storytellers. To the episode of Paul's departure in Acts 20:36-38 and 21:5-6 should be compared a similar scene in Chariton: "When the designated day of sailing arrived, the crowd ran in a body toward the harbor, not only men but also women and children, and there were mingled together prayers, tears, groans. . . . Ariston, Chaereas's father, was carried down. . . . He put his arms about the neck of his son and clinging there, he wept. . . ." (3.5.3 [second-century C.E.]) (Pervo, *Profit*, 68)

At first it didn't sound like a trick. Paul was the first to stick up for the foreigners, but he still loved his own heritage. Just don't bash people saying that they have to be exactly like you before they can be considered a Christian. He had, in fact, made a few vows of his own during his years on the road, and it would be nice to get closure on them at this homecoming in the temple itself.

But the outskirts were home now. And all these new converts needed an advocate in the boardrooms where the apostles were making or breaking an inclusive church without the foreigners' having a vote. And he wasn't planning on shutting up after paying up.

Paul scowled at the fundamentalists across the temple yard whom he knew were secretly keeping an eye on him. He looked around for a water-seller, and thought about the little kids skipping stones at the water's edge and the believer's beach picnics at the different ports of call he had visited while sailing toward Jerusalem. At each gathering he told them of his plans, and that the Spirit was telling him to go. And at each port they said that their own prayers had told them that he shouldn't go. How could both be true? Best to trust his own instincts and stay the course.

Paul shifted the sticky coins for his appointment tip from one hot hand to another, and wiped the trickle of sweat from his wrists. That made him think of that crazy prophet Agabus who had crashed into his visit at Philip's house and gotten a free lunch for himself. But in the middle of the meal he had reached over and grabbed Paul's own belt and hog-tied his own ankles and wrists with it. Agabus had yelled that Paul's spirit was likewise going to get belted in Jerusalem, and that he was going home just to get kicked out of his own house.

His little performance had worked. Everyone started up again begging him to not go. "You don't need this!" "Why give them the satisfaction?" "You don't need their permission!" "You know they can't stop what the Holy Spirit is doing by yelling at you!"

Paul's thoughts were cut short by the arrival of the petty temple official who took the information he needed and gave Paul a future appointment. Paul stamped his left foot awake and turned quickly to get out of the crowds. He gave a cold glance at those fundamentalists who had feigned their warm welcome when he had gone up to see James and all the elders, and he hurried down the steps away from their smirking and out of their sight.

Paul had been smirking right back at them the other day when he was superciliously polite and reported the whole story about what was happening with his work among the foreigners. As if he needed to report to them. And they had been polite right back, praising his work but hedging that while there may be room for both traditional and more contemporary kinds of fellowships, "we certainly have to be careful that we're not just watering everything down to bring in new members, now don't we?" Apparently the traditional crowd was spreading rumors that he was throwing the baby out with the bath water, by telling the new Christians that they didn't need the Law or the Prophets.

The voices in his head continued to mock him as he relived that distasteful little interview. "Let's make a deal, " they had sniveled. "Of course we're not saying that you need to be purified of any of your recent behavior, but since we need a sponsor anyway for a few of our young men going on retreat, wouldn't it be convenient if you just could help out and make yourself really look like one of us? Then the rumors could die down."

Philip's four daughters became famous in Christian legend. Eusebius quotes an ancient source as follows: "The four daughters of Philip who were prophetesses were at Hierapolis in Asia. Their grave is there and so is their father's." (*Ecclesiastical History*, 3.31.4 [fourth-century C.E.])

Hog-tied by pig-headed people. He laughed and snorted. If this was all that was going to happen to him in Jerusalem—these little political restraints and cautionary tethers—he still had a lot of rope. He'd been accused of being stubborn as a donkey by a better authority than these. The Lord himself had teased him back on the Damascus Road about his being an ass kicking against the goads. They may not like it, but this was the main part of his résumé now! He'd been belted a lot worse than this. This little handful of maneuvers was going to be a picnic. It was going to be a kick.

(Margie Brown)

The Best-Laid Plans

Mobbed in the Temple and rescued by Roman soldiers, Paul addresses both the general public and the Sanhedrin, but he must eventually be evacuated from Jerusalem for his own safety.

The Story

BUT just before the seven days were up, the Jews from the province of Asia saw him in the temple. They stirred up all the crowd and seized him, shouting, 'Help us, men of Israel! This is the fellow who attacks our people, our law, and this sanctuary, and spreads his teaching the whole world over. What is more, he has brought Gentiles into the temple and profaned this holy place.' They had previously seen Trophimus the Ephesian with him in the city, and assumed that Paul had brought him into the temple.

The whole city was in a turmoil, and people came running from all directions. They seized Paul and dragged him out of the temple, and at once the doors were shut. They were bent on killing him, but word came to the officer commanding the cohort that all Jerusalem was in an uproar. He immediately took a force of soldiers with their centurions and came down at the double to deal with the riot. When the crowd saw the commandant and his troops, they stopped beating Paul. As soon as the commandant could reach Paul, he arrested him and ordered him to be shackled with two chains; he enquired who he was and what he had been doing. Some in the crowd shouted one thing,

some another, and as the commandant could not get at the truth because of the hubbub, he ordered him to be taken to the barracks. When Paul reached the steps, he found himself carried up by the soldiers because of the violence of the mob; for the whole crowd was at their heels yelling, 'Kill him!'

Just before he was taken into the barracks Paul said to the commandant, 'May I have a word with you?' The commandant said, 'So you speak Greek? Then you are not the Egyptian who started a revolt some time ago and led a force of four thousand terrorists out into the desert?' Paul replied, 'I am a Jew from Tarsus in Cilicia, a citizen of no mean city. May I have your permission to speak to the people?' When this was given, Paul stood on the steps and raised his hand to call for the attention of the people. As soon as quiet was restored, he addressed them in the Jewish language:

'Brothers and fathers, give me a hearing while I put my case to you.' When they heard him speaking to them in their own language, they listened more quietly. 'I am a true-born Jew,' he began, 'a native of Tarsus in Cilicia. I was brought up in this city, and as a pupil of Gamaliel I was thoroughly trained in every point of our ancestral law. I have always been ardent in God's service, as you all are today. And so I persecuted this movement to the death, arresting its followers, men and women alike, and committing them to prison, as the high priest and the whole Council of Elders can testify. It was they who gave me letters to our fellow-Jews at Damascus, and I was on my way to make arrests there also and bring the prisoners to Jerusalem for punishment. What happened to me on my journey was this: when I was nearing Damascus, about midday, a great light suddenly flashed from the sky all around me. I fell to the ground, and heard a voice saying: "Saul, Saul, why do you persecute me?" I answered, "Tell me, Lord, who you are." "I am Jesus of Nazareth, whom you are persecuting," he said. My companions saw the light, but did not hear the voice that spoke to me. "What shall I do, Lord?" I asked, and he replied, "Get up, and go on to Damascus; there you will be told all that you are appointed to do." As I had been blinded by the brilliance of that light, my companions led me by the hand, and so I came to Damascus.

There a man called Ananias, a devout observer of the law and well spoken of by all the Jews who lived there, came and stood beside me, and said, "Saul, my brother, receive your sight again!" Instantly I recovered my sight and saw him. He went on: "The God of our fathers appointed you to know his will and to see the Righteous One and to hear him speak, because you are to be his witness to tell the world what you have seen and heard. Do not delay. Be baptized at once and wash away your sins, calling on his name."

'After my return to Jerusalem, as I was praying in the temple I fell into a trance and saw him there, speaking to me. "Make haste," he said, "and leave Jerusalem quickly, for they will not accept your testimony about me." "But surely Lord," I answered, "they know that I imprisoned those who believe in you and flogged them in every synagogue; when the blood of Stephen your witness was shed I stood by, approving, and I looked after the clothes of those who killed him." He said to me, "Go, for I mean to send you far away to the Gentiles."'

Up to this point the crowd had given him a hearing; but now they began to shout, 'Down with the scoundrel! He is not fit to be alive!' And as they were yelling and waving their cloaks and flinging dust in the air, the commandant ordered him to be brought into the barracks, and gave instructions that he should be examined under the lash, to find out what reason there was for such an outcry against him. But when they tied him up for the flogging, Paul said to the centurion who was standing there, 'Does the law allow you to flog a Roman citizen, and an unconvicted one at that?' When the centurion heard this, he went and reported to the commandant: 'What are you about? This man is a Roman citizen.' The commandant came to Paul and asked, 'Tell me, are you a Roman citizen?' 'Yes, said he. The commandant rejoined, 'Citizenship cost me a large sum of money.' Paul said, 'It was mine by birth.' Then those who were about to examine him promptly withdrew; and the commandant himself was alarmed when he realized that Paul was a Roman citizen and that he had put him in irons.

THE following day, wishing to be quite sure what charge the Jews were bringing against Paul, he released him and ordered the chief priests and the entire Council to assemble. He then brought Paul down to stand before them.

With his eyes steadily fixed on the Council, Paul said, 'My brothers, all my life to this day I have lived with a perfectly clear conscience before God.' At this the high priest Ananias ordered his attendants to strike him on the mouth. Paul retorted, 'God will strike you, you whitewashed wall! You sit there to judge me in accordance with the law; then, in defiance of the law, you order me to be struck!' The attendants said, 'Would you insult God's high priest?' 'Brothers,' said Paul, 'I had no idea he was high priest; scripture, I know, says: "You shall not abuse the ruler of your people." '

Well aware that one section of them were Sadducees and the other Pharisees, Paul called out in the Council, 'My brothers, I am a Pharisee, a Pharisee born and bred; and the issue in this trial is our hope of the resurrection of the dead.' At these words the Pharisees and Sadducees fell out among themselves and the assembly was divided. (The Sadducees deny that there is any resurrection or angel or spirit, but the Pharisees believe in all three.) A great uproar ensued; and some of the scribes belonging to the Pharisaic party openly took sides and declared, 'We find no fault with this man; perhaps an angel or spirit has spoken to him.' In the mounting dissension, the commandant was afraid that Paul would be torn to pieces, so he ordered the troops to go down, pull him out of the crowd, and bring him into the barracks.

The following night the Lord appeared to him and said, 'Keep up your courage! You have affirmed the truth about me in Jerusalem, and you must do the same in Rome.'

When day broke, the Jews banded together and took an oath not to eat or drink until they had killed Paul. There were more than forty in the conspiracy; they went to the chief priests and elders and said, 'We have bound ourselves by a solemn oath not to taste food until we have killed Paul. It is now up to you and the rest of the Council to apply to the commandant to have him brought down to you on the pretext of a closer investigation of his case; we have arranged to make away with him before he reaches you.'

The son of Paul's sister, however, learnt of the plot and, going to the barracks, obtained entry, and reported it to Paul, who called one of the centurions and said, 'Take this young man to the commandant; he has something to report.' The centurion brought him to the commandant and explained. 'The prisoner Paul sent for me and asked me to bring this young man to you; he has something to tell you.' The commandant took him by the arm, drew him aside and asked him, 'What is it you have to report?' He replied, 'The Jews have agreed on a plan: they will request you to bring Paul down to the Council tomorrow on the pretext of obtaining more precise information about him. Do not listen to them; for a party more than forty strong are lying in wait for him, and they have sworn not to eat or drink until they have done away with him. They are now ready, waiting only for your consent.' The commandant dismissed the young man, with orders not to let anyone know that he had given him this information.

He then summoned two of his centurions and gave them these orders: 'Have two hundred infantry ready to proceed to Casarea, together with seventy cavalrymen and two hundred light-armed troops; parade them three hours after sunset, and provide mounts for Paul so that he may be conducted under safe escort to Felix the governor.' And he wrote a letter to this effect:

From: Claudius Lysias
To: HIS EXCELLENCY
THE GOVENOR Felix.
Greeting.

This man was seized by the Jews and was on the point of being murdered when I intervened with the troops, and on discovering that he was a Roman citizen, I removed him to safety. As I wished to ascertain the ground of their charge against him, I brought him down to their Council. I found that their case had to do with controversial matters of their law, but there was no charge against him which merited death or imprisonment. Information, however, has now been brought to my notice of an attempt to be made on the man's life, so I am sending him to you without delay, and have instructed his accusers to state their case against him before you.'

Acting on their orders, the infantry took custody of Paul and brought him by night to Antipatris. Next day they returned to their barracks, leaving the cavalry to escort him the rest of the way. When the cavalry reached Caesarea, they delivered the letter to the governor, and handed Paul over to him. He read the letter, and asked him what province he was from; and learning that he was from Cilicia he said, 'I will hear your case when your accusers arrive.' He ordered him to be held in custody at his headquarters in Herod's palace.

Comments on the Story

On that seventh and final day Paul entered the temple for the last time, where the whole plan backfired when some Asian Jews, who had viewed Paul's mission close at hand and were not amused, caught sight of him. Experience in Ephesus may have offered them the equivalent of a graduate course on fomenting riots. In any event, they convulsed the crowd, reiterating charges once laid against Stephen (chap. 6), iniquities they claimed Paul had widely disseminated. To ice that incendiary cake, they alleged that he had brought gentiles onto the holy ground—an error the narrator says, rather than a fabrication. City and temple erupted. After removing their quarry from the sanctuary —death defiles—they slammed the gates and got down to action. Word of these turbulent proceedings wended its way to the commandant of the Roman constabulary. With the appearance of soldiers, the riot abated. Arresting the source of the disturbance, the commandant had him secured and began an inquiry. The answers were too numerous and clamorous to comprehend, so he abandoned the first of what will be a number of attempts to clarify the facts.

He will instead have the prisoner interrogated, a process that went far beyond the third degree. Paul's injuries, even before torture, were so grievous that he had to be carried by soldiers, serenaded all the way by the unrequited mob.

On the very portal of painful torture Paul politely begged permission to speak, in words and accent that proclaimed him a gentleman. The astonished commandant assumed that he had captured an insurgent leader. This case of mistaken identity opens the door for a famous response. Paul is indeed a Jew, but nonetheless a citizen of one of Hellenism's cultural citadels. This comes as news to both the officer and the hearers. Paul has kept this card in his pocket for a necessitous moment. He could not have selected a better time to play it. With this revelation Paul took the initiative. Oratory is one charm that can soothe the savage beast. The commandant told him to go ahead and speak. The situation was less than ideal. Paul has no laboriously crafted address to be delivered in the peak of conditioning to an expectant audience. The audience is, of course, a howling mob. The orator is not only unprepared but the victim of a very recent and quite savage beating. Still, opportunity beckons. Like Jesus (Luke 21) and Peter (chap. 3), Paul will speak in the temple. Having established his Greek credentials, Paul will see if he has any luck in a plea aimed at Jews.

At first his luck was in. Since the reader knows that Paul was engaged in purification rather than desecration and that he has not traveled the world to trash the temple, the speech can largely ignore the specifics. After a typically respectful and flattering opening, the accused began with his credentials. They are impressive and, once again, new information for the readers, who learn that Paul had studied with Gamaliel of chapter 5. Pious and zealous, he took up the role of persecutor. In fact, zeal, especially when accompanied by rage, can be problematic, as Paul learned through his conversion.

The first account of that famous event was told by the narrator (chap. 9). In this second rendition (a third is yet to come), the story is Paul's own and is acquiring a different slant, with less emphasis upon punishment and the role of Ananias. His commission to the gentiles is now said to have been given while he was rapt in ecstasy in the midst of worship in this very temple. The conversion of Saul is becoming the call of Paul (cf. Isa. 6:1-9). Prophets normally object to their calls and lose the argument. So here. The climax is, of course, the word "gentiles," at which the simmering coals of wrath burst once more into flame. The notion that gentiles could share in the promises was utterly odious.

Renewed riot moved the commandant to revert to his earlier plan, extraction of information by torture. So his subordinates got back to work, dragging off the once-more humiliated Paul to be stripped and strung up for the whip. Just as the lash was about to fall, the prisoner raised a technical question about the legality of whipping uncondemned Roman citizens. Rationalists may object that he should have raised this point earlier, but storytellers understand the merits of last-second delivery. So much for our objection. Paul's had a rather chilling effect on the proceedings. Realizing that he has been induced to commit a possible offense, the centurion in charge moved up the chain of command to reprimand his superior. That officer then came to the scene (one should imagine the classic gloomy dungeon, with dripping walls and smoking lamps) to investigate. Can this be true? It is. Illegal purchase of citizenship is rather costly, noted the apparently still skeptical commandant. So it may be, Paul might concur. He wouldn't know about any of that, for he held the franchise by birth. That fact reduced the whole detachment, including their commander, to abject fear. The most they could hope for is that word would not get out. Good treatment of the prisoner is one preventative.

By education, experience, and status Paul has the equipment to stave off both "religious" and "criminal" charges. Hearers have every reason for optimism. No one can present sound evidence that he introduced gentiles. Among the potential witnesses in his behalf will be James and those with whom he undertook the vow. Removed from the threat of the mob, Paul will be able to rely upon Roman justice.

Still seeking clarification of Jewish legal questions that were understandably beyond his interest and ken, the commandant ordered a meeting of the Sanhedrin the next day, before which he presented Paul, no longer in irons. Good as these plans appear, they have placed Paul in a precarious situation, for the commandant has led his charge into the lions' den, to those who had executed Stephen without benefit of a formal sentence. The reader will notice that 22:30–23:5 and 23:6-10 are parallel and complimentary paragraphs. The first pits Paul in a one-to-one confrontation with the chief priest. In the second, the two major parties have a falling out. In both cases Paul grasps the initiative and is able to keep his opposition off balance and thus ineffective. This is a clever and courageous performance in which Paul saved his own life, fending off the lions until the commandant caught on. The suspense has its origin in different kinds of knowledge, as the hearer is well aware of what the Sanhedrin can do, while the commandant is not. After Paul has exposed the chief priest as a brute and the Council as no more restrained than a mob, the percipient Roman officer removed his charge to safety. The following vision brings both consolation and worry. Has the Sanhedrin had enough?

A number of Paul's opponents vow to abstain from food and drink until they have killed Paul. (Vows, it seems, bring nothing but trouble.) This group of more than forty conspirators came before the Sanhedrin to repeat their oath and summarize their plan. Since the leaders know that Paul would be most vulnerable while being transported by his small escort, they agree to request another hearing so that the group will get their opportunity to strike. The plan has the advantages of both simplicity and accordance with the commandant's object of discovering facts. Those who expect the high priest and his compatriots to rudely reject a proposal that they become co-conspirators in, and accomplices to, a murder will be disappointed. Readers are left to assume that, given the difficulty of nailing Paul with valid evidence, they found the idea splendid.

A secret known to both a large band of assassins and the Sanhedrin's leaders is hard to keep. Word got out. Paul, it transpires, had a nephew in Jerusalem, who learned what was going on and came to inform his uncle, who, in turn, directed an available centurion to escort the youth to his commandant. This order, as readers may see and hear, the centurion obeyed. The commander, for his part, was wise enough to offer the young man privacy. Soldiers know a bit more about security than even the most zealous civilians. The ambush is fixed for the next day, logically enough for those who are going without water in the Middle Eastern heat.

The commandant acted swiftly. He orders one centurion to add to the size of Paul's guard, then gives another centurion a letter to be given to the governor. Security concerns recommend a nocturnal operation. The size of the opposition calls for a substantial force: two hundred regulars, seventy horses, and another two hundred armed men. He won't send a boy to do a man's job. By Roman standards this was a large force (much, in fact, of the garrison). Paul's safety justifies any risk. The extent of the measures taken to protect him sends a very clear message about his importance in the eyes of the commandant. The objective is the capital, Caesarea, and its governor, who will assume custody. With this task force goes a communication from the commandant, whose name, we learn, is Lysias. Readers will find Lysias's self-exculpation amusing. He reports that Paul had been seized by Jews and rescued by the soldiers as a Roman citizen in need of protection. As far as the commandant is concerned, the charges are minor, at most.

The combination of superior force and speed paid off. The nighttime march reached Antipatris, beyond the murderers' reach. The infantry returned to its barracks the next day, leaving the cavalry to escort Paul to the coast. The governor, Felix, learns the basic facts and promises a hearing when the complainants arrive. Trial by a procurator is vastly preferable to the kind of kangaroo courts over which high priests preside. There are some grounds for hope, now that Paul has eluded a truly fiendish plot. What of the conspirators? The narrator is silent here, permitting those so inclined to feast their minds upon the dilemma of scrupulous zealots, torn between the horns of conscientious vow and physical necessity. In all likelihood, nature will win, as, one by one, a pair here, a group there, they surreptitiously dispense themselves of their solemn vow. If not, good riddance.

Retelling the Story

The following night the Lord appeared to him and said, 'Keep up your courage! You have affirmed the truth about me in Jerusalem, and you must do the same in Rome.' (Acts 23:11)

The first volley came at Paul when he wasn't even looking. Rumors flared and shot through the air, bursting into falling sparks of more little rumors. "There he is! We heard that someone saw him come into town with some strangers, and now what's he doing in the Temple area?"

"Isn't he that idiot who keeps stirring up people against those of us who practice real religion? He and his convert half-breeds who think you can do or not do anything you feel like. He used to be one of us, but I bet that two-tongued snake has even taken some of his precious foreigners into the Temple area with him! Why wouldn't he?"

"Hey, let's get him! Grab him before he contaminates the Temple with his filth! You know he's going to!"

A lit fuse spread quickly through the city, which erupted into a mob and a lynching in progress. But when the commander heard about it, he yelled for some soldiers to hustle down there. When the rioters saw them getting close, they dropped Paul like a hot potato and the commander slapped handcuffs on him and asked questions later. As they hauled him off to the barracks, everyone was yelling bloodthirsty nonsense so the soldiers had to heave Paul up and carry him over their heads to get him out of there.

When they dumped him on the ground to open the barrack gates, Paul had a chance to catch his breath and get his own ammunition ready. He hollered at the commander in Greek, "Can I say something here?"

"Hey, you're a Greek just like me!" They chatted, and when the commander was satisfied that Paul wasn't an outside instigator, he gave him the OK to speak to the crowd for a minute.

"Hey, I'm a Jew just like you!" he yelled. The noise level died down as he tried to explain to them that he was as religious as they were, and even more so, because he'd gotten quite a reputation for harassing this new religious cult that everyone knew was dangerous because they kicked traditional values right in the face.

There was some hooting and jeering when he tried to tell them about the day when a bright light knocked him down

> The encounter with the Roman officer follows a widely used storytelling motif: mistaken identity. The confusion of the officer about whether or not Paul is "the Egyptian" is cleared up when he hears Paul speak Greek. The reference is to an ancient stereotype about the barbarism of Egyptians. Lucian, the second-century C.E. Greek satirist, makes such a reference to an Egyptian servant: "He spoke in a slovenly manner, one long, continuous prattle; he spoke Greek, but his accent and intonation pointed to his native land" (*Navigium* 2). In contrast, the storyteller here in Acts has Paul stand out as one with an impressive command of the language, thus indicating that he is actually a person of status, not a mere rabble-rouser. (Conzelmann, 183)

on the road and Jesus himself yelled at Paul to stop harassing him! Everyone laughed when he got to the part where the people with him had seen the light too, but didn't hear the voice and just saw Paul talking to myself. "Déjà vu!" someone shouted. But Paul kept on talking as fast as he could, about how he'd been blinded but a man healed him and baptized him and told him that from now on he'd have to tell everybody what he saw and heard that day. Except the Lord had warned him that here in this so-called religious town the people wouldn't be able to take what he had to say, so he was better off taking God out to the foreigners!

That started the next skirmish as Paul was hit with a barrage of dirt balls and mud. The commander yelled at Paul to shut up and at the crowd to go home and at the soldiers to take Paul in and flog him.

> Luke's picture of Paul's ability to quiet the crowd with a gesture marks him as an individual of the sort that Virgil describes in the *Aeneid* 1.148-53: "When rioting breaks out in a great city, and the rampaging rabble goes so far that stones fly, and incendiary brands—for anger can supply that kind of weapon—if it so happens they look round and see some dedicated public man, a veteran whose record gives him weight, they quiet down, willing to stop and listen. Then he prevails in speech over their fury by his authority, and placates them" (first-century B.C.E.). (Pervo, *Profit*, 35)

"Hey, I'm a Roman citizen just like you!" Paul scolded the guard who was trying to tie him to the table. That brought about the next battle of wits as Paul was dragged right back to the commander, because a citizen had more pretrial rights than the riffraff.

The commander taunted Paul. "So I hear you've been saying that you're a Roman citizen. How convenient. Can you prove it? Did you have to pay as much as I did for that quasi-citizenship?"

But when he found out that Paul was a citizen from birth, he hastily cleared the room. "Everybody out! Right now! No, wait, first get those chains off him! I'm sorry, sir, we'll get this cleared up. Let's go, everybody! Centurion, bring his accusers here first thing in the morning so we can find out what their problem is."

> Unruly crowds were a regular feature of ancient Greek novels, as in this example from Apuleius 2.27: " 'On your honors, fellow Roman citizens . . . take severe vengeance on this wickedly plotting woman. . . .' The mob grew restive, excited into crediting the charge on mere grounds of probability; they shouted for firebrands; they looked for stones; they encouraged the lads to lynch the woman" (second-century C.E.). (Pervo, *Profit*, 39)

"Hey, I'm a Sanhedrin just like you!" Paul began as the religious leaders assembled. "I follow the laws as well as anybody has in this room!"

Somebody slapped him hard in the face, and Paul yelled, "You cheap facade! You want to judge me, but you punch me and so break the law yourself!"

Others yelled at him to shut up because he was talking to the high priest himself, so he sarcastically offered a pretend apology. As he glanced around the room, he recognized some of his own party affiliates present, so he shifted tactics and blurted, "Hey, I'm a Pharisee just like you! And my dad was a Pharisee, too! They're just tormenting me because you and I believe in the resurrection of the dead. Aren't you sick of the Sadducees badgering us about this? What's it to them if I say that a resurrected angel spoke to me? They're just jealous!"

This time Paul ducked as the two sides had at it among themselves, and they all got so unruly that Paul had to once more be rescued by being locked up.

In the middle of the night, a cluster of antagonists met in the dark and swore a hunger strike until Paul was killed. Then a clique of religious leaders wrote an obsequious petition to the commander to get Paul back in their hands. Paul's nephew overheard the scheme and got word to the commander, who wrote his own ingratiating letter to the governor, saying that he was sending Paul to him along with a protective posse. He might as well win points with the governor as well as get Paul off his hands.

Paul sensed the Lord standing next to his barrack bunk and whispering into his dreams. "You did it! You told the truth about me in this town. We have troubled times ahead, and opportunities, too. Be brave!"

Slumbering, Paul felt both a wave of peace and a twitch of adventure. "I'll be brave," he promised. "Hey, I'm a messenger just like you!" *(Margie Brown)*

Paul in Court

Once more faced with a lethal plot against his life, Paul appeals to the emperor.

The Story

FIVE days later the high priest Ananias came down, accompanied by some of the elders and an advocate name Tertullus, to lay before the governor their charge against Paul. When the prisoner was called, Tertullus opened the case.

'Your excellency,' he said to Felix, 'we owe it to you that we enjoy unbroken peace, and it is due to your provident care that, in all kinds of ways and in all sorts of places, improvements are being made for the good of this nation. We appreciate this, and are most grateful to you. And now, not to take up too much of your time, I crave your indulgence for a brief statement of our case. We have found this man to be a pest, a fomenter of discord among the Jews all over the world, a ringleader of the sect of the Nazarenes. He made an attempt to profane the temple and we arrested him. If you examine him yourself you can ascertain the truth of all the charges we bring against him.' The Jews supported the charge, alleging that the facts were as he stated.

The governor then motioned to Paul to speak, and he replied as follows: 'Knowing as I do that for many years you have administered justice to this nation, I make my defence with confidence. As you can ascertain for yourself, it is not more than twelve days

since I went up to Jerusalem on a pilgrimage. They did not find me in the temple arguing with anyone or collecting a crowd, or in the synagogues or anywhere else in the city; and they cannot make good the charges they now bring against me. But this much I will admit: I am a follower of the new way (the "sect" they speak of), and it is in that manner that I worship the God of our fathers; for I believe all that is written in the law and the prophets, and in reliance on God I hold the hope, which my accusers too accept, that there is to be a resurrection of good and wicked alike. Accordingly, I, no less than they, train myself to keep at all times a clear conscience before God and man.

'After an absence of several years I came to bring charitable gifts to my nation and to offer sacrifices. I was ritually purified and engaged in this service when they found me in the temple; I had no crowd with me, and there was no disturbance. But some Jews from the province of Asia were there, and if they had any charge against me, it is they who ought to have been in court to state it. Failing that, it is for these persons here present to say what crime they discovered when I was brought before the Council, apart from this one declaration which I made as I stood there: "The issue in my trial before you today is the resurrection of the dead." '

Then Felix, who was well informed about the new way, adjourned the hearing. 'I will decide your case when Lysias the commanding officer comes down,' he said. He gave orders to the centurion to keep Paul under open arrest and not to prevent any of his friends from making themselves useful to him.

Some days later Felix came with his wife Drusilla, who was a Jewess, and sent for Paul. He let him talk to him about faith in Christ Jesus, but when the discourse turned to questions of morals, self-control, and the coming judgement, Felix became alarmed and exclaimed, 'Enough for now! When I find it convenient I will send for you again.' He also had hopes of a bribe from Paul, so he sent for him frequently and talked with him. When two years had passed, Felix was succeeded by Porcius Festus. Wishing to curry favour with the Jews, Felix left Paul in custody.

THREE days after taking up his appointment, Festus went up from Caesarea to Jerusalem, where the chief priests and the Jewish leaders laid before him their charge against Paul. They urged Festus to support them in their case and have Paul sent to Jerusalem, for they were plotting to kill him on the way. Festus, however, replied, 'Paul is in safe custody at Caesarea, and I shall be leaving Jerusalem shortly myself; so let your leading men come down with me, and if the man is at fault in any way, let them prosecute him.'

After spending eight or ten days at most in Jerusalem, he went down to Caesarea, and next day he took his seat in court and ordered Paul to be brought before him. When he appeared, the Jews who had come down from Jerusalem stood round bringing many grave charges, which they were unable to prove. Paul protested: 'I have committed no offence against the Jewish law, or against the temple, or against the emperor.' Festus, anxious to ingratiate himself with the Jews, turned to Paul and asked, 'Are you willing to go up to Jerusalem and stand trial on these charges before me there?' But Paul said, 'I am now standing before the emperor's tribunal; that is where I ought to be tried. I have committed no offence against the Jews, as you very well know. If I am guilty of any capital crime, I do not ask to escape the dealth penalty; if, however, there is no substance in the charges which these men bring against me, it is not open to anyone to hand me over to them. I appeal to Caesar!' Then Festus, after conferring with his advisers, replied, 'You have appealed to Caesar: to Caesar you shall go!'

Some days later King Agrippa and Bernice arrived at Caesarea on a courtesy visit to Festus. They spent some time there, and during their stay Festus raised Paul's case with the king. 'There is a man here,' he said, 'left in custody by Felix; and when I was in Jerusalem the chief priests and elders of the Jews brought a charge against him, demanding his condemnation. I replied that it was not Roman practice to hand a man over before he had been confronted with his accusers and given an opportunity of answering the charge. So when they had come here with me I lost no time, but took my seat in court the very next day and ordered the man to be brought before me. When his accusers rose to speak, they brought none of the charges I was expecting; they merely had certain points of disagreement with him about their religion, and about someone called Jesus, a dead man whom Paul alleged to be alive. Finding myself out of my depth in such discussions, I asked if he was willing to go to Jerusalem and stand trial there on these issues. But Paul appealed to be remanded in custody for his imperial majesty's decision, and I ordered him to be detained until I could send him to the emperor.' Agrippa said to Festus, 'I should rather like to hear the man myself.' 'You shall hear him tomorrow,' he answered.

Next day Agrippa and Bernice came in full state and entered the audience-chamber accompanied by high-ranking officers and prominent citizens; and on the orders of Festus, Paul was brought in. Then Festus said, 'King Agrippa, and all you who are in attendance, you see this man: the whole body of the Jews approached me both in Jerusalem and here, loudly insisting that he had no right to remain alive. It was clear to me, however, that he had committed no capital crime, and when he himself appealed to his imperial majesty I decided to send him. As I have nothing definite about him to put in writing for our sovereign, I have brought him before you all and particularly before you, King Agrippa, so that as a result of this preliminary enquiry I may have something to report. There is no sense, it seems to me in sending on a prisoner without indicating the charges against him.'

Agrippa said to Paul: 'You have our permission to give an account of yourself.' Then Paul stretched out his hand and began his defence.

'I consider myself fortunate, King Agrippa, that it is before you I am to make my defence today on all the charges brought against me by the Jews, particulary as you are expert in all our Jewish customs and controversies. I beg you therefore to give me a patient hearing.

'My life from my youth up, a life spent from the first among my nation and in Jerusalem, is familiar to all Jews. Indeed they have known me long enough to testify, if they would, that I belonged to the strictest group in our religion: I was a Pharisee. It is the hope based on the promise God made to our forefathers that has led to my being on trial today. Our twelve tribes worship with intense devotion night and day in the hope of seeing the fulfilment of that promise; and for this very hope I am accused, your majesty, and accused by Jews. Why should Jews find it incredible that God should raise the dead?

'I myself once thought it my duty to work actively against the name of Jesus of Nazareth; and I did so in Jerusalem. By authority obtained from the chief priests, I sent many of God's people to prison, and when they were condemned to death, my vote was cast against them. In all the synagogues I tried by repeated punishment to make them commit blasphemy; indeed my fury rose to such a pitch that I extended my persecution to foreign cities.

'On one such occasion I was travelling to Damascus with authority and commission from the chief priests; and as I was on my way, your majesty, at midday I saw a light from the sky, more brilliant than the sun, shining all around me and my companions. We all fell to the ground, and I heard a voice saying to me in the Jewish language, "Saul, Saul, why do you persecute me? It hurts to kick like this against the goad." I said, "Tell me Lord, who you are," and the Lord replied "I am Jesus, whom you are persecuting. But now, get to your feet. I have appeared to you for a purpose: to appoint you my servant and witness, to tell what you have seen and what you shall yet see of me. I will rescue you from your own people and from the Gentiles to whom I am sending you. You are to open their eyes and to turn them from darkness to light, from the dominion of Satan to God, so that they may obtain forgiveness of sins and a place among those whom God has made his own through faith in me."

'So, King Agrippa, I did not disobey the heavenly vision. I preached first to the inhabitants of Damascus, and then to Jerusalem and all the country of Judaea, and to the Gentiles, calling on them to repent and turn to God and to prove their repentance by their deeds. That is why the Jews seized me in the temple and tried to do away with me. But I have had God's help to this very day, and here I stand bearing witness to the great and to the lowly. I assert nothing beyond what was foretold by the prophets and by Moses:

that the Messiah would suffer and that, as the first to rise from the dead, he would announce the dawn both to the Jewish people and to the Gentiles.'

While Paul was thus making his defence, Festus shouted at the top of his voice, 'Paul, you are raving; too much study is driving you mad.' 'I am not mad, your excellency,' said Paul; 'what I am asserting is sober truth. The king is well versed in these matters, and I can speak freely to him. I do not believe that he can be unaware of any of the facts, for this has been no hole-and-corner business. King Agrippa, do you believe the prophets? I know you do.' Agrippa said to Paul, 'With a little more of your persuasion you will make a Christian of me.' 'Little or much,' said Paul, 'I wish to God that not only you, but all those who are listening to me today might become what I am—apart from these chains!'

With that the king rose, and with him the governor, Bernice, and the rest of the company, and after they had withdrawn they talked it over. 'This man,' they agreed, 'is doing nothing that deserves death or imprisonment.' Agrippa said to Festus, 'The fellow could have been discharged, if he had not appealed to the emperor.'

Comments on the Story

Within five days the accusers make their appearance, including the high priest (who rarely left Jerusalem). They came equipped with a professional orator, Tertullus. Paul, it scarcely need be said, will be competent to speak for himself. There follows a brief rhetorical duel, which would have been pleasing to ancient readers, for whom oratory was a major form of entertainment. Brevity is desired here, to the relief of modern hearers. That need to be succinct leaves Tertullus room for no more than a summary of the basics, all of which are lies. Paul, he claims, is an obnoxious agitator. Hearers of Acts know better.

All of this is most offensive, but it tosses Paul a ball he can smash out of the park. After a brief summary of the actual facts, Paul opens the subject of resurrection. This not being the occasion for a missionary sermon, Felix halts the proceedings, noting that Lysias will be needed. Since the readers know where Lysias stands, things are looking up.

While awaiting the commandant's opportunity to extricate himself from the press of duties and vindicate Paul, readers of Acts may pass the time by watching their hero help a governor and his wife while away some of the dreary hours of life in a backward provincial capital. The ethical strictures of Paul's doctrine did not find a warm reception in the heart of a greedy procurator, who soon found that the press of his duties precluded his attendance. Evidently what he really wanted to hear was the sound of money. Whatever the cause, the initial suggestion of speedy justice has been disappointed. Paul languishes for two whole years. Acts has a roller-coaster plot.

The advent of a new governor, Porcius Festus, renews hope. No more than three days after taking office he visits Jerusalem, meets the priestly and other aristocracy, and learns of a thorn in their flesh: Paul. Would His Excellency be so kind as to send him back to Jerusalem, where the trial may more easily be conducted? Since, as we need not be told, an ambush is in the offing, this is quite frightening. Festus, fortunately, does not take the bait but invites the accusers to present whatever charges they have at the capital. His apparent skepticism sends a signal of renewed hope.

Within a week they appeared for what seems to be a repeat performance of the trial reported in chapter 24. Those who would like witnesses and evidence will be disappointed. Still, the trial has come to an end and the verdict is at hand. At this point Festus betrays the reader's hope, his proper role, and Paul. "Anxious to ingratiate himself with the Jews," he wonders if the accused will accept a change of venue. Something has gone wrong. Swayed by either the winds of political expediency or the clangor of coins, Festus is now willing to do what the accusers want. Neither Paul nor the reader have any doubt about the outcome of that little jaunt to Jerusalem. Implying that he is being sold out, Paul claims the right of trial before the emperor's bench.

This is a stunning development. Readers expect Paul to answer the question with the single word "no." Instead he plays the highest trump a citizen of his standing holds: appeal to Rome. No doubt equally surprised and quite possibly in need of professional advice, Festus went into conference with his staff. That consultation held, he delivered a verdict of two crisp phrases: "You have appealed to Caesar: to Caesar you shall go!" Paul is, indeed, destined for Rome (19:12). What on the surface has the aroma of corruption is, in fact, the very plan of God.

While Paul awaited his fate, a royal couple, Agrippa and Bernice dropped in to pay their respects. (Agrippa II was a member of the Herodian family. His sister, Bernice, would be romantically involved with the emperor Titus.) One of Festus's leading concerns is the case of Paul, about which he provides an interesting summary. To his mind this is nothing but a (boring) theological debate, reasonable settlement of which had been aborted by Paul's appeal. Since Agrippa *is* interested, Festus arranges an audience for the following day. Paul's final defense will take place in a setting of considerable splendor, before an audience including not only a client king and a governor, but all those of prominence who could squeeze in the time to attend a gala affair. Since this is not a trial, there need be no worry about the outcome.

In a brief introductory speech Festus set the background, including the role of the mob, his view of the matter, and his object: the development of a concise report to advise the imperial court. Agrippa, with his knowledge of Judaism and his experience in worldly affairs, will be of great value in this endeavor. (Only spoilsports will wonder why Agrippa does not hold a private interview. Few will be able to disentangle themselves long enough to ask why Festus does not simply free one he regards as innocent.)

Thus invited, Agrippa takes the chair and invites Paul to address the distinguished crowd. In this speech Paul exhibits, to the best of the author's ability, all the mannerisms and skill of a trained orator. His self-defense is appropriately autobiographical, summarizing the highlights of his career. Since this amounts to but one more story of his "conversion," hearers may be tempted, like Eutychus (20:7-12), to doze off. Those who do so will miss a good oration. This is Paul's most important speech. For yet a third time the "conversion" is related. These repetitions show how important the story is for Luke, not solely out of concern for Paul, but because the legitimacy of the church Luke knows stands or falls with the legitimacy of the Pauline mission. By this third telling the account has become the story of a prophet's call. The missionary commission now occurs on the Damascus Road. There is no reference to the blinding of Paul. As a prophet, Paul stands firmly within an Israelite line of succession.

As Paul began to expound the resurrection, Festus pressed the buzzer. His dramatic interruption registers both the enchantment of Paul's rhetoric and his own religious density. After a polite acknowledgment, Paul returned to his primary hearer, Agrippa. This movement cannot have escaped the attention of a devout and informed Jew. The faith Paul presents is anything but the babble of a backwoods revival. Agrippa must acknowledge that Paul has been quite persuasive. This was a bit awkward, so Paul saved the day and got the last word, a well-phrased wish for the salvation of all. This is his last word in the Holy Land. As all politely rise to leave with the king, we overhear their "verdict": innocent of any serious crime. Agrippa assures Festus that, were it not for the (evidently nonretractable) appeal, Paul could have been freed. Acts 26 is Luke's story of how Paul defended himself before the kings and rulers of the earth. Whatever may come, which, given the wiles and determinations of unprincipled opponents, could be quite unfortunate, the verdict that really counts is in.

Retelling the Story

Agrippa said to Festus, "The fellow could have been discharged, if he
had not appealed to the emperor." (Acts 26:32)

The trample of horses still thundered through Paul's headache. Fleeing in a
cloud of soldiers to escape the ambush was a living nightmare five nights ago,
but now in his jail cell it all just continued as deadly dreams. Hordes of skeletons, those enemies who had vowed to go on hunger strike until Paul was dead,
chased him in his sleep.

He saw himself running on foot, led by the quick shadow of a nightingale,
which he knew was his young nephew who had discovered the plot and flown
with the news to the barracks commander. And where was the letter sent by the
commander to the governor pleading for Paul's safekeeping? He lurched
through the woods, repeatedly losing the letter and his way and his breath as
the skeletons pursued.

With the morning sun, a gaggle of religious elders traveled in Paul's own
footprints toward Governor Felix's castle. Their lawyer wet his lips and
smoothed his hair as he rose to present his case before Felix.

"We know you have a busy schedule, Your Honor, but please hear us out
briefly. This man is a troublemaker, a riot-monger, and a ringleader of that
troublesome Nazarene sect. We caught him in the act of trying to desecrate the
temple itself!"

The gaggle at the prosecution table all quacked and honked with more
details, but the governor waved them down and motioned for Paul to speak.

"Your Honor, I simply came back home for a visit! They are the ones who
started it all by picking a fight with me and throwing me in court for no reason!
All I said to them was that I believe in resurrection!"

Felix rolled his eyes. He didn't want to spend his day in a roomful of different brands of religious fanatics. He glanced at the letter from the barracks commander that the prisoner had brought in with him. This man might have some
powerful connections. He'd better keep him around, at least until he could pass
the buck to someone else to judge this case.

Paul sat in prison for two years, occasionally being brought out as the
evening entertainment for Felix and his wife who intended it as a hint to him
that a bribe might be in order for his release. Finally Felix was replaced by the
new governor Festus, who got no further in getting rid of this pesky prisoner.
As soon as Festus opened up an inquiry to see why this guy was really in his
dungeon, Paul's enemies showed up and made an incomprehensible ruckus
once more. Festus was stuck. If he freed Paul, these apparently influential
subjects would be upset. If he handed Paul over to them, Rome would be
upset with him. Finally Paul gave him an out. "You can't push me off on a

lower court made up of my accusers themselves," Paul pronounced. "I appeal to Caesar!"

"Fine," sighed Festus. "That's just where you'll go!"

Some time passed before it was again a convenient evening to bring out the prize prison rat to provide the evening's entertainment for a visiting king and queen.

Festus had come up with a plan to make himself look good to his guests, so he said with great solemnity, "I have found this man guilty of no crime, but since he appealed to the emperor, that's where he must go. Perhaps if you hear his case, you can suggest what I might say in my letter to the emperor."

Paul launched into his story once again. He told how it was a mystery story; how could God raise someone from the dead? He told how it was a murder story; he himself had been a ravenous wolf devouring these new believers in the Way. He told how it was a comedy; he was simply walking down the road when a light blinded him and a voice shouted at him that he was impossible to work with, like a donkey kicking against the harness! He told how it was a love story; that Jesus of Nazareth was suffering with love for the whole world and had died to tell them all to come home to God. Even the Gentiles.

Festus taunted Paul that he was insane! The governor jeered, "Do you really think that with just a few minutes of jabber you're going to talk me into being one of these Christians?"

As the governor bade his guests good-bye and they left the hall, they conferred. "He may be crazy, but he's not a criminal. Even though he's a pain, he doesn't deserve the death penalty. Pity! If he hadn't opened his mouth and appealed to Caesar, you could have just let him go. But since he has made this appeal, that wouldn't look good on your record. Get him out of here. Give him his one-way ticket to Rome."

> "To kick against the goad" is a Greek proverb frequently quoted in Greek literature. It does not occur in a Semitic form. Its meaning is summarized in this way: "It is useless, being human, to strive against fate" (*Scholia Vetera in Pindari Carmina* 2.60 [fifth-century B.C.E.]). Why would a voice from heaven, which is speaking in Aramaic quote a Greek proverb? Such a question would likely not occur to an audience listening to this story being recounted in their native Greek language. Rather they would recognize the practical wisdom in the heavenly advice, made more powerful by the fact that it is spoken in their own idiom. Consequently the storyteller is seen here to make the story more directly relevant to the audience through the creative use of anachronism. (adapted from Conzelmann, 210-11)

The rustle of spies tiptoed through Paul's headache. Fleeing from city to city had been a living nightmare these last few years, but now in his jail cell he couldn't flee his dreams. Shipwrecks and earthquakes and floggings ran amok through his tossing and turning. Caesar himself and his legions mocked him in his sleep. He would leave this prison tomorrow in chains, bound for Rome and who knows how many more prisons. He saw himself running on foot but in harness and bridle, led only by a quick shadow and a voice that he recognized. And where was the letter giving him his commission to the Gentiles? He lurched through the woods, repeatedly losing the letter and his way and his breath as angels pursued. *(Margie Brown)*

When Paul appeals to Caesar, he lays claim to a right he presumably has as a Roman citizen. The appeals procedure in Roman law is not entirely clear, so we cannot be sure how accurate Luke's account is. Two procedures are relevant: 1) the *provocatio,* or the right of a citizen to demand the verdict of the people rather than that of the government official, and 2) the *appellatio,* or appeal for intercession to a superior magistrate. It is unclear if either of these would have applied in Paul's situation or whether either would imply a change in venue to Rome as is assumed here. But in any case, in terms of the plot of the story, Paul's appeal gets him to Rome, which is his goal all along. (Conzelmann, 203-4)

Hell and High Water

Despite extreme perils by land and by sea, Paul completes the voyage to Rome, saving all those with him.

The Story

WHEN it was decided that we should sail for Italy, Paul and some other prisoners were handed over to a centurion named Julius, of the Augustan Cohort. We embarked in a ship of Adramyttium, bound for ports in the province of Asia, and put out to sea. Aristarchus, a Macedonian from Thessalonica, came with us. Next day we landed at Sidon, and Julius very considerately allowed Paul to go to his friends to be cared for. Leaving Sidon we sailed under the lee of Cyprus because of the head winds, then across the open sea off the coast of Cilicia and Pamphylia, and so reached Myra in Lycia.

There the centurion found an Alexandrian vessel bound for Italy and put us on board. For a good many days we made little headway, and we were hard put to it to reach Cnidus. Then, as the wind continued against us, off Salmone we began to sail under the lee of Crete, and, hugging the coast, struggled on to a place called Fair Havens, not far from the town of Lasea.

By now much time had been lost, and with the Fast already over, it was dangerous to go on with the voyage. So Paul gave them this warning: 'I can see, gentlemen, that this voyage will be disastrous; it will mean heavy loss, not only of ship and cargo but also of life.' But the centurion paid more attention to the captain and to the owner of the ship than to what Paul said; and as the harbour was unsuitable for wintering, the majority were in favour of putting to sea, hoping, if they could get so far, to winter at Phoenix, a Cretan harbour facing south-west and north-west. When a southerly breeze sprang up, they thought that their purpose was as good as achieved, and, weighing anchor, they sailed along the coast of Crete hugging the land. But before very long a violent wind, the North-easter as they call it, swept down from the landward side. It caught the ship and, as it was impossible to keep head to wind, we had to give way and run before it. As we passed under the lee of a small island called Cauda, we managed with a struggle to get the ship's boat under control. When they had hoisted it on board, they made use of tackle to brace the ship. Then, afraid of running on to the sandbanks of Syrtis, they put out a sea-anchor and let her drift. Next day, as we were making very heavy weather, they began to lighten the ship; and on the third day they jettisoned the ship's gear with their own hands. For days on end there was no sign of either sun or stars, the storm was raging unabated, and our last hopes of coming through alive began to fade.

When they had gone for a long time

without food, Paul stood up among them and said, 'You should have taken my advice, gentlemen, not to put out from Crete: then you would have avoided this damage and loss. But now I urge you not to lose heart; not a single life will be lost, only the ship. Last night there stood by me an angel of the God whose I am and whom I worship. "Do not be afraid, Paul," he said; "it is ordained that you shall appear before Caesar; and, be assured, God has granted you the lives of all who are sailing with you." So take heart, men! I trust God: it will turn out as I have been told; we are to be cast ashore on an island.'

The fourteenth night came and we were still drifting in the Adriatic Sea. At midnight the sailors felt that land was getting nearer, so they took a sounding and found twenty fathoms. Sounding again after a short interval they found fifteen fathoms; then, fearing that we might be cast ashore on a rugged coast, they let go four anchors from the stern and prayed for daylight to come. The sailors tried to abandon ship; they had already lowered the ships boat, pretending they were going to lay out anchors from the bows, when Paul said to the centurion and the soldiers, 'Unless these men stay on board you cannot reach safety.' At that the soldiers cut the ropes of the boat and let it drop away.

Shortly before daybreak Paul urged them all to take some food. 'For the last fourteen days,' he said, 'you have lived in suspense and gone hungry; you have eaten nothing. So have something to eat, I beg you; your lives depend on it. Remember, not a hair of your heads will be lost.' With these words, he took bread, gave thanks to God in front of them all, broke it, and

began eating. Then they plucked up courage, and began to take food themselves. All told there were on board two hundred and seventy-six of us. After they had eaten as much as they wanted, they lightened the ship by dumping the grain into the sea.

When day broke, they did not recognize the land, but they sighted a bay with a sandy beach, on which they decided, if possible, to run ashore. So they slipped the anchors and let them go; at the same time they loosened the lashings of the steering-paddles, set the foresail to the wind, and let her drive to the beach. But they found themselves caught between cross-currents and ran the ship aground, so that the bow stuck fast and remained immovable, while the stern was being pounded to pieces by the breakers. The soldiers thought they had better kill the prisoners for fear that any should swim away and escape; but the centurion was determined to bring Paul safely though, and prevented them from carrying out their plan. He gave orders that those who could swim should jump overboard first and get to land; the rest were to follow, some on planks, some on parts of the ship. And thus it was that all came safely to land.

Once we had made our way to safety, we identified the island as Malta. The natives treated us with uncommon kindness: because it had started to rain and was cold they lit a bonfire and made us all welcome. Paul had got together an armful of sticks and put them on the fire, when a viper, driven out by the heat, fastened on his hand. The natives, seeing the snake hanging on to his hand, said to one another, 'The man must be a murderer; he may have escaped from the sea, but divine justice would not let him live.' Paul, however, shook off the snake into the fire and was none the worse. They still expected him to swell up or suddenly drop down dead, but after waiting a long time without seeing anything out of the way happen to him, they changed their minds and said, 'He is a god.'

In that neighbourhood there were lands belonging to the chief magistrate of the island, whose name was Publius. He took us in and entertained us hospitably for three days. It so happened that this man's father was in bed suffering from recurrent bouts of fever and dysentery. Paul visited him and, after prayer, laid his hands on him and healed him; whereupon the other sick people on the island came and were cured. They honoured us with many marks of respect, and when we were leaving they put on board the supplies we needed.

Comments on the Story

Any hopes raised by the splendors of chapter 26 quickly fade in what seems to be a terse and matter-of-fact account of the shipment of some prisoners to Rome. Also present, in some capacity, are Aristarchus (cf. 20:4), and at least one other person. Through the first-person plural hearers are drawn into the company and share their experience. Ancient ships tended to hug the coast, putting in at night as often as possible. For some time the trip was uneventful. At Myra (later the home of a famous saint, Nicholas), the centurion in charge of the prisoners found passage on a grain ship bound for Italy. These were oceangoing vessels serving a well-regulated trade, since emperors wished to keep the large populace of Rome distracted and well fed.

Adverse winds (tacking was unknown, and rudders were primitive) made progress disappointingly slow, so they took refuge in an insecure Cretan harbor. Mid-October was the normal end of the sailing season. At this point Paul intervened with a combination of nautical advice and prophecy. The professionals had reason for disagreeing with him. Unwisely so, since a savage nor'easter soon broke upon them, requiring major efforts to maintain the ship's integrity and raising the danger that they would be wrecked on the shoals of North Africa. The sailors soon had to surrender effective control of the ship to the seemingly interminable storm. As one dark day followed another, at least some of the cargo had to be jettisoned (waterlogged wheat would swell and possibly burst the vessel). Unable to navigate, their mission in ruins, the crew gave up. So also did the passengers. At this last and gloomiest moment, Paul intervened once more. Despite difficulties raised by wind and wave, loose gear and howling storm, he was able to gain the attention of all. After no more than the briefest of "I told you so's," he offered a message of hope for all, anchored in a vision and concluded with a practical proposal.

They had been adrift for two weeks before signs of land, quickly confirmed by repeated soundings, appeared. In order to prevent running aground in the dark, anchors were dropped. The company ardently prayed for day to come. Faithless sailors chose this moment to abscond in the ship's boat. Alert as ever,

Paul detected this desertion and informed the centurion. Keeping the crew meant losing the boat. How would they get ashore?

When the prayed-for day arrived, Paul took the initiative again, with the sound suggestion that all have something to eat. After two weeks of constant worry and limited food, morale was low. After he had set a personal example, the others followed suit. At this point the narrator gives a head count: 276. Where do such data normally come? At the end of miracle stories.

Light revealed a bay with a beach. The vessel soon ran aground and began to break up. Since prisoners might take advantage of the confusion to escape, the soldiers deemed it best to liquidate them. The centurion Julius, determined to rescue Paul, countermanded this suggestion. By hook, crook, or packing case every single person got ashore. For the final time in Acts, Paul has eluded a plot. Since chapter 21, his rescuers have been Roman soldiers or officials.

The island was named Malta. With an urban sophisticate's disdain for "natives" (who were, in fact, liable to supplement meager incomes by viewing shipwrecks as windfalls, the passengers and crew of which were best executed or enslaved), the narrator reports the surprising hospitality of the locals. Storytellers could raise the suspense here by withholding the good news and pointing to the potential dangers.

Never one to remain idle, Paul busied himself with contributing to the bonfire. This provoked the attack of a viper that had been lurking in the driftwood. The superstitious natives saw the hand of providence at work. Justice will out. When, to their surprise, he shrugged off this irritant without injury, they leapt to the contrary conclusion: a god was among them. Primitive as such views may be, the estimates of these natives were not unflattering. Barbarian assistance presently yielded to more suitable hospitality provided by the local ruler. In turn, Paul visited his ailing father and healed him. As the news of this spread, other opportunities presented themselves. Beneficiaries returned hospitality and became the rewarded benefactors of their hosts.

Since, as generations of teachers have recognized, this long account of adventure requires no glazing to give it appeal, why look a gift horse in the mouth? One should be grateful that the New Testament has, for once, made the storyteller's role easy. Scholars, for their part, may wonder why Luke has devoted so much space to this tale. It is certainly the most spectacular miracle story in Acts. Paul will testify at Rome, come hell or high water. There is no dearth of high water. Scarcely less abundant are hell's symbols: darkness certainly, serpent probably, and, most specifically, death, the very essence of hell.

Good as this story is, it can become even more appealing when, prompted by the observation that this material has the same (concluding) structural position in Acts held by the passion and resurrection of Jesus in Luke 23–24, one begins to look for indications that 27:1–28:10 describes, in symbolic fashion, Paul's "death" and "resurrection," similarly to the story of Peter in chapter 12. Ancient writers employed imprisonment, shipwreck, and winter as tropes for death. The author of Acts knew that both Peter and Paul had perished. He does not tell these stories, but he is convinced that death was not the end. Through his good stories Luke can both foreshadow their deaths and intimate their triumphs over the last enemy. Those who begin to search for links between Acts 27 and the story of Jonah, for example, as well as similarities to Luke 23–24 will find ample reward. (For some stimulus see Pervo, *Luke's Story of Paul*, 92-93.)

Yet another approach to this lengthy journey is to note that the preferred Lukan image for "Christianity" is "The Way," a word often translated "movement." It may also mean "road" or "journey." Many of the famous teachings of Jesus take place in the course of his journey to Jerusalem in Luke (9–19). The famous journeys of Acts are not just accounts of missionary travels. They are models of the journey undertaken by each believer and the community of faith. Acts 27 says that the voyage of faith will be arduous but eventually victorious.

In this story Paul has come very close to his master, the beginning of whose ministry he roughly duplicates (cf. 28:7-10 with Luke 4:38-41). By any account Paul is a real hero in this passage, not just a good preacher, but a vigorous, wise, and energetic master of all he beholds. For us such heroes belong mainly in comic books, too good to be true. Luke had nothing against comic-book heroes, but he wished to accomplish something more. Paul, himself, is a kind of symbol for a universal church, a "renaissance man" at home in all situations, among Jews and gentiles, Greeks and Romans, in danger and at work, leading a life marked by adventure amidst the ordinary. Christians in the U.S. today need more than the kind of comic-book theology a superficial reading of Acts may suggest, but the notion of Christian life as an adventure is not without merit.

Retelling the Story

> In that neighbourhood there were lands belonging to the chief magistrate of the island, whose name was Publius. He took us in and entertained us hospitably for three days. (Acts 28:7)

Publius picked his way through the shards of wood and the shivering bodies on the beach. The sun was barely up, and villagers were already rushing down with blankets and dry clothing as soon as they heard about the shipwreck. "What a way to wake up," he thought, shaking off the last wisps of sleep to make room for the fingers of terror that were gripping villagers and victims alike. "There must be nearly three hundred people washed to shore and crawling their way like drunken crabs spilled from the ship's wreckage, seeking the solidness of sand."

Publius started to bark orders as soon as he could think of some. Being the chief official of this island was like being assigned to a vacation paradise moated with piranhas. Far from the violence of Roman capriciousness, it was nature itself that ruled with a harsh hand, and the natives were equally suspicious of both the government and the gods. Was he privileged or imprisoned by living in the fanciest house on the island? Either way, it was his job to deal with this new panic. It was now evident to him that it had been a prison ship that shipwrecked on the bay's sandbar, and he began to untangle the waves of intimidation between soldiers and sailors and convicts. He was in charge now.

Here and there campfires flared up along the beach. As he walked among them, snatches of stories drifted in his footprints. No corpses had been found yet. It would be a miracle if all of them had made it. There was grumbling about a man named Julius, apparently a centurion in the elite Imperial Regiment. There were curses toward a few of their own convicts who apparently ranked a smattering of special privileges. Publius immediately focused on trying to locate this Julius so that an appropriate chain of command could accompany this chaos.

Publius found Julius both arguing and wheedling with a convict named Paul. Apparently the two of them were also trying to take charge of this mayhem. Exhaustion, frustration, and starvation were ruling over any semblance of sanity, and they were both relieved when Publius ordered them toward a campfire and some food so that he could question them.

Their Alexandrian ship had set sail from Asia bound for Italy. They had made slow headway through the rough, unprotected waters to the lee of Crete, and the weather had made it impossible to dock until they got as far as Fair Haven Harbor. By this time their timetable was completely off. The sailing season was practically over. They should have wintered there, but the harbor town was far too small for their hordes, so they had tried to make a break for it and get as far as Phoenix. They'd been caught by a nor'easter of hurricane force and had to luff their sails and just let the wind take them.

> Shipwreck stories were very popular in ancient literature, including biblical tradition (see Jonah). They were so common, in fact, that Lucian found them an easy target in his essay ridiculing educated Greeks who served in Roman households. Luke would not have won any points with Lucian; he had heard this story much too often. "So it was not without interest and attention that I listened to them while they spun yarns about their shipwreck and unlooked-for deliverance, just like the men with shaven heads who gather in crowds at the temples and tell of third waves, tempests, headlands, strandings, masts carried away, rudders broken, and to cap it all, how the Twin Brethren [Castor and Pollux, protectors of seamen] appeared . . . or how some other *deus ex machina* sat on the masthead or stood at the helm and steered the ship to a soft beach where she might break up gradually and slowly and they themselves get ashore safely by the grace and favour of the god." (*De Mercede [On Salaried Posts in Great Houses]* 1 [second-century C.E.])

195

An argument erupted again, something about the lifeboat. Publius looked around. He hadn't noticed before that in all the wreckage there was no lifeboat pulled ashore.

Julius explained that it had come loose and was smashing against the side of the ship, so they had lashed it tight by passing ropes under the belly of the ship, hoping also that those ropes would help hold the ship together. Then they lowered anchor and just tried to ride it out, but the storm battered them so badly that first they threw all the cargo overboard, and then later ripped out the ship's tackle with their bare hands and tossed it, too.

They guessed that they had been at least two weeks in the raging storm, slowly starving to death. Paul interjected now that he was the one who'd come up with a plan. An angel had told him that he had to make it to Rome, and if they all stayed together, they'd all be saved even if the ship was lost. Julius snarled that that wasn't much of a plan, and why should the fate of three hundred people revolve around Paul's own itinerary, anyway? Paul shouted back that there was nothing wrong with getting them all to work together, and Publius barked at them to get on with their story.

Finally a midnight calm had overtaken them, and the sailors sensed that there was land nearby. Soundings showed the water to be a hundred and twenty feet deep, and then ninety. Now there was the danger of smashing up against rocks, so they dropped four anchors down from the stern and waited for dawn.

Paul explained defensively that he had found some sailors untying the ropes that lashed the lifeboat to the hull, saying they needed the rope to lower some more anchors from the bow. But he was suspicious that they were really trying to escape. No one would make it if they didn't all make it together! So he hastily alerted Julius, who just as hastily ordered the soldiers to slash the ropes and let the boats and the ropes fall into the sea. Julius retorted that after crying wolf, Paul didn't even stay around for the fight that broke out between the soldiers and sailors after that happened! And the ship captain was livid that Julius had given orders to the sailors behind his back!

Publius sighed and snapped his fingers for more food to be brought to their little campfire. He appreciated the silence as the two drenched rats turned their attention to food for a few blessed minutes. But it did not last long. Soon they were at it again, arguing about that infernal lifeboat incident.

Publius interceded one more time, and diverted their attention to the more pressing task of seeing to the other survivors. Julius was to oversee the aid to the injured, and Paul was to organize the gathering of food and firewood. After finding and consulting with the ship captain and his belligerent crew, Publius ordered them the task of piling up the ship's debris. Then he turned to go home and check on his own problems. His father was sick with fever and dysentery and was probably waiting for him up at the big house.

196

Publius continued receiving progress reports and gossip throughout the day. The stories about Paul continued to escalate, to which Publius mused to himself, "Why am I not surprised?"

The latest juicy account told of Paul's encounter with a snake. The word was that he had been tending the fire when a snake crawled out of the woodpile and latched its fangs into Paul's hand. Some of the yokels jumped to the conclusion that there must be a curse on this prisoner of unknown crime. He survived the shipwreck, but see how the gods were still out to get him! Paul just shook the snake off into the fire, and when he showed no ill effects, most of them changed their minds and began to treat him like a god or something, tugging at him to come and do magic and miracles for them at their house.

Publius laughed and gave the command to have Paul brought up the hill

The shipwreck motif was also taken up in the apocryphal acts of the apostles. In the second-century C.E. *Acts of Peter* 5, for example, when Peter boards the ship for his final voyage to Rome, the captain of the ship, Theon, relates to him a vision he has received: "In the middle of the night while I was steering the ship and had fallen asleep, it seemed that a man's voice said to me from heaven, 'Theon, Theon!' It called me twice by my name and said to me, 'Of all those who sail with you let Peter be highest in your esteem; for through him both you and the others shall escape uninjured from an unexpected mischance.' " Not only is the ship saved from harm, but Theon is baptized as well.

so that they'd leave him alone. For three days Publius hosted Paul and his little group, all the while secretly relishing the jealousy of both Julius and the ship captain, and joking that they should be glad to have Paul out of their hair for awhile if the scuttlebutt he'd heard was true.

It was Paul who picked his way through the shards of sadness and to the shivering body of Publius's father. "What a way he has," Publius thought, shaking from his mind the gossip and gibes that clung to Paul in order to make room for this gift of healing that had unexpectedly entered his house. As word spread like a crashing wave that Publius's father was beginning to get better, every sick person on the island washed up onto his porch hoping to be cured.

As winter passed, Publius hosted his guests with graciousness and gratitude. The viper of discontent that had latched its fangs into his heart was being shaken off into a fire now burning there. But a cloud still clung to him as he directed everyone's eagerness to share throughout the winter and to gather supplies for the group's sailing in the spring. He could barely fathom the knowledge that his final gift would be to send them off as prisoners once again.   *(Margie Brown)*

The End Is Where We Start From

Once in Rome Paul has the freedom to proclaim his message, but few of his Jewish co-religionists are convinced.

The Story

Three months had passed when we put to sea in a ship which had wintered in the island; she was the *Castor and Pollux* of Alexandria. We landed at Syracuse and spent three days there; then we sailed up the coast and arrived at Rhegium. Next day a south wind sprang up and we reached Puteoli in two days. There we found fellow-Christians and were invited to stay a week with them. And so to Rome. The Christians there had had news of us and came out to meet us as far as Appii Forum and the Three Taverns, and when Paul saw them, he gave thanks to God and took courage.

WHEN we entered Rome Paul was allowed to lodge privately, with a soldier in charge of him. Three days later he called together the local Jewish leaders and when they were assembled, he said to them: 'My brothers I never did anything against our people or against the customs of our forefathers; yet I was arrested in Jerusalem and handed over to the Romans. They examined me and would have liked to release me because there was no capital charge against me; but the Jews objected, and I had no option but to appeal to Caesar; not that I had any accusation to bring against my own people. This is why I have asked to see and talk to you; it is for loyalty to the hope of Israel that I am in these chains.' They replied, 'We have had no communication about you from Judaea, nor has any countryman of ours arrived with any report or gossip to your discredit. We should like to hear from you what your views are; all we know about this sect is that no one has a good word to say for it.'

So they fixed a day, and came in large numbers to his lodging. From dawn to dusk he put his case to them; he spoke urgently of the kingdom of God and sought to convince them about Jesus by appealing to the law of Moses and the prophets. Some were won over by his arguments; others remained unconvinced. Without reaching any agreement among themselves they began to disperse, but not before Paul had spoken this final word: 'How well the Holy Spirit spoke to your fathers through the prophet Isaiah when he said, "Go to this people and say: You may listen and listen, but you will never understand; you may look and look, but you will never see. For this people's mind has become dull; they have stopped their ears and closed their eyes. Otherwise, their eyes might see, their ears hear, and their mind understand, and then they might turn again, and I would heal them." Therefore take note that this salvation of God has been sent to the Gentiles; the Gentiles will listen.'

He stayed there two full years at his own expense, with a welcome for all who came to him; he proclaimed the kingdom of God and taught the facts about the Lord Jesus Christ quite openly and without hindrance.

Comments on the Story

With winter's end the journey resumes, marked by a VIP reception at the outskirts of the city. Ensconced in Rome, Paul is once more treated as a prisoner, albeit quite leniently. His first step was to seek support from leaders of the Jewish community, to whom he explained his situation and protested his innocence of any offense against their shared traditions. Despite the injustice of the situation, he harbors no grudge. In response, the delegation notes that no negative reports about him, official or otherwise, have come to their attention. They do, however, observe that no one has anything positive to say about the sect he represents. They are nonetheless interested. Paul is obviously just the right person to offer a full exposition.

That he will certainly do, after a suitable day has been selected. Paul used the day in question to make his case before a large crowd. Some found his exposition of Scripture convincing; others did not. None of this is surprising. The narrator has given Paul a clean slate and permitted him to make a fresh case. As often happened, his audience was divided and left without making a collective decision. At this point Paul laid down the law, or rather the prophets, with a harsh quote from Isaiah that has the ring of finality. Paul's last word reflects the failure of the Jewish mission. Whereas verse 17 spoke of "our people," verse 25 says "*your* fathers" (emphasis added). Jews have, once more, become "the other." Verse 28 describes the future: "the Gentiles will listen." One story, painful for the author for several reasons, and painful for us because of the use we have made of it, has come to an end.

But the story is not over. Prisoner Paul may have been rebuffed by those to whom the promises were first made, but he did not abandon his mission. For two years he evangelized all who were willing to come. The mission at Rome was no less open or more impeded than that at Ephesus (19:10). This is a good end for a story. Two years might not be happily ever after, but it is about as close as most people get to that state, and there is much to be said for "quite openly and without hindrance" (v. 31) as stirring words with which to ring down a curtain.

As a conclusion to the *whole* story of Acts, this passage has disappointed many. Scholarly theories include the suggestion that Luke intended to write another book but was unable to do so (many scholars fail to deliver promised books), or that the work was written when those two years were up, so that the information was current (keeping publications current is a scholarly burden), or, finally, that the author wished to end at this point. The last solution appeals to an age that admires open endings. It is surely the best answer. If there is anything that demands an open ending, it is the reign of a God who never ceases to open the door of hope to human beings.

Retelling the Story

WHEN we entered Rome Paul was allowed to lodge privately, with a soldier in charge of him. . . . [H]e proclaimed the kingdom of God and taught the facts about the Lord Jesus Christ quite openly and without hindrance. (Acts 28:16, 31)

The Three Taverns' owner wiped down the bar and set up another round. The frothy sounds of laughter and lies bubbled over the tables. Dribbles of dares could be heard over in the darts area.

Soldiers and sailors jibed roughly with one another, and each of the few tourists in the corner stared and hung onto his glass like it was a ship's railing.

One of the soldiers was regaling the crowd around his table with stories of his last three months wintering hard on a spit of an island that took a shipwreck to find. "A prison scow, nearly three hundred aboard, and we got all wrapped up for two weeks in a hurricane and nearly starved to death! When the wind died and we finally figured out where land was, we wanted to bump off all the prisoners so they wouldn't escape, but the commander was mollycoddling some of them. Big cases, you know, en route to the emperor's court. Some hotshot wanna-be named Paul kept getting in the way, putting his nose in everyone's business, telling the ship captain how to sail, when to sail. . . .

A sailor burst into the yarn with shouts of agreement and enhancements of his own. "Yeah, told the captain that God had told him that if Paul made it safely, we'd all make it out alive! Even convinced the captain to cut away the lifeboats when he thought some of us were trying to escape! We were so glad to ship him off again on another prison ship. If I ever see that little twerp again, I'll. . . ."

A burst of invective rushed over from the closest table. "So you're to blame for foisting him onto Rome!" Some of the religious leaders sharing the table tried to shush this unseemly outburst from one of their own, while others chuckled behind their hands. "He comes into town and calls a meeting. We show up and first he boasts, "I'm Paul, the one you've heard so much about!"

Another quickly joined into the caricature. "You never heard of me? No letters? No rumors even? Well, anyway. . . ."

The first grumbler picked it up again. "He babbles, 'first of all, I want to say that I've done nothing wrong, even though I am under house arrest waiting to see the emperor. Second, I want to say that you people have done everything wrong by not being convinced that Moses and the Prophets were all trying to tell you about Jesus of Nazareth!' "

His tablemate continued. "And he even throws Isaiah's own words at us as an insult! Us, hard-hearted? Hard-headed Paul, is more like it!"

A gentler voice from their group interceded. "Remember, though, that some of our own were convinced by what he was saying."

These quieter words sank into the sawdust on the floor. The smoke of heated words continued to swirl to the rafters. Some unspoken thoughts hovered around the memories of that recent meeting, as Paul's intensity clashed with the leaders' own internal dissension.

A small group of Christians ducked into the tavern door and headed directly to the proprietor. As they placed a take-out order, they talked quietly among themselves about the discussion group that was converging this evening at Paul's rented house. One of them had heard that even the landlord, who'd been curious about their discussions, might show up! They joked among themselves about the Roman guard stationed to live with Paul as he awaited trial. Even now that guard was with the group who had detoured to the bakery and with whom they would rendezvous momentarily at the corner of Appian Way.

By ending his story where he does, Luke follows a biblical pattern, as seen in 2 Kings 25:27-30, where King Jehoiachin was released from prison by the king of Babylon. "He released him [King Jehoiachin] from prison, treated him kindly, and gave him a seat at table above the kings with him in Babylon. Jehoiachin, discarding his prison clothes, lived as a pensioner of the king for the rest of his life. For his maintenance, as long as he lived, a regular daily allowance was given him by the king." Such stories were attempts to make the best of a bad situation in the saga of a people.

As they gathered up their parcels, they reflected on their role as sheep among wolves in Rome. Jews, gentiles, Christians, Romans, authorities and nobodies could be friend or foe these days. The world was cracking in two, between those who refused to listen and those who would keep on listening! Paul's legs were in chains, but his words weren't! But now, for safety, they gathered up their talking along with their packages and quickly left the dark tavern into the brilliant sunlight. *(Margie Brown)*

According to the *Acts of Paul,* Paul was beheaded in Rome by order of Nero: "Then Paul stood with his face to the east, and lifting up his hands to heaven prayed at length; and after communing in prayer in Hebrew with the fathers he stretched out his neck without speaking further. But when the executioner struck off his head, milk spurted upon the soldier's clothing. And when they saw it, the soldier and all who stood by were amazed, and glorified God who had given Paul such glory. And they went off and reported to Caesar what had happened." (*Martyrdom of the Holy Apostle Paul* [*Acts of Paul* 11.5] [late-second-century C.E.])

Selected Bibliography

References in the text are cited by author.

Barrett, C. K. *A Critical and Exegetical Commentary on the Acts of the Apostles.* International Critical Commentary. Vol. 1. Edinburgh: T. & T. Clark, 1994.

Boring, M. Eugene, Klaus Berger, and Carsten Colpe. *Hellenistic Commentary to the New Testament.* Nashville: Abingdon Press, 1995.

Cadbury, Henry J. *The Making of Luke–Acts.* 1927. Reprint, London: S.P.C.K., 1958.

Conzelmann, Hans. *Acts of the Apostles.* Hermeneia. Philadelphia: Fortress, 1987.

Donceel, Robert and Pauline Donceel-Voûte. "The Archaeology of Khirbet Qumran." In *Methods of Investigation of the Dead Sea Scrolls and the Khirbet Qumran Site: Present Realities and Future Prospects,* 1-38, edited by Michael O. Wise, et al., eds. New York, N.Y.: Annals of the New York Academy of Sciences 722, 1994.

Elliott, J. K., ed. *The Apocryphal New Testament.* Oxford: Clarendon, 1993.

Ferguson, John. *The Religions of the Roman Empire.* Ithaca, N.Y.: Cornell University Press, 1970.

Foakes Jackson, F. J. and Kirsopp Lake, eds. *The Beginnings of Christianity. Part I: The Acts of the Apostles.* 5 vols. Reprint edition. Grand Rapids: Baker Book House, 1979.

Gamble, Harry Y. *Books and Readers in the Early Church: A History of Early Christian Texts.* New Haven: Yale University Press, 1995.

Haenchen, Ernst. *The Acts of the Apostles: A Commentary.* Philadelphia: Westminster, 1971.

Jeremias, Joachim. *Jerusalem in the Time of Jesus: An Investigation into Economic and Social Conditions During the New Testament Period.* Philadelphia: Fortress, 1969.

Krodel, Gerhard A. *Acts.* Augsburg Commentary on the New Testament. Minneapolis: Augsburg, 1986.

Musurillo, Herbert. *The Acts of the Christian Martyrs.* Oxford: Clarendon, 1972.

_____ . *The Acts of the Pagan Martyrs.* Oxford: Clarendon, 1954.

Nock, A. D. *Conversion: The Old and the New in Religion from Alexander the Great to Augustine of Hippo.* Oxford: Clarendon, 1933.

Parsons, Mikeal, and Richard Pervo. *Rethinking the Unity of Luke and Acts.* Minneapolis: Fortress, 1993.

Pervo, Richard I. "The Ancient Novel Becomes Christian." In *The Novel in the Ancient World,* 686-711, edited by G. Schmeling. Leiden: E. J. Brill, 1996.

_____ . *Luke's Story of Paul.* Minneapolis: Fortress, 1990.

_____ . *Profit with Delight: The Literary Genre of the Acts of the Apostles.* Philadelphia: Fortress, 1987.

Seim, Turid Karlsen. *The Double Message: Patterns of Gender in Luke and Acts.* Nashville: Abingdon Press, 1994.

Tannehill, Robert C. *The Narrative Unity of Luke–Acts: A Literary Interpretation.* Vol. 2. Minneapolis: Fortress, 1990.

Tyson, Joseph B. *Images of Judaism in Luke–Acts.* Columbia: The University of South Carolina Press, 1992.

White, L. Michael. *Building God's House in the Roman World.* Baltimore: Johns Hopkins University Press, 1990.

Winter, B. W., and A. D. Clarke, eds. *The Book of Acts in its Ancient Literary Setting.* Vol. 1. Grand Rapids: Eerdmans, 1993.

Index of Readings from
The Revised Common Lectionary

204

Index of Parallel Stories

GREEK AND ROMAN LITERATURE

PAPYRI